YOU HAVE NOT YET
BEEN DEFEATED

YOU HAVE NOT YET BEEN DEFEATED

SELECTED WORKS 2011–2021

ALAA ABD EL-FATTAH

Foreword by
NAOMI KLEIN

Translated by
A COLLECTIVE

SEVEN STORIES PRESS
NEW YORK • OAKLAND

Copyright © Alaa Abd el-Fattah, 2021
Translation copyright © Collective, 2021

Published in North America by Seven Stories Press in 2022

All rights reserved.
No part of this book may be reproduced, stored in a retrieval system, or transmitted in any
form or by any means, including mechanical, electronic, photocopying, recording, or otherwise,
without the prior written permission of the publisher.

SEVEN STORIES PRESS
140 Watts Street
New York, NY 10013
www.sevenstories.com

College professors and high school and middle school teachers may order free examination
copies of Seven Stories Press titles. Visit https://www.sevenstories.com/pg/resources-academics
or email academics@sevenstories.com.

Library of Congress Cataloging-in-Publication Data

Names: Abd el-Fattah, Alaa, 1980- author. | Klein, Naomi, 1970- writer of foreword.
Title: You have not yet been defeated : selected works 2011-2021 / Alaa Abd
   el-Fattah ; translated by A Collective.
Description: New York : Seven Stories Press, 2022.
Identifiers: LCCN 2021056463 | ISBN 9781644212455 (trade paperback) | ISBN
   9781644212462 (ebook)
Subjects: LCSH: Abd el-Fattah, Alaa, 1980- | Political
   prisoners--Egypt--Biography. | Political activists--Egypt--Biography. |
   Bloggers--Egypt--Biography. | Egypt--Politics and government--2011- |
   Egypt--History--Protests, 2011-2013.
Classification: LCC DT107.828.A366 A5 2022 | DDC 365/.45092
   [B]--dc23/eng/20220107
LC record available at https://lccn.loc.gov/2021056463

Printed in the USA.

9 8 7 6 5 4 3 2 1

CONTENTS

CHRONOLOGY: EGYPT 1952–2021

23 JULY 1952: Mid-ranking army officers stage a coup, depose King Farouq and take control of the state. Mohammed Naguib is their figurehead and the Revolution Command Council is established as the ruling authority.

AUGUST 1952: Workers' protest for better conditions in Kafr al-Dawwar is brutally repressed, and two of the workers are sentenced to death and executed.

SEPTEMBER 1952—JANUARY 1953: The Agrarian Reform Law initiates a major land redistribution programme, bolsters popular support for the revolution. The Constitution of 1923 is abrogated. All political parties are dissolved and banned.

JANUARY 1954: After a short honeymoon period with the revolution, the Muslim Brotherhood is outlawed.

MARCH 1954: Naguib, who favoured a return to constitutional government, is sidelined. Gamal Abdal Nasser consolidates power.

OCTOBER 1954: Nasser survives an assassination attempt. The Brotherhood are blamed and a brutal crackdown begins.

MARCH 1956: A new election law grants women the right to vote.

JULY 1956: Egypt nationalizes the Suez Canal.

OCTOBER 1956: Israel invades Egypt's Sinai Peninsula, under agreement with France and the UK, but international pressure forces their withdrawal. A major political victory for Nasser. Control of the canal is cemented.

1959: Arrests of communist intellectuals and activists begin. Hundreds are detained, some are tortured, at least two are killed, most are not released until 1964.

JANUARY 1960: Construction begins on the Aswan High Dam, Nasser's landmark development project.

SEPTEMBER 1961: Nasser—with Nehru of India and Tito of Yugoslavia—initiates the International Non-Aligned Movement.

JUNE 1967: War between Israel and Egypt, Syria, and Jordan. Israel occupies the Palestinian West Bank, the Gaza strip, the Syrian Golan Heights, and Egypt's Sinai Peninsula. A humiliating defeat. A war of attrition begins against Israeli forces now occupying the east bank of the Suez Canal.

SEPTEMBER 1970: Nasser dies of a heart attack. His successor is Vice-President Anwar El-Sadat.

MAY 1971: Sadat purges powerful opponents with the 'Corrective Revolution', announces the closure of political detention centres, and starts releasing detained activists, mainly Muslim Brotherhood members.

JANUARY 1972: A student uprising demanding democracy, press freedom and a popular war to liberate Sinai, occupies Tahrir Square and is expelled by police with force.

OCTOBER 1973: Egypt and Syria launch war against Israel in an effort to regain lands lost in 1967.

APRIL 1974: Members of an Islamist group break into the Technical Military Academy in Cairo: the first step in a planned coup to announce the birth of an Islamic State. Security forces engage, killing eleven.

APRIL 1974: Sadat's October Paper sets the stage for a complete reversal of economic policy: promoting entrepreneurship over central planning, and the dismantling of the public sector.

JANUARY 1977: A price hike of basic commodities triggers massive riots across the country. The army is deployed, a curfew imposed and more than 100 people are killed.

AUGUST 1978: Sadat establishes the National Democratic Party (NDP) which inherits the assets, resources and status of the state political party, the Socialist Union.

1977–79: Sadat visits Jerusalem to address the Knesset. He signs the Camp David Accords with Jimmy Carter and Menachem Begin. In response, Egypt is boycotted by most Arab countries, the headquarters of the Arab League are moved from Cairo to Tunis and Egypt's membership is suspended.

1979: Soviet forces invade Afghanistan, triggering a guerrilla war with local Islamist mujahideen. The CIA begins covert operations in support, which Sadat is heavily involved with: supplying Soviet weapons to the fighters, training insurgents, and allowing Egyptian militant Islamists to travel to Afghanistan to join the war.

MAY 1980: Sadat openly denounces the Coptic Church, accusing it of trying to establish a state within a state.

SEPTEMBER 1981: Sadat deposes the Coptic Pope. He orders the arrests of 1,536 people—who fall across the entire political and professional spectrum. This is accompanied by asset freezes, professional expulsions and the closure of certain newspapers.

OCTOBER 1981: Sadat is assassinated by members of a militant Islamist group while attending a military parade. The group begins a simultaneous insurrection in Asyut and takes control of the city for a few days before paratroopers from Cairo restore government control. Sadat is succeeded by his Vice-President Hosni Mubarak and a state of national emergency is declared. It will be continually renewed throughout the coming thirty years of Mubarak's rule.

SEPTEMBER 1984: Workers demonstrate and stage a sit-in at Kafr el-Dawwar Spinning & Weaving Factory (public sector), protesting rising food prices and demanding increased pay. The sit-in is violently broken up by police forces, leaving three workers dead. Several more strikes will follow, protesting rising prices, low pay, corruption, neglect of the public sector and the complicity of the official workers' unions.

NOVEMBER 1987: The Arab boycott of Egypt ends, Egyptian membership of the Arab League will be restored, and its headquarters return to Cairo.

AUGUST 1989: Workers occupying the Iron & Steel Factory in Helwan are attacked by Central Security Forces. One worker is killed, tens are wounded, and about 600 are arrested and tortured at police stations.

FEBRUARY 1990: Islamist militants attack a bus carrying Israeli tourists in Egypt, killing eleven. Eight months later, they assassinate Rifaat el-Mahgoub, Speaker of Parliament, in Cairo.

JANUARY 1991: Egypt sends 35,000 troops to join the US-led war on Iraq. As a reward, $14bn of Egypt's $46bn foreign debt is dropped.

MAY 1991: Egypt agrees its first structural adjustment loan with the International Monetary Fund: $380m, conditional on the removal of price controls, reduced subsidies, introduction of sales tax and an accelerated privatization programme for state-owned enterprises.

1993: Several militant Islamist attacks on tourists, senior police officials shot dead in daylight ambushes, and failed assassination attempts on the Interior Minister and the Prime Minister.

OCTOBER 1994: 15,000 workers in Kafr el-Dawwar strike and occupy the factory. Security forces lay siege, cut off water and electricity. In the eventual dispersal, violence spreads across the town, injuring sixty and killing four.

JUNE 1995: Mubarak survives an assassination attempt in Addis Ababa by a militant Islamist group from Sudan.

SEPTEMBER 1995: Egypt becomes the first country to cooperate with the CIA's extraordinary rendition programme. Abu Talal al-Qasimi is illegally captured by the CIA in Croatia and taken to Egypt. He will later be executed in Egypt.

1994–1997: Islamist attacks continue to escalate: Nobel laureate Naguib Mahfouz is stabbed in the neck, a bomb attack on the Egyptian embassy in Islamabad kills seventeen, tourists are attacked and killed in separate attacks at the Pyramids, the Egyptian Museum and in Luxor.

FEBRUARY 2000: Gamal Mubarak, Hosni Mubarak's son, is appointed member of the ruling National Democratic Party's general secretariat.

SEPTEMBER 2000: The second Palestinian Intifada erupts. In Egypt, it triggers widespread demonstrations supporting the Palestinians, denouncing Mubarak's position, and demanding a reversal of Egypt's normalization with Israel.

SEPTEMBER 2001: After 9/11 Egyptian intelligence acquires a new importance to the US in light of their long experience with Islamist groups. The CIA's 'extraordinary rendition' programme is expanded and Egypt becomes a principal collaborator in the reception and torture of suspects.

MARCH 2003: The US invasion of Iraq triggers large demonstrations protesting Egypt's subservience to US foreign policy—as well as rising prices, corruption and economic policies. Tens of thousands of protestors occupy Tahrir Square for a few hours before being violently dispersed by police.

OCTOBER 2004: Three coordinated bombs are detonated in tourist spots around Taba, South Sinai, killing 38 people.

DECEMBER 2004: The first demonstration by the Kefaya ('Enough') movement against Mubarak, rejecting the extension of his presidency and the grooming of Gamal Mubarak to succeed him. 'No Succession' will become a regular anti-Mubarak slogan from now on, and Kefaya demonstrations will steadily gain traction.

JULY 2005: Three bombs in Sharm el-Sheikh kill 88 people, mostly Egyptians.

SEPTEMBER 2005: Mubarak's presidency is renewed for a fifth term. The constitution had been amended to allow multiple presidential candidates to compete in elections, though with very restrictive conditions for candidacy. Mubarak wins 88 per cent of the vote. Two months later, despite rampant violations, the Muslim Brotherhood win 20 per cent of seats in parliamentary elections.

MARCH 2006: Around 1,000 judges stage a silent protest demanding the full independence of the judiciary. Alaa is arrested from a protest in solidarity with the judges and spends forty-five days in prison.

JUNE 2007: In January of the previous year elections were held in the West Bank and Gaza from which Hamas emerged the victor. Fatah did not cede power which resulted in a split in the Palestinian leadership. Now, Hamas officially take control of Gaza, Israel imposes a blockade, and Egypt supports it by closing its border crossing at Rafah.

APRIL 2008: Landmark strike in the massive textile factories in al-Mahalla receives support from a wide spectrum of popular organizations and groups: workers' unions, political move-ments and parties, student unions, and academics. Clashes with security forces escalate and spread through the city. A group of human rights centres, NGOs, and independent lawyers team up to form The Front for the Defence of 6 April Demonstrators. The 6 April Youth Movement, a grassroots activists group, is also formed.

DECEMBER 2008: Israel launches an air and ground war against the Gaza strip triggering large demonstrations in Egypt denouncing Mubarak for his friendly policies towards Israel, and demanding the permanent opening of the Rafah border crossing.

SEPTEMBER 2009: A coalition of Egyptian human rights organizations issue a report stating that after eighteen years of ruling under Emergency Law 'Egypt has been turned into a police state.'

JUNE 2010: Khaled Said, 28, is dragged from a cybercafé near his home in Alexandria by two plainclothes policemen and beaten to death. The police report claims he suffocated as he tried to swallow a bag of hashish he was caught with, but Said's family manage to take a photograph of his corpse in the morgue. His face is battered beyond recognition. They release the photograph online, along with a claim that he was killed for having video material implicating policemen in a drug deal.

A new Facebook page, 'We are all Khaled Said', attracts hundreds of thousands of followers in a few days, becoming Egypt's largest dissident group online.

DECEMBER 2010: 'We are all Khaled Said' calls for a protest on 25 January, a national holiday: Police Day. Inspired by the recent Tunisian revolution and encouraged by comments posted on the page, the admins change the event title to 'A revolution against torture, unemployment, corruption, and injustice'.

25 JANUARY 2011: On Police Day, demonstrations erupt in several Egyptian cities and towns. Security forces respond violently, killing at least one protester in Suez.

27 JANUARY 2011: In anticipation of planned protests the following day, the Mubarak regime orders the internet be shut down.

28 JANUARY 2011: Tens of thousands of demonstrators across the country march towards the centres of their cities after Friday prayers. In the ensuing battles with the police, at least 800 people are killed and 99 police stations are burned to the ground. By sunset, the revolutionists have won—and occupied Egypt's main city centres. The police retreat to desert barracks and the military deploy, taking up positions around key buildings. Protestors lead chants of 'The People, the Army, One Hand' but it is not clear what the military's stance is.

29 JANUARY 2011: Mubarak dismisses the cabinet of Ahmad Nazif, and directs Ahmad Shafiq, Minister of Civil Aviation, to form a new cabinet. For the first time in his thirty years in power he appoints a Vice-President, Omar Suleiman, the Intelligence chief well known in Washington for his cooperation with the CIA's rendition programme.

31 JANUARY 2011: In a further bid to appease protestors, Minister of the Interior, Habib El-Adly, is dismissed.

1 FEBRUARY 2011: Mubarak announces that he will not run for reelection at the end of his term in September 2011.

2 FEBRUARY 2011: The Battle of the Camel: several thousand Mubarak supporters—some paid—attack Tahrir. First with horses and a camel, then with rocks, and ultimately with live rounds from the tops of surrounding buildings. The Brotherhood now appear with full organizational force in defence of Tahrir. The battle lasts until the morning, the square holds.

11 FEBRUARY 2011: After eighteen days of protest that have paralyzed the country and fixed the world's attention on Tahrir

Square, Mubarak steps down and tasks the Supreme Council of the Armed Forces (SCAF) with running the country.

13 FEBRUARY 2011: SCAF suspends the constitution and dissolves Parliament.

18 FEBRUARY 2011: Habib El-Adly and other NDP figures are arrested by order of the Public Prosecutor.

5 MARCH 2011: Hundreds storm the buildings of the feared State Security agency in several cities, including the headquarters in Cairo, after word spreads that papers, case files and evidence of torture was being destroyed inside.

19 MARCH 2011: National referendum on constitutional amendments. A 'yes' vote—promoted by the Brotherhood—would mandate holding parliamentary elections before drafting a new constitution. First major rift between Islamist and revolutionary groups. 'Yes' takes 77 per cent of the vote.

13 APRIL 2011: Mubarak and his sons, Alaa and Gamal, are arrested by order of the Public Prosecutor.

4 MAY 2011: A Palestinian reconciliation agreement brokered by Egypt is signed by Hamas and Fatah in Cairo. The interim government's successful mediation indicates that Egypt no longer adheres to Mubarak's policy of isolating Hamas. The Rafah border will soon be re-opened.

5 MAY 2011: Habib el-Adly is sentenced to twelve years in prison for financial corruption, the first Mubarak-era official to be convicted and sentenced.

3 AUGUST 2011: Mubarak's trial, for corruption and complicity in the killing of some 900 protesters, begins and is aired live on television. Mubarak is wheeled into court on a hospital bed.

9 OCTOBER 2011: The Maspero massacre. Thousands of Coptic Christians gather in Cairo to protest the burning of a church in Upper Egypt and the state's failure to protect Copts. The army attacks, killing 26 and injuring 350.

20 OCTOBER 2011: Alaa publishes 'To Be with the Martyrs, for that is Far Better' in national broadsheet, al-Shorouk.

30 OCTOBER 2011: Alaa is arrested by the Military Prosecutor.

19–24 NOVEMBER 2011: The Battle of Mohammed Mahmoud Street. A sit-in held by families of the injured of the revolution in Tahrir is attacked by police. Thousands flock to the square and engage in a five-day battle that leaves sixty dead and several thousand injured. The Muslim Brotherhood are absent, concerned the unrest could disrupt upcoming elections.

24 NOVEMBER 2011: SCAF announces the appointment of Mubarak-era figure, Kamal El-Ganzouri, as Prime Minister. Some protestors split from Tahrir and begin an occupation of the street outside the Cabinet Building.

28 NOVEMBER 2011: Parliamentary elections begin.

16–20 DECEMBER 2011: The army violently disperses the sit-in at the Cabinet Building, sparking four days of clashes that leave 17 dead and some 2000 injured.

25 DECEMBER 2011: After an extended hunger strike by his mother, Laila Soueif, Alaa and all the accused in the Maspero case are released by a civil judge.

21 JANUARY 2012: Parliamentary elections announced, with the Brotherhood winning 47 per cent of the seats and the Salafists, 25 per cent.

1 FEBRUARY 2012: The Port Said Massacre. 74 fans of Cairo football club al-Ahly, whose ultras are known as revolutionaries, are killed in al-Masry SC's stadium.

31 MARCH 2012: Breaking an earlier pledge, the Muslim Brotherhood announces Khairat el-Shater—de facto leader of the organization and a known hardliner—will run in the upcoming presidential election, with Mohammed Morsi as a reserve candidate.

14 APRIL 2012: The Supreme Presidential Election Commission disqualifies ten presidential candidates, including el-Shater and Omar Suleiman.

2 JUNE 2012: Mubarak and Habib el-Adly are sentenced to life in prison for ordering the killing of protesters.

24 JUNE 2012: Mohammed Morsi is declared winner of the presidential election, with 51.7 per cent of the vote. Ahmad Shafiq—the establishment's candidate—immediately leaves the country for the United Arab Emirates.

12 AUGUST 2012: Morsi replaces Minister of Defence Hussein Tantawi with General Abdel Fattah el-Sisi, and removes Army Chief of Staff, Sami Anan.

22 NOVEMBER 2012: Morsi makes a unilateral power grab, declaring his decisions immune from judicial review and precluding the courts from dissolving a new Constituent Panel. Massive protests ensue.

15–22 DECEMBER 2012: The new constitution hastily drafted by Islamists amid protests is approved by referendum with 63.8 per cent of the vote, but a turnout of 32.9 per cent.

JUNE 2013: As Morsi's first anniversary in power approaches, attention turns to calls for protests on 30 June. Discontent in almost all quarters is high: reforms have ceased altogether, police violence continues unabated, sectarian attacks are on the rise, promised cooperation with the revolutionary groups that helped win the election has not materialized, and the country is ravaged by increasingly frequent electricity cuts due to mismanagement of fuel supplies. A new campaign by the name of Tamarrod ('Rebellion') claims to have gathered millions of signatures calling for Morsi's resignation and early elections.

30 JUNE 2013: Millions take to the streets demanding Morsi's departure. Counter demonstrations are organized by Morsi supporters, developing into two sit-ins in Rabaa and el-Nahda Squares in Cairo.

3 JULY 2013: Defence Minister General el-Sisi removes Morsi from power and installs Chief Justice of the Constitutional Court, Adly Mansour, as interim president.

24 JULY 2013: Sisi calls for people to take to the streets to give him a 'mandate' to deal with 'terrorism': the Brotherhood. Tens of thousands oblige.

14 AUGUST 2013: Police attack the sit-ins at Rabaa and el-Nahda squares. More than 900 people are killed. At least 42 churches are attacked in response by Islamist mobs around the country. A roundup of Brotherhood leaders and supporters begins; opposition television channels are shut down or forced into exile.

4 NOVEMBER 2013: Morsi appears for the first time since his removal, on trial charged with inciting violence, the first of several court cases against him. Some charges carry the death penalty.

26 NOVEMBER 2013: A protest is held outside the Shura Council protesting the re-activation of a British-era law outlawing protest. It is attacked by police, who make dozens of arrests.

28 NOVEMBER 2013: Alaa is arrested and charged—among other things—with organizing the protest at the Shura Council. Protest is now effectively outlawed and those arrested at, or in the vicinity of, protests are handed lengthy prison sentences.

25 DECEMBER 2013: The Muslim Brotherhood is officially designated a terrorist organization.

29 DECEMBER 2013: Three al-Jazeera English journalists are arrested from the Marriot Hotel in Cairo on terrorism charges. The al-Jazeera channels, owned by Qatar, are aligned with the Brotherhood.

28 MAY 2014: Sisi wins presidential election with 96.9 per cent of the vote.

30 NOVEMBER 2014: In a retrial, Mubarak's case is dismissed and Habib el-Adly acquitted over the killing of protestors in 2011.

21 APRIL 2015: Morsi is sentenced to twenty years for charges relating to the killing of protesters in 2012.

9 MAY 2015: Mubarak and his sons are sentenced to three years on corruption charges.

29 JUNE 2015: A bomb kills the Prosecutor General, Hisham Barakat, as he leaves home on his way to work.

25 JANUARY 2016: Italian academic Giulio Regeni is killed in police custody under torture. He had been researching contemporary labour issues.

15 APRIL 2016: Thousands demonstrate against Egypt's transfer of the two Red Sea islands, Tiran and Sanafir, to Saudi Arabia, in the largest protests since Sisi's election.

11 NOVEMBER 2016: Egypt devalues its currency, the most drastic among several liberalization measures required to secure a $12bn loan from the IMF.

2017: Egypt becomes the world's third highest importer of weapons. Foreign debt rises to 103 per cent of GDP.

24 MARCH 2017: Mubarak is released from prison.

6 SEPTEMBER 2017: Human Rights Watch estimates some 60,000 political prisoners now held in Egypt and that 'widespread and systematic torture by the security forces probably amounts to a crime against humanity'.

JANUARY 2018: Presidential elections for Sisi's second term. All potential opponents are arrested or pull out.

30 MARCH 2019: Alaa is released from prison, but sentenced to spend every night in his local police station, Doqqi, for the next five years.

17 JUNE 2019: Mohammad Morsi collapses during a court session and dies. All national newspapers report the story with the same news bulletin of forty-three words on page three.

20 SEPTEMBER 2019: Small street protests erupt, the first in years, triggered by a building contractor revealing shocking details about government corruption. A massive sweep of activists begins.

29 SEPTEMBER 2019: Alaa is arrested from inside Doqqi police station.

FOREWORD

The text you are holding is living history. Many of these words were first written with pencil and paper in a cell in Egypt's notorious Torah Prison, and smuggled out in ways we likely will never understand. One was drafted in collaboration with another political prisoner, the two men shouting ideas to each other across the dark ward. A few texts were written in relative freedom, on the eve of repeated imprisonments, or during probationary release, in an isolation cell at a police station where the author was required to spend his nights.

At every stage, and whichever form they take—essay, letter, interview, tweet, speech—they exist only because of extraordinary risks taken by the writer, intellectual, technologist and Egyptian revolutionary Alaa Abd el-Fattah. Those risks include the ever-present threat that Alaa would face further ludicrous charges, and prolonged detention. In the case of texts written during stints on the outside, or during probation, the threat—made explicit in night-time visits from state security officers—was that these writings would lead directly to his re-imprisonment, or worse. And still, he wrote.

The fact that these words are before us now, in book form, many for the first time in translation, is a result of further risks, these ones taken by friends, family, and comrades in Egypt's luminous but brutally extinguished revolution. The ones who camped outside the prison to demand communication with the prisoner; who smuggled out hidden slips of paper; who selected the texts from Alaa's huge body of work; who edited, translated, and contextualized them in these pages.

This careful work has taken place against the backdrop of

continuous and escalating state repression against the regime's political opponents. That opposition is politically and ideologically diverse. Alaa and his comrades are part of the left, internationalist, anti-sectarian, youth-led movement that is part of a global confrontation with transnational capital and its national organs, a movement that has seen expressions from Tahrir Square to Occupy Wall Street. And because this strain has refused to fully surrender its hopes for a liberated Egypt, it too has faced the wrath of the vengeful regime of General Abdel Fattah el-Sisi.

As I write, Alaa is re-imprisoned, as he feared he would be, and the silence from his cell is harrowing. His sister, Sanaa Seif, a prominent organizer in her own right, is also in jail, most recently for 'spreading false news'. His editors at *Mada Masr*, where many of Alaa's writings first appeared, have also faced harassment and detention for their commitment to independent thought in a sea of state propaganda.

Alaa, as you will read, is a student of the South African freedom struggle, and in particular the Freedom Charter—a document that laid out a roadmap for collective freedom written under one of the most repressive periods of Apartheid rule; a document whose meaning and import were magnified by the raw difficulty of bringing the text into being. This text is also a product of revolutionary effort, of subterfuge and hope. In the age of 'frictionless' everything, it is born of pure friction.

All of this makes the book's very existence remarkable—and yet none of this friction is why it must be read. It must be read for the precision of its language, for its bold experimentations with form and style, and for the endlessly original ways its author finds to express disdain for tyrants, liars and cowards. Most of all, it must be read for what Alaa has to tell us about revolutions—why most fail, what it feels like when they do, and, perhaps, how they might still succeed. It is an analysis rooted as

much in a keen understanding of popular culture, digital technology, and collective emotion as it is in experiences confronting
tanks and consoling the families of martyrs.

So, for instance, in the handful of months when Alaa was on
probationary release from prison in 2019, before his reimprison-
ment, he shared several reflections on how the outside world had
altered during his years of incarceration. When, he wondered,
did otherwise serious adults start communicating with one
another via emojis and gifs? Why, amidst the constant online
chatter, was there so little actual discourse—engaged people
building on each other's knowledge of history and current events
to create shared meaning?

In an interview with journalists at *Mada Masr*, Alaa observed
that, 'Getting out [of jail], I feel like we've gone back to the
Stone Age. People speak in emojis and sounds—ha ha ho ho—
not text. Text and the written word are great. So I'm disturbed.'
He describes a debate about whether veterans of Tahrir Square
have anything to teach youth in Sudan, who were, in 2019,
waging a courageous uprising of their own. 'And you're in these
circles of people sending gifs and heart emojis . . . This medium
is stifling. It's very strange that the entire world knows that
these tools and mediums are defective and they have no faith in
them and are suspicious of them, but they just keep using them.
There's a need for an alternate imagination.'

This critique of the ways corporate communication platforms
systematically infantilize and trivialize consequential subjects
carries particular weight because Alaa is no technophobe. On
the contrary, he is a programmer, a world-renowned blogger, as
well as a social media aficionado with close to a million followers across platforms. He came to activism as a teen in the late
1990s and 2000s, surfing the liberatory promise of the pre-social
media internet, a time when email lists and Indymedia networks
were weaving together emergent movements across continents

and oceans, converging to show solidarity for Palestine and the Zapatistas; to oppose corporate globalization from Seattle to Genoa to Porto Alegre; and to try to stop the 2003 US-UK invasion and occupation of Iraq. As a worker, the internet was Alaa's day job; as an activist, it was one of his key weapons.

And yet in his own life, he had watched these networked technologies—filled with so much potential for solidarity, increased understanding, and new forms of internationalism—turn into tools of aggressive surveillance and social control, with Big Tech collaborating with repressive regimes, governments using 'kill switches' to black out the internet mid-uprising, and bad-faith actors seizing on out-of-context tweets to slander reputations and make activists markedly easier to imprison. Interestingly, it is not these explicitly repressive applications that most preoccupy Alaa in these pages. As he wrote in 2017, 'My online speech is often used against me in the courts and in smear campaigns, but it isn't the reason why I am prosecuted; my offline activity is.' This insight may come from being raised in a family of revolutionaries, with his father, the renowned human rights lawyer Ahmed Seif el-Islam, behind bars during Alaa's early years. He knows well that authoritarian states will always find ways to surveil and entrap the figures that pose a material threat to their hold on power, whether through digital tools or analogue ones.

Nor was he under any illusion that Silicon Valley was a partner in his people's liberation. In one of this book's most prescient passages, Alaa, writing without Internet access in a prison cell in 2016, predicted the Covid-19 lockdown lifestyle almost to the letter, with its attendant attacks on public education and labour standards. Mimicking the breathless techno-utopian tone, he wrote:

Tomorrow will be a happy day, when Uber replaces drivers with self-driving cars, making the trip to university cheaper;

and the day after will be even happier when they abolish
the university, so you're spared the trip and can study at
Khan Academy from the comfort of your own home. And
the day after will be even happier still when they do away
with your trip to work and have you doing piecework from
home in a flexible, sharing-based labour market, and the
day after will be happier and happier when they send you
off for early retirement because you've been replaced by a
robot.

This kind of analysis of the workings of capital meant that,
while others enthused about 'Facebook Revolutions' and 'Twitter
Uprisings', Alaa was able to remain clear-eyed about who these
companies were and whose interests they served. In 2011, in an
interregnum before his long prison sentences began, Alaa travelled to California to keynote RightsCon, the inaugural Silicon
Valley human rights conference which now takes place every
year. The crowd surely expected this hero of Tahrir to flatter
them with tales of how their companies had aided in Egypt's
revolution and how they could further advance their mutual
goals of democracy and liberation. Instead, as we read in a tran-
script of that speech, he declared himself 'quite cynical' about
the gathering's entire premise. Sure, it would be nice if the giants
of Silicon Valley were dedicated to protecting and advancing
human rights, but corporations are not really likely to do any of
that.' What they are built to do is

> monetize every single transaction . . . I don't expect either
> Twitter or Facebook or the mobile companies to change
> their business models just for activists, so that is not going
> to happen . . . What needs to happen is a revolution.
> What needs to happen is a complete change in the order of
> things, so that we are making these amazing products, and

we're making a living, but we're not trying to monopolize, and we're not trying to control the internet, and we're not trying to control our users, and we're not complicit with governments.

Over the subsequent decade, events would bear out these insights so thoroughly that it's easy to forget that in 2011 Silicon Valley, they were close to heresy.

Rather than treating these companies like revolutionary comrades, Alaa chose to discuss the subtler impacts of social media and platform communications on daily life, the quality of discourse, and on the formation of fragile and vulnerable identities. He would return to the theme often because it has at least as much of an impact on movements as state surveillance and censorship. After all, if the groups and individuals who want political change find themselves unable to speak to each other in productive ways, what does it matter what the censors do?

When he emerged, briefly, from prison in 2019, his concerns had only deepened. And it must have been jarring. Four and half years behind bars had trained him in the painful skills of patience, disengagement and deferral. Now here he was, plunged back into the waters of instant digital gratification and continuous digital input. And he was, quite understandably, appalled. Not just by the replacement of carefully chosen words by crude emoticons, but, one senses, by the dissonance between the enormous stakes of the struggle for liberation against the military regime—fallen comrades, thousands of political prisoners, tortured bodies, death sentences—and the light-hearted, absurdist tone that characterizes how pretty much everything now gets discussed online, in Egypt and beyond. The subtext seems clear: he had lost his liberty, missed his son's birth and early years, been absent for his father's death—in large part because he believed, and the Egyptian military state agreed, that words had power.

So why were so many frittering away their relative freedom of expression by treating words so lightly?

'I feel like there has been a regression,' he said, 'even in two-way conversation, not just collective—in the ability to deal with complex topics.'

REGRESSION AND MATURITY

It's fitting that Alaa would zero in on regression when he was able to re-engage online after what he described as his 'deep freeze'. Fitting because inducing a regressed state in the incarcerated person is the goal of prisons like the one that swallowed him up, as it had his father before him. Isolation, humiliation, continuous changing of the rules, severed connections with the outside world—all of it is designed to achieve a numbed and nullified state of submission. Which makes it all the more remarkable that prison did not succeed in inducing regression in the author, quite the opposite. This book is surely testament to that.

In addition to the dexterity of its prose, as well as the acuity of its ideas, this book is remarkable for its consistent political maturity. Mature because it does something very rare in the canon of movement writing: look squarely at just how much has been lost.

Since becoming part of the alter-globalization movements in the late 1990s, a global network that Alaa joined as a teen, I have been struck by how hard it is, from inside an uprising's nucleus, to even know when a revolutionary moment has passed. Among core organizers, there are still meetings, still strategy sessions, still hopes for a new opening just around the corner—it's only the masses of supporters who are mysteriously absent. But because their arrival was always a little mysterious to begin with, that too can feel like a temporary state rather than a more lasting setback. Indeed we leftists have been known to spend years staggering

around like golems inside the husks of our movements, unaware
that we have been drained of our animating life force.

Alaa speaks to this eerie, undead stage of political organization, writing, with his devastating precision, of a time when 'the
revolution did not yet believe itself to be over'. Or of the period,
in 2013, when the liberatory spirit of Tahrir had been supplanted
by a battle between the Muslim Brotherhood and security state:
'My words lost any power and yet they continued to pour out of
me,' he writes. 'I still had a voice, even if only a handful would
listen.'

Alaa is no longer on that kind of political autopilot. Instead,
he has spent years probing the toughest of questions: Have we
actually lost? How close did we get? What can we learn going
forward so we stop losing? His assessments in this collection
are utterly devoid either of easy boosterism or self-indulgent
doomerism. He recognizes the movement's glories, honours the
life-altering 'togetherness' of Tahrir Square. And yet, he acknowledges, Egypt's revolution failed in its most minimal common
goals: to secure a government that rotates based on democratic
elections and a legal system that protects the integrity of the
body from arbitrary detention, military trials, torture, rape, and
state massacres.

It also failed, at the peak of its popular power, 'to articulate
a common dream of what we wanted in Egypt. It's fine to be
defeated,' Alaa writes, 'but at least have a story—what we want
to achieve together.' Reading his earlier, more programmatic
essays, it's clear that this was not for lack of ideas. Inspired by
the extraordinary grassroots process that led to the drafting of
South Africa's Freedom Charter, Alaa had a vision for how the
movement that found its wings in Tahrir Square could fan out
across the country and engage in 'intensive discussions with
thousands of citizens' to democratically develop a vision for their
collective future. 'Since we've agreed that the constitution is one

of the key goals of our ongoing revolution, why not include the revolutionary masses in its drafting?' Trapped between top-down political parties who wanted no part of this kind of participatory democracy and by street activists who were dismissive of state power, the idea died on the vine.

'But,' Alaa adds to his stark assessments, 'the revolution did break a regime.' It defeated much of Mubarak's machine, and the new junta that is in its place, while even more brutal, is also precarious for the thinness of its domestic support. Openings, he tells us, remain. In this way, Alaa acts as the revolution's toughest critic and its most devoted militant. Which makes sense, given where he is. This is a writer for whom every outward communication is a risk, and who therefore cannot afford either the delusion of over-inflating his movement's power or the finality of discounting its latent potential. He has time only for words that hold out the possibility of materially changing the balance of power.

We who have been part of those uprisings that kicked off with alter-globalization in the late nineties and early aughts, and that continued through the movements of the squares and subsequent climate and racial justice reckonings, could learn a great deal from Alaa's model of intellectual honesty. Because wherever we live, there is a very good chance that we have lived through some major political losses, even if they took subtler, more sanitized forms than in counter-revolutionary Egypt. Yet many contemporary organizing models have managed to insulate us from direct confrontations with those defeats, and repressed the waves of grief from their attendant material losses. There are plenty of factors that aid in this avoidance: at times we have made no demands of power, so how could we fail to have those demands met? At other times, our demands have been so sweeping and all-encompassing that the moment of reckoning could be perpetually deferred. And, of course, there is always the next crisis demanding our attention, helpfully delaying difficult introspection once again.

This is not to say, by any means, that those who identify with this global uprising have all been on identical trajectories. When North Americans and Europeans occupied squares and parks, inspired in large part by Tahrir, we were already living in liberal democracies and did not face the same risks of a resurgent military state. When our occupations failed, many of us were able to throw ourselves into the ultimately unsuccessful campaigns of Bernie Sanders and Jeremy Corbyn, or in the electoral experiments of Syriza in Greece and Podemos in Spain. Bolivians, meanwhile, have managed to repel a foreign-backed coup and protect their left government. In short, national contexts differ, and some activists pay far higher prices, in blood and freedom, for political setbacks—inside our highly unequal nation states, and between them.

Yet as we confront the conflagration of the global climate crisis, of surging fascist political forces, as well as the rapid consolidation of wealth by the transnational billionaire class even during a global pandemic (made exponentially more lethal by their greed), none of us, no matter where we live, have a right to claim that we are winning. Sure, left movements have changed the public discourse in profound ways in recent years, discovering just how many millions hunger for deep change. Profound reckonings have been sparked about the ongoing violence of colonialism, white supremacy, patriarchy and of course capital. Material victories continue to be won every day—in the schools, in the courts, and beyond. And yet, if we check the ledger, it is also true that we have failed to stop the steamroller of hyper-polluting and exploiting trade. We have failed to keep global emissions from steadily rising. We failed to stop the invasion of Iraq, Afghanistan or the war in Yemen. Our resistances, however heroic, however effervescent, have not brought justice to Palestine, or protected the most minimal democracy in Hong Kong. I could go on, but will spare us.

The blame lies with the perpetrators—not with the millions of overwhelmingly unarmed activists who tried to stop these juggernauts. Yet Alaa's model here should remind us, wherever we reside, that though it may not be our fault, it *is* our duty to make time in our organizing and theorizing to confront our defeats. Not to wallow, but because such confrontations are our only hope of seeing the new terrain of struggle clearly.

As a committed internationalist, Alaa has words that are specifically addressed to those of us living in very different political contexts. He may have been defeated, or at least taken temporarily out of commission by a regime utterly unconcerned with the law or human rights. But 'you,' he says, seemingly addressing those who are part of rights-based movements in liberal democracies, 'have not yet been defeated.' This is the sentence that forms the book's title, and it sits on the page as a challenge to anyone free enough to see it.

In this challenge, he leaves us with no miracle cures. Just hard-won clarity about what many of us already know in our bones. Here are a few of his most urgent messages:

—That serious stakes demand intellectual seriousness. Resist the algorithmic pull of the trivial, absurdist and mocking, as well as the delusion that they constitute meaningful resistance. Yes, laughter is a necessary tool of survival—and Alaa can be very funny indeed. 'I wanted to keep watching *Game of Thrones*' he tweeted right before disappearing into prison, once again, in 2014. And then, on his brief release, much more darkly: 'I'm the ghost of spring past.' Yet he insists that, in the 'post-truth' age, an information ecology in which truth and meaning are valued and defended is a threat to power, which is why elites actively encourage our sense of the absurd.

—That movements must be avowedly internationalist and

feminist, which means rejecting the temptations to deploy easy nationalism and the 'trap of masculinity' as tools of struggle. Alaa acknowledges that in the fire of revolutionary conflict, it can be seductive to believe that these forces can be harnessed towards liberatory ends. But given how thoroughly state actors have defined both The Nation and The Man, once the potent forces of nationalism and masculinity are summoned, he warns, we 'open the door to relics of the past looking both to ride the wave of revolution and steer it off its course'.

—That movements need a captivating vision of the world they are fighting for, and not only rage at the system they are desperate to overthrow. 'Our rosy dreams will probably not come to pass,' he writes, with typically brutal honesty. 'But if we leave ourselves to our nightmares we'll be killed by fear before the Floods arrive.'

—That freedom, however limited, must be exercised to its maximum potential. Alaa understandably rejects the common formulation that Egypt is one large prison: no, he writes, prison is a very specific place, with specific cruelties and barbarities. And while it's true that many liberal freedoms are denied to all Egyptians, the freedoms possessed by those on the outside—control over their bodies, time and relationships—are immense compared to the life of an incarcerated person. Still, while refusing the idea of prison as metaphor, he is, throughout, preoc-cupied with the ways technically free people are nonetheless confined and entrapped—by black box algorithms and, more profoundly, by the way capitalist logics constrain imaginations, preventing contemporary movements from meeting our most urgent crises.

—That bodies, movements, and the natural world are capable of regeneration—even if past losses and wounds mean that they regenerate into something different, more scarred and less conventionally perfect. We must be willing to become, he says, borrowing from Donna Haraway, a new, more beautiful kind of monster, 'for only the monstrous can hold both the history of dreams and hopes, and the reality of defeat and pain together.'

It is this kind of softness that makes Alaa an evolved movement leader: his refusal to romanticize or glorify imprisonment or suffering in any way, his insistence on his own fragility, his right to sadness. And yet, no matter the physical and psychic mutilations, his belief that healing and regeneration remain possible.

And there is a final, related lesson. Our movements must urgently defend the integrity of the body. We must defend all bodies against imprisonment, indefinite detention, torture, rape and state-sanctioned massacre. Because we are human, and without a shared belief in the body's right to integrity, transcendent movements will continue to be crushed by the raw power of states willing to inflict violence without limit. And that is precisely how we lose voices like Alaa's to the muffled darkness of the prison cell. It cannot stand. #FreeAlaa.

Naomi Klein, July 2021

INTRODUCTION

Alaa Abd el-Fattah has spent seven of the eight years since the counter-revolution led by General Abdel Fattah el-Sisi in prison. He is in prison for his ideas and his words. Here, for the first time, a collection of Alaa's work is brought together, assembled and translated by his family and friends.

The reader is introduced to Alaa at the peak of the energies unleashed by the 2011 revolution in Egypt as he surveys the constitutional history of South Africa. Writing for a national broadsheet, *al-Shorouk*, he is setting the stage for the following day's launch of the 'Let's Write Our Constitution' campaign, an initiative in mass democracy inspired by South Africa's Congress of the People of 1955, and an attempt to turn the opportunities following the fall of Mubarak four months earlier into irreversible legislative gains.

Three short months later, the military kill twenty-six protestors at Maspero and we follow Alaa into the massacre's aftermath in 'To Be With the Martyrs, for that is Far Better', his account of the night spent in the Coptic Hospital, fighting for autopsies to be performed. Two weeks after its publication he is summoned by the Military Prosecutor.

Imprisoned while his wife delivers their first child, Khaled, and his mother is on hunger strike, Alaa's writings from prison in this period are urgent and impassioned yet always connected to broader political developments and attuned to their minutiae.

Following Alaa's release, we find ourselves in the swirling waters of 2012–13: relentless street protests and industrial actions, parliamentary and presidential elections, constitutional crises, the Muslim Brotherhood's victory and catastrophic year in power. In this period Alaa writes very few long-form essays, instead tweeting and posting to Facebook, hosting public fora, appearing on television talk shows and speaking at rallies. We tried to use Alaa's social media output to tell the story of 2012–13, but we must bear in mind the sheer volume of his output. He has tweeted a total of 290,000 times since 2007—about 100 books' worth of tweets.

Our social media selections are an attempt instead to show how he uses the internet: as a medium not only for transmission outwards, but of collecting information, combining and disseminating, as a space for debate, a personal diary, a public diary, a podium and a comedy stage. Alaa writes relentlessly, his brain always engaged with a multitude of topics simultaneously, his patience for engagement with other people seemingly inexhaustible: there is no opinion that is not worth engaging with.

August 2013 brings the massacre at Rabaa el-Adaweya Square in Cairo. The public killing of hundreds of supporters of ousted Muslim Brotherhood President Mohamed Morsi is designed to silence a country that considered itself in an ongoing state of revolution. But Alaa refuses to be silenced, and his Facebook posts, 'Above the Sound of Battle' 'What Happened at Abu Zaabal?' and 'You Know the Killing Was Random' are widely remembered as beacons in the reeling darkness of those days.

In August 2012 Mohamed Morsi had appointed General Abdel-Fattah el-Sisi as the new Minister of Defence, replacing the aged and unpopular Field Marshall Hussein Tantawi. Tantawi had held the position for the previous twenty years, had overseen the removal of Mubarak the previous year, and as head of the Supreme Council of the Armed Forces (SCAF) had been de-facto in charge of the country through the transitional period up to Morsi's electoral victory. Tantawi's removal by the newly elected civilian was greeted as a revolutionary act—but the president had sealed his own downfall by elevating the ambitious and ruthless Sisi to the position from which he would soon overthrow him.

Once the police had decimated the Muslim Brotherhood—
with the massacre at Rabaa, the round-up of the leadership, the
arrest of thousands of men and women, and the total clampdown
on media—they turned their attention to the revolutionary youth.
A colonial-era British law outlawing protest was re-animated and
turned against the street, and in November 2013, three months
after Rabaa, Alaa was arrested again. He was among the very first
targets, along with two of the co-founders of the 6 April Youth
Movement, Ahmed Maher and Mohammed Adel.

In this next spell inside, Alaa writes four major essays in four
months ('Graffiti for Two', 'Autism', 'Everybody Knows' and
'Lysenko Country'). His pieces are read widely, published in
multiple newspapers simultaneously, reported on as news in the
national press. The revolution did not yet believe itself to be
over. But the machinery of the state, the police, the judiciary,
the media, have set to work on grinding the disobedience out of
the people. Alaa's trial, ostensibly for organizing a protest, is long
and complex. One judge recuses himself, and his replacement
has Alaa arrested as a fugitive as he stands outside the courthouse, barred from entering. Over 2014 he is released briefly
twice—for two months in the spring, and one month in the
autumn. But it was in the summer that Alaa's father died.

Ahmed Seif el-Islam was a key figure in his son's life. A
member of a militant communist cell who was imprisoned and
tortured in the 1980s and emerged from incarceration with a
profound attachment to the idea of the law and the opportunities that it might present, even within a dictatorial police state.
He went on to found the Hisham Mubarak Law Centre and
his clients ranged from the young men charged with the Taba
terrorist bombings of 2004, to dissident bloggers, to striking
workers, to the men persecuted for their perceived sexuality in
the notorious Queen Boat Case. The positions he took, and
the organizations he helped build played a part in creating the

conditions for the 2011 revolution. But, in 2014, exhausted by his years on the frontlines, and with two of his children in prison (Alaa's sister, Sanaa, had been arrested recently at a protest for prisoners), his heart gave out.

Eighteen days later, Alaa was briefly released from prison, long enough to deliver an address at the memorial for his father, but one month later, on 27 October, was sentenced to five years in prison. Inside, he went quiet for a year.

He appears for us again in 2016—first with a short reflection written for the *Guardian*, then with three major pieces on the changing economics of the digital revolution. 'The Birth of a Brave New World' trilogy is a breathtaking display of how wide-ranging and original a thinker Alaa is. Written from prison, almost entirely from memory, he writes a precise and prescient critique of the relationship between Silicon Valley, venture capital, labour and technology that remains relevant and illuminating. Alaa's imprisonment does not only deprive Egyptians, or Arabic speakers, of one of their most important voices: we are all the poorer for his absence.

2017's 'A Portrait of the Activist Outside his Prison' lays out Alaa's personal history and the lessons he learned as a 'techie' activist in the years leading up to the 2011 revolution. This is followed by a letter to the RightsCon conference in California where Alaa had given the keynote address in 2011 before returning to Egypt to face the Military Prosecutor. 'You Have Not Yet Been Defeated' is one of the few pieces addressed specifically to an international audience, and puts forward his ideas on how to tackle the feeling of helplessness taking hold during the global authoritarian surge of the late 2010s.

Alaa does not write again until he's released, under strict parole conditions, in March 2019. We find a different writer now, one emerging into a world under the brutal and complete control of the Sisi regime, condemned to spend every night in his local police station for the coming five years, overwhelmed by all the re-adjustments he has to make to his new half-life outside prison. He is angry, funny, revealing, scarred. He begins to write at night, locked in what he calls his Kiosk of Solitude, a wooden structure in the courtyard of Doqqi police station that he occupies from 6 p.m. to 6 a.m. He writes about the unfolding revolutions in Sudan and Algeria, and about the climate crisis, but is really gearing up to publish a monumental fourteen-part essay on life in prison: 'Vengeance in Victory: A Personal Introduction'.

Shortly afterwards he completes a playful, unorthodox text about healing and regeneration, 'Five Metaphors on Healing', and we feel that we are in the hands of a writer experimenting in public, experimenting *with* his public. The openness and com-mitment to truth that made him into a revolutionary leader is searching for expression in a new world, sharing himself and his attempts to reconstitute himself with a vanquished public also unable to meaningfully reconstruct itself under the Sisi regime.

Around this time some small street protests erupt, triggered by a building contractor revealing details about government corruption—details shocking even to a populace that expects a high level of corruption. Seeing these small protests as a security failure, Sisi re-organizes the divisions of power and responsi-bility between the state apparatuses. A massive sweep of activists begins, Alaa is one of dozens of targeted arrests (among thou-sands of people arrested randomly from the street) and is taken from inside the police station where he was already detained every night. Everyone arrested is charged with 'belonging to a terrorist organization' and 'spreading false news', and none are sent to trial but are kept instead in a state of 'preventive deten-tion pending trial', that can be renewed without trial. Legally, this is subject to a two-year limit. We will cross that threshold as this book goes to print, though we expect that, as with the majority of political prisoners in Egypt today, Alaa's imprisonment will, one way or another, continue uninterrupted.

For the first five months, the prisoner is brought before the prosecutor every fifteen days to be interrogated and, if necessary, have their detention renewed. It is in these sessions that Alaa creates a new form of public delivery. Though he is deprived of pen and paper, of newspapers or a radio, of any correspondence, Alaa turns the sessions before the prosecutor, in the presence of his lawyers, into a public platform in which he addresses—literally—the state. Afterwards, his lawyers would reconstruct from memory what he said as best they could to be published on social media by his family.

On one reading, the progression of pieces in the book mirrors the overall flow of history since 2011: optimism, ideas and public engagement are besieged by the unrelenting military state until its prisons have swollen to consume all existence and intellect. Alaa's imprisonment is a lived and live metaphor for a country imprisoned. But Alaa is never content to be a metaphor—even from deep inside the carceral state he engages practically, logically, with his captor. When prison underwrites an entire system of governance, when prison is the answer to every one of a government's problems, then the existential question is: how do you actually close that prison? Beginning with ideas he first sketches out in 2013's 'Who Represents the Bourgeoisie?', picking up again in his 'Interview with *Mada Masr*' on brief release in 2019, and then fully and powerfully expressed in his 'Statements to the Prosecutor' we find him returning to the question of how history materializes; how to break out of a political system in which accommodation of opposing thought—from all sides—has become impossible; how to chase reformist goals with revolutionary zeal—because anything more ambitious will, right now, only perpetuate an inescapable cycle of coups, massacres, polarization and insurgency.

Alaa is a radical idealist *and* a practical organizer; a writer able to talk about both the grand sweep of history and minor bureaucratic procedures, as coherent in the middle of an angry crowd or giving condolences in a martyrs' house or on stage at a tech conference in California; a voice that speaks not only as 'Alaa'— an individual endlessly persecuted—but as an agent of historical change, that speaks knowing that it will pay the price, yet *must* speak. He exists as multiple things at once, as an anti-capitalist considering how to bring the bourgeoisie into the balance of powers against a military authority; as a captive of a deaf, dysfunctional state, advising that state on how better to govern; as a prisoner who is always trying to look beyond the warden.

Readers who know Alaa's work in its original Arabic will know that his language is as multi-layered as his thinking, as poetic as his ideals and dense with historical and cultural references that assume a shared, comradely intelligence. We've done what we can to help the English reader with footnotes, without getting in the way of Alaa's texts.

Dozens of people have volunteered their time to bring this book into being, and we are presenting it without any names because the chains of transmission from prison are unnamed, because authoritarianism relies on consequences being unforeseeable, and because our only wish is to present Alaa's words to you.

Alaa is currently allowed one visit from one family member for twenty minutes once a month. It takes place behind glass and through monitored headsets. He knows that this book is being published. He approves, and he likes the title. Beyond that, it has been left in the hands of his editors, our hands, and we can only hope that it does justice to the scale of his thought, the agility of his mind and the bravery of his words.

The Editors, July 2021

2011

WHO WILL WRITE THE CONSTITUTION?

It's been four months since the revolution toppled Hosni Mubarak, President of Egypt for the previous thirty years, and the Supreme Council of the Armed Forces assumed official control of the country as a transitional body to oversee a democratic transfer of power.

26 June 1955, Kliptown, near Johannesburg: thousands of people gather in a space much like our Tahrir squares,[1] fanning out in a field to take part in the Congress of the People and to vote on the Freedom Charter. A revolutionary takes to the stage and poetically recites the charter. The packed square thunders with chants of 'Africa! Africa!'

For two days, Kliptown lived the most important democratic experiment in history—before it was subdued by apartheid police forces. But, as usual, the police arrived too late to suppress freedom. The charter was adopted and became the Constitution of the South African liberation movement. Four decades later, it was the principal reference for the new constitution of the free South Africa.

We, the people of South Africa, declare for all our country and the world to know: the people are the authority, all groups shall have equal rights and the country's wealth belongs to the people. The people will share in the land that they work, and all will be equal before the law. All will have equal rights. There will be work and security and the doors of culture and learning will be opened. There will be

---

[1] Plural because there were multiple revolutionary squares in Egypt, but Tahrir was their centre.

housing, security and comfort, peace and friendship. These
freedoms we will fight for, side by side, throughout our
lives, until we have won our liberty.

These articles were not written from the stage, nor did the
thousands gathered in the square claim to speak in the name of
the people out of nowhere. Months of preparation preceded the
Congress, during which some 50,000 volunteers travelled the
length and breadth of the country asking every person they met
a simple question: *What is the South Africa you dream of?*

The volunteers collected responses and sent them to elected
committees in each local area who then compiled them into
lists of demands, which were then sent to elected committees
representing each district, which collated and summarized them
before forwarding them to the committee drafting the Freedom
Charter. The Congress was attended by all elected committee
members, as well as representatives of trade unions, revolutionary parties and other grassroots organizations.

The people—all of them—wrote the charter and, in turn, the
Constitution.

The idea was born when the African National Congress
(ANC—Nelson Mandela's party) found itself at an impasse.
With participation in the anti-apartheid struggle declining,
young party leaders decided to expand the struggle into social
and economic issues and started a campaign for a fair minimum
wage. They quickly realized the gulf separating them, the political activists and elites, from the masses—so they decided to
organize the Congress and draft a charter that gave the grassroots
a leading role. They decided on a campaign of political awareness
in which the masses would be the teacher, and the politicians
and activists would be the students.

The Congress and the charter radically transformed the party.
Firstly, no one party could have organized such a process, the

sheer scale of the proposal forced various anti-regime parties and movements to come together across ideological, ethnic, class and religious lines—which then gave birth to an inclusive national liberation movement.

Secondly, on the ideological level, the Congress settled the debate within the ANC between an Afrocentric vision that saw the liberation of black South Africans as part of the larger fight against colonialism on the continent, and a belief that the solution was a common struggle for equality among everyone who lived in the nation regardless of ethnicity, including white South Africans.

Third, the Congress offered the first genuine opportunity for the political elite to become familiar with the problems and aspirations of farmers.

The adoption of the charter changed history. In the minds of the people, the regime fell that day—though it would take another four decades to actually come down. After having been divided by apartheid and by colonialism into separate ethnicities and tribes, the people were reborn as a unified entity with a single goal and vision that was passed down through generations—generations that were willing to pay the price in torture and imprisonment and martyrdom. The people protected the legitimacy of the charter until the apartheid regime fell and the people remained. The legitimacy of the square became embodied in an excellent constitution inspired by the Freedom Charter, and the people continued to protect their charter and their constitution.

Today, in another square, we are arguing about the drafting of a new constitution for the Second Egyptian Republic, gripped by a logic that says those who will draft the constitution will themselves represent the people. So our debate is limited to when the constitution will be drafted and the best way to select our representatives. Naturally, the elites think it's their destiny and their right to be elected, and sometimes confuse being an elected representative with being a guardian of the people. Honestly, there's no difference here between the Constitution First camp and the Parliament First camp and I worry that they've already agreed that the people's role ends at the ballot box.

It's assumed that if there's a consensus in place between the different political forces then all the people are represented. The evidence, however, is that all major political groups in Egypt—including the most popular, the Brotherhood—are out of touch with the masses. This was apparent in Tahrir, where the political parties, movements and activists found themselves to be a somewhat isolated minority, even if they played leading roles at times. This distance from the people, if it is not recognized, will have a negative effect on the drafting of the constitution.

There is a lesson for us in the experience of our 'Wefaq' committees.[2] Popular participation leads to a revolutionary charter composed in lyrical language calling for the doors of education and culture to be thrown open, while a closed-door meeting of experts results in a noted judge suggesting that the votes of educated people should carry more weight. Can you imagine such an idea coming out of a national consensus that included those not fortunate enough to have got an education? This is guardianship, then—not representation, nor consensus.

Yes, Mubarak tailored the old constitution to his political order. But the truth is that many of the crimes of his regime were in direct and flagrant contradiction with articles of that constitution. Even the worst constitution doesn't sanction torture. The Constitution itself did not protect us.

It's on us to ask: what value is a constitution drafted without

---

2   'Wefaq Committee' or 'The Conference for National Accord'. One of many initiatives launched by the SCAF to produce guiding directives and recommendations for the upcoming constitution. It was composed of several committees, e.g. the electoral system committee, the public freedoms committee, the legislation committee, and the armed forces committee. The criteria for selection of participants was unclear and the internal working processes were loose. It was boycotted and criticized by several political groups, including the Muslim Brotherhood.

genuine popular participation? Even an exemplary text is nothing more than ink on paper without a balance of power to apply and protect it. The Freedom Charter was written by the people. Together with the constitution that emanated from it, they gave rise to a real social contract and became a part of the people's identity passed down through the generations. And the people became the protectors of their constitutional and revolutionary legitimacy.

Here we have the opposite. 'The 'Wefaq' Assembly has had disastrous consequences, such as enshrining the army as guardian of the civil state. This 'sovereign' institution, with vast repressive capacities and a long record of violations and interference in governance, will no longer be subject to any oversight by elected bodies.

Let us be more humble. Mandela and his comrades needed the public to educate them politically. Why assume that we're any better? Since we've agreed that the constitution is one of the key goals of our ongoing revolution, why not include the revolutionary masses in its drafting? Do we need to try and emulate the South African experiment and build a collective project to sketch out the Egypt we all dream of? What would happen if tens of thousands of people were involved in assembling this dream? Maybe we will come to a genuine consensus and be unified again. We might find priorities that have been overlooked. Political parties, for example, typically ignore, or only pay lip service to, environmental issues. But maybe if we listened to the fishermen on our lakes and heard their complaints about the destruction of fisheries by multinational corporations, we'd discover how urgent this issue is, how it's linked to social justice and in need of genuine constitutional protection. Maybe we need to give the people of Burullus, who have long fought for potable water, a chance to educate us about what it means to be denied fresh water, and to remind us that water is a basic human right.

Our current debate over who will draft the constitution should not be focused on content, but rather on how we select the Constituent Assembly. The constitutional amendments and the constitutional declaration did not provide details. We can agree, for example, on proportional representation for women, youth, and religious minorities, as well as representation from each governorate, quotas for representatives of professional syndicates, labour and farmers' unions, seats for activists, rights advocates, artists, and so on. But even more important is agreeing on how the Constituent Assembly will operate.

We first need to abandon the idea that drafting a constitution is a simple matter, one that a few experts can make short work of by referring to existing constitutions. A single major issue—such as the question of having a presidential system versus a parliamentary one—requires extensive, perhaps weeks-long, discussions. The discussions must be public and hearings should be held to allow citizens, civil society, and our grassroots and political movements to take part.

If we combine a popular document that reflects our shared aspirations and dreams, a representative Constituent Assembly elected by the people (directly or via Parliament), and operating mechanisms open to civil society, we will indeed establish a second republic based on a genuine social contract, real national consensus, and full constitutional, popular and revolutionary legitimacy. Then we can say that power is truly with the people.

Published on 10 July 2011 in *al-Shorouk*

———

The next day, Alaa and a coalition of partners launch the 'Let's Write Our Constitution' initiative, an attempt to mobilize thousands of volunteers across Egypt to create mass participation in the writing of the new constitution.

TO BE WITH THE MARTYRS,
FOR THAT IS FAR BETTER

On Friday, 30 September 2011, a mob of Islamists set fire to a church in Marinab, a village in the Edfu district of southern Egypt, and set about terrorizing local Coptic families. While Christian leaders were calling for help, the Governor of the province, General Mostafa al-Sayyed, appeared on several television channels denying anything was happening. This sparked a wave of anger among Egyptian Christians, Copts, and in the following days thousands of protestors—mostly Coptic, but with Muslim and secular allies—occupied the space outside the National Television & Radio Building, also known as Maspero. This sit-in was violently dispersed on 4 October.

A new march set out for Maspero from Cairo's Shubra district five days later. Though it was pelted with bottles and stones by onlookers and plainclothes agitators, the march made it to Maspero. There, it was attacked by soldiers with live ammunition, and protestors were run over by Armoured Personnel Carriers (APCs).

National television announced that Coptic demonstrators were attacking the Army, had killed three soldiers, and called on Egyptians to take to the streets to defend the military. Meanwhile, army troops raided the offices of two independent TV channels, al-Hurra and 25 January, that were streaming live coverage from outside Maspero, and cut their feeds.

26 protestors and one soldier were killed that night. 350 people were injured and several hundred were arrested. This came to be known as the Maspero Massacre.

The title of the article that follows, published ten days later, refers to St Paul's Epistle to the Philippians: 'My desire is to depart and to be with Christ, for that is far better.' The phrase, in its Arabic version, is commonly used at the beginning of obituaries of Egyptian Christians.

Two days in the morgue, two days with corpses struggling to hold on to the glory of martyrdom in a crumbling government hospital, struggling against the whole of Mubarak's unfallen regime, against Mubarak's soldiers who ran them over, Mubarak's prosecutors who declined to investigate, Mubarak's media who branded them not martyrs but murderers. Struggling against Mubarak-era superstitions that claim autopsies violate the dead and can never bring justice, against the clerics and priests of Authority who preach that those who seek justice in this life abandon the right to it in the next, struggling against Mubarak's sectarianism that turns poor against poor and hides who has stolen their daily bread.

Two days in the company of merciful death and merciless shame. Why, Lord, do you take mostly the poor? How does the bullet, the tank, know the difference? The blood's the same, the grave's the same, but we have cheated martyrdom again and again.

Egypt is a heartbreaker, she only chooses the most precious— and Mina Daniel[3] was the best of us. Without him, we would never have prevailed in the morgue.

BLESSED ARE THE MEEK

They came to the hospital in their hundreds, searching for wounded bodies to treat and murdered bodies to bury. They came to the hospital searching for shelter from the night all their fears came to life. They came to the hospital searching for people to share in their rage, for strength in numbers. They came as the church's flock—and, outside, a mob laid siege to the hospital

---

3   Mina Daniel was a prominent youth activist, a Copt, who sought to unify the energies of Coptic disenfranchisement with the wider demands of the revolution. He was killed at Maspero.

(maybe these are the 'honourable citizens' who Mubarak's soldiers are addressing day and night), backed-up by the army, the
self-proclaimed Defenders of the Revolution—to make it clear
that the church is the only flock they'll ever be part of.

We came looking for our comrade from our square, the one
with the charming smile, Mina, who belongs to us and to whom
we belong. Martyrdom chose Mina because he belongs to the
flock of the square and the revolution. That's what his family
told us, as they insisted we, his friends, be part of every decision
in the hospital—*because they're his friends from the square*. Mina
struggled from the afterlife to open the martyrs' families hearts
to us and bind us into a shared struggle. The blood's the same,
the tears are the same: and as we saw the truth in the tears of the
martyr's mothers—truth that was completely absent from the
television coverage—they saw the truth in ours. They understood that we were Mina's comrades, and forgot to check our
names' provenance with the usual wariness.

The hospital issued its report in line with state television's
broadcasts: did they die of heart failure, or was it a fight? The
priests urged that they be buried quickly—it was hot and there
are no fridges in the morgue. Here, we intervened, with the
square's ego and innocence: but what about justice? What about
retribution? Their bodies are the last chance to prove guilt, so we
need a forensic medical report.

What madness is this, to cut open our children's bodies
looking for a justice that we've never seen? Not even by accident? What justice when we are poor? What justice when we are
Copts? What justice when murder reigns? Don't you understand
that we are the weak?

But in our ranks was Mina, and it was his sister who first
agreed to an autopsy, and then one by one they were convinced,
reluctantly, as friends insisted and lawyers gave courage. Hours
of tears and debates and embraces. We fought time with slabs

of ice and miserable fans, hoping our love would be enough to preserve the sanctity of the bodies.

By the morning of the second day the prosecutor found half the families now demanding autopsies, so the judge issued his decree: he either issues burial permits for all, or requests autopsies. Are we not all equal in death?

And of course the priests didn't hold back: *the Bishop will soon pray over their comrades, if you delay he'll have returned to his quarters. Have mercy on your children. Their reward in heaven will be great.*

We stood firm, a unified front against the regime, but this time the vanguard was in the mind, the firing line across the hearts and as we'd defeated them with chants and bricks, so we defeated them with solidarity. After a long fight, the prosecutor produced the autopsy order for all the bodies, on condition that we guarantee the security of the forensic team.

Yes, first we were responsible for securing our demonstrations; then we were responsible for securing public facilities; and here we are today, responsible for the security of state employees when asking the state to act as a state. We didn't bother to ask about the role of the police and the army: the answer was clear on the martyrs' bodies.

We told the families the autopsies would take time, let's move the bodies to the Chief Coroner's morgue at Zeinhom where the facilities are better. The fear returned to their eyes: yes, Mina had made them believe in their country, but the rumour mill never stopped turning and the gang of Honourable Citizens at the gate kept everyone on edge. They were too polite to say it to us, but we understood: they would not leave the safety of the Coptic Quarter. We could not know what evil waited for us outside.

And so it was on us to secure the hospital, and guarantee suitable working conditions for the forensic team. We needed to evacuate thousands of scared people, and hold back the thousands enraged. We were but a handful of outsiders but it was on us, ironically, to act like a kind of riot police. All our new coalition had to hold on to was its unity.

The forensics team began its work under our protection, watched by our doctors and our lawyers, our unknown soldiers, who know far more of killing, torture and massacres than any medical examiner. The team started their work and we were on alert in case a family member entered and saw the knife cutting into their son's body; in case our unified front would break in the face of the mob outside, or the rage of the bereaved.

MY KINGDOM IS NOT OF THIS WORLD

Vultures can't pick at a unified front. The worst are the ambulance chasers, their poisoned, honeyed words: *are you sure about this lawyer? She's just a kid. I've got years of experience. And who are these guys? Who are these Muslims? How can you trust them?*

You'd been warning us for months, Mina: Maspero must join Tahrir, the Copts' demands must be the people's demands, and the people's must be the Copts'. The way is hard, Mina. The regime's violence rains randomly, but these guys know where to cut. We spent the whole day quelling rumours and accusations, winning back the crowd's confidence, calming them.

At first we thought our role was like the riot police, but we soon saw how different it really was. After that day I'll never understand how any security agency, anywhere in the world, can think that violence is an effective way to deal with a crowd— whether furious or terrified. Who convinced every government on earth that armed confrontation calms the masses down? We had no weapon to face down their rage but our embraces, and with tears of mourning we managed to drive out the fallacy of a militaristic sectarian reality with the truth of the dream of a free Egypt.

Oh Mina, our revolution is so fragile a stray bullet could end it. Oh Mina, our revolution is so strong, an embrace could

save it. Oh Mina, with you I understood the lessons of the
prophets—but when will the military understand?

From the start, the forensic experts complained about the
conditions, the lack of equipment, the people watching over
them—but in the end they did their jobs. When the team was
close to completing the autopsies and started writing the causes
of death a rumour exploded that they were faking the report. A
report can record a single wound as the cause of death though
these bodies bear several, and so a rumour took hold, the crowd
rose up, and our front was broken.

From the brink of victory to the depths of distress. The families
believed in a dream of justice and let us cut into their children's
bodies, missed the honour of the Bishop praying over them,
risked delaying their burials further: they sacrificed all that we
asked them to sacrifice even though they weren't with us in the
beginning—and now they demand a guarantee. They need to *feel*
justice—but we're offering them technical words and legal jargon.
Why does the report say they were run over with a 'heavy vehicle'
when we all know it a was a military APC? What's this 'explosive
projectile'? Why not write 'military bullets'? Didn't you promise us
justice? Where's the name of the killer that we all know?

We were so drowning in minutiae of details that I didn't
realize when we'd actually won. But at some point I looked up
and saw that the hospital staff, the doctors and the priests had
all switched over to our side. Mina, what did you do? Did the
weakness and poverty of your family fire their conscience, or
did your strength open their minds? Did we really clear all those
hurdles in just a few hours? Even the forensics team came over
to our side. The only solution was to sit with each family one by
one, explain the meaning of 'causes of death' and the details to
be added to the forensic reports, explain the role of the prosecutor, and the role of the lawyers. The forensic doctor caught
the bug and was transformed from a bureaucrat into a guardian

of justice: maybe when forced to translate the language of the report—a language he was used to filing for the powerful—to the language of the weak, he remembered that justice is always with the weak? I saw them describe the features of the martyrs to their families to assure them that they were not just corpses to them, that they cared about them and their memory. I saw that which you had given your life for, if only for a moment.

On our way to the church, the triumph was complete. No one checked the names of those carrying the martyrs or leading the chants. Was it a Muslim who led us in chanting:

We'll do right by them
Or we'll die like them!

What a question. The blood's the same, the tears are the same.

TURN THE OTHER CHEEK

Before the Coptic Hospital we were in another hospital, far from the action, waiting for an x-ray on Ahmad's foot, who was shot with a live round.

We found Ahmad on Talaat Harb Street, trying with his comrades to save the homeland by returning to Tahrir Square. It had been only a few hours since the killing, but they didn't think about asymmetries of power, whether they had the numbers, or how to deal with the 'unarmed' (according to the international press conference) forces shooting at them. Ahmed and his comrades were only concerned about leaving the square to the paid-up mob marching under the blessing of the police and the army, chanting for Islam. We all knew it was an orchestrated protest: an attempt to cover up a military massacre with a sectarian story and frame the Salafis.

Ahmed was like a mythical hero, refusing to go to hospital, telling his friends the wound is light, probably just birdshot.

But we convinced him to go to a private hospital away from the action, and carried him away on our shoulders. In the taxi he told us how he had been arrested by the Army, tasted their torture, faced the 'integrity' of their military courts. He told us about his injuries from the treacherous Battle of Abbaseya. The wounds did not stop him from going down to face the bullets again.

At the hospital, once it was confirmed he had been shot with a live round and not just a shotgun pellet, a policeman appeared. Ahmed impressed us with his answers, cool but challenging; he impressed us even more with his disgust at the cop's comment, 'so you're a Muslim?' If Ahmed were a Christian, would he have arrested him?

We didn't see that Ahmed could be weak, like us, until he collapsed into our arms and wept as the doctor sterilized his wounds. We only noticed how young he was when he answered his phone nervously: 'What Maspero, mama? What's that got to do with me? I'm just out with my friends.'

Does General Hamdy Badeen[4] realize that in our unified front are those who fear their loving mothers more than they fear bullets and APCs? Can Tantawi hear us when we carry Mina to pay his last respects to the square, can he hear us chanting *'Ya Musheer, ya Musheer! We cheer the bridegroom from Tahrir!*[5] Does anyone from the Army understand the true meaning of the mother of Khaled Said paying her respects to the mother of Mina Daniel? Or have they forgotten the blood and the tears and the embraces and the dream—and so can never again have a place among us, though we have harboured so many who have wronged us before.

Published on 20 October 2011 in *al-Shorouk*

---

4   Member of the Supreme Council of the Armed Forces and the ranking general at the Maspero massacre.

5   *Al-Musheer* is the rank of Field Marshal, commander of the Armed Forces: General Tantawi. The bridegroom is entering the afterlife.

———

Al-Ahram Online, 24 October 2011: Egyptian bloggers and activists Alaa Abd el-Fattah and Bahaa Saber have been summoned by the military prosecution for questioning.

Abd el-Fattah is out of the country but is expected to appear in front of the military prosecution tomorrow, Tuesday 25 October 2011.

It is as yet unclear why the two activists have been summoned by the military prosecution, although speculation abounds that they will be asked to testify as eye witnesses to the 9 October Maspero clashes.

24 October 2011

@Alaa: Detention is a lot easier if you're with friends. I'm warning you, I'll snitch on all the best twitterati so I'm not on my own :-P

KEYNOTE ADDRESS TO RIGHTSCON 2011

Alaa has travelled to California to give a keynote address at the RightsCon conference in Silicon Valley, which he delivers in English. While there he learns he has been summoned to the military prosecutor.

Hi. Let me just take thirty seconds off topic and talk about extraordinary justice, which is what I'm going to be facing, Military Prosecutors. There's obviously no due process. Civilians shouldn't be facing that. I urge you to find ways to stand in solidarity with anyone who is facing extraordinary justice. You've had your share of it with the Guantanamo detainees here in this country. So, if you care about human rights, you know what it's like, and you know why it's important. There are around 12,000 civilians in Egypt who are currently in military prison. Some of them for participating in the revolution that the military pretends to have protected and sided with, some for very minor offenses. Mostly, they've been randomly detained around major events in which it is the military who has committed the crimes and not the civilians. So, I urge you to find ways to stand in solidarity with anyone who is facing extraordinary justice. Thank you.

[*Applause*]

Now, for the topic. So I guess I'm here as an activist, as a footsoldier in a revolution to talk about how tech companies can find ways to maintain and promote and protect and respect the human rights of their users. Now, that's a topic I'm quite

cynical about. Companies are not really likely to do any of
that. Corporations are not really likely to do any of that. The
conflicts . . . it's not exactly that there is a conflict of interest. I
think we're all here because we know that it's actually possible
to go about our business without infringing on people's rights
and without allowing in tools that are being used to infringe
on people's rights, but the relationships, the structure of relationships between power is such that even if it's possible, even
if it doesn't cost much, even if it's not going to affect the profit
margins, it's probably not going to happen, but it also sometimes
conflicts with the profit margin in very funny ways. So, from the
perspective of an activist, some very normal features can be quite
annoying, can be quite problematic. Real name policies, rate
limits on Twitter, real name policies on Facebook or anything
like that, that is actually problematic. If you're trying to mobilize people the way mobile companies are trying to monetize
every single transaction: that limits what we can do. But this is
the business model. I don't expect either Twitter or Facebook or
the mobile companies to change their business models just for
activists, so that is not going to happen.

But here's something that could happen:

Companies . . . If governments are trying to pass legislation or
change regulation and it's going to affect their profit, then companies *do* stand up, do make a noise, do try and change things.
But if the same governments are doing something sinister that's
going to affect humans, that's going to affect their users, they're
not likely to talk about it. So, we've all heard about the 'kill
switch', how Egypt was completely cut off from the internet for
a few days during the first uprising in the revolution. Vodafone
and Co., their defence, their constant defence, is that this was
the law, that there was nothing that they could do. But they
knew about that law two years in advance. And they never made
a noise.

We, in Egypt, had ways of fighting unjust laws. We could take it to the Constitutional Court, we could do a campaign against it, it might have been possible for us to get rid of that law before the revolution happened *if* the companies had chosen to actually expose the fact that it had happened. That law was almost secret. But they knew about it because there were meetings and a process was set up with them so that they could figure out how to do a kill switch. There were test runs that were done in small cities. But they failed to object. They failed to object publicly, and they failed to object to the government.

The reason why they failed to object, in my opinion, is that it's actually a conspiracy. It's not a conspiracy in which they sit in a dark room and agree to screw us, but it's a conspiracy in which interests coincide. In which interests that should not exist coincide. The market is highly centralized, highly monopolized, and that is done to maintain the privilege that these corporations have. In exchange, these corporations will also extend the privilege to the government and allow them to be more in control. The conspiracy doesn't happen because people decide. It just happens because their interests happen to coincide in this way.

Now, the same company, Vodafone, claims that they are powerless against government. They are a poor defenceless company that can't resist an order—but is actually able to resist paying tax in the UK. So, they *do* have leverage over government. So, here's the first thing you could do: you could act like any normal citizen, like any organization that is made of people, and engage with government normally. If you hear about plans, or if you're getting orders that you do not like, challenge them. Challenge them *legally*. I'm not expecting corporations to become revolutionaries, but you *can* do things. You can take it to court, you can resist, you can ask for due process.

We're not even sure that Vodafone—of course, I'm just using them as the example, but all the communications companies—that they got a proper order. The law existed, but it was a moment of chaos. We suspect that they just got a phone call, and they started implementing it. There is a process probably, a written order should have been issued and so on. They could have stalled this operation if they wanted to. They didn't choose to do it. So, that's something that is easy that you can do. But you're not likely to do it anyway, right? That's not going to happen. Let's be honest. What needs to happen is a revolution. What needs to happen is a complete change in the order of things, so that we are making these amazing products, and we're making a living, but we're not trying to monopolize, and we're not trying to control the internet, and we're not trying to control our users, and we're not complicit with governments, we're not Amazon who's removing WikiLeaks, and we're not Vodafone who is happily cutting off tax and cutting off people's communication and so on.

So, here's another thing that you could do: go occupy somewhere. But you're not likely to do that because that's not likely to succeed, right? It's a small movement, and it doesn't look like it's going anywhere and so on. So, what *can* you do? What *can* you do realistically that takes into account what you are about?

Well, here's what you can do. Ignore the activists. Ignore the revolutionaries. We have to face bullets. We have to face military trials. It doesn't matter really what you do. It doesn't matter if Facebook is going to reveal my information or not. I have to assume that I'm being constantly watched, that everything about me is public. It doesn't matter. But what *matters* is ordinary users, ordinary users who use your products to practise their agency. When you decide that they cannot decide to choose a pseudonym, then you are negating them the right to negotiate their identity. The right to negotiate your identity is—it's not in the Charter of Human Rights, but it's actually essential to most rights—women know what I'm talking about because you have to negotiate your identity constantly: you are someone else in the home, and you're someone else in the workplace, you have to negotiate who you are, sometimes I have to be nice and the mother type, sometimes I have to be the bitch at the office. If you're gay, if you're from a religious minority, if you're *whatever*, negotiated identity is very important. I get to *choose* whether to reveal who I am and how to reveal who I am, and decide who I am on my own terms and on my own basis.

When you design products that help me assert my agency but then interfere in how I get to assert my identity, then you're denying me something very important. Then you're making teenagers threatened because their parents—and their peers— can continue their pressure in ways that aren't even possible in the physical world. I can hide from my mom and smoke, but I can't hide my Facebook from my mum. Then what's going on there? How do I retain that right? So, think about the rights of the ordinary users. Think about them in ways that go beyond *privacy / government is going to see this / what's going on*. This is about who I am. This is about my identity. This is about how I express myself. This is about how I communicate with the world, and that is a place in which I don't think your profit conflicts with the rights of your users, and I don't think your government really cares that much.

You *can* do a better job at it.

As for the activists, we always find a way.

Thank you.

Delivered on 25 October 2011 in California

———

Two days later Alaa flies back to Egypt. In Cairo he holds a small council at his parents' apartment to decide what his position will

*be in front of the Military Prosecutor. Since SCAF took power in
February at least twelve thousand people have been tried in military
courts, by military prosecutors, in front of military judges. Alaa's
sister, Mona Seif, is the head of a growing national campaign group
called 'No to Military Trials' that is increasingly generating public
awareness about—and outrage against—this parallel penal system
that is being used to repress the constant demonstrations and labour
actions going on across a country that considers itself in an ongoing
state of revolution.*

RETURN TO MUBARAK'S PRISONS

30 October: Alaa presents himself to the Military Prosecutor but refuses to answer their questions, arguing that he is a civilian and should not be tried by the military, and that the military are themselves accused of the violence at Maspero.

He is arrested.

His charges include unlawful assembly, stealing military hardware, damage to military property and assaulting a soldier. The mainstream media is rife with stories of Alaa ripping doors of APCs and hurling caches of weapons into the Nile.

The next night, several thousand people march through Downtown Cairo and surround the Appeals Prison in Bab al Khalq, calling for Alaa's freedom. But they ultimately go home. Two days later he is moved to Torah Prison.

He and his partner, Manal Hassan, are eight months into their first pregnancy, their child conceived shortly after Mubarak's fall.

I'd never have guessed I'd be repeating the experience, five years later. That after a revolution that overthrew a tyrant, I'd return to his prisons.

They come back to me, the memories, all the details. The skill of sleeping on the floor with eight colleagues in a cell four metres long and two wide, the songs of prison and the conversations of the convicted. But I cannot remember how I kept my glasses safe while I slept. They've been stepped on three times in one day. I realize they're the same ones that were with me last time, when I was imprisoned in 2006, and that I'm locked up again now, again 'pending trial', on similarly flimsy charges—the only difference is we've swapped a National Security Prosecutor for a Military Prosecutor: a change in keeping with the military moment we're living.

Last time, my imprisonment was shared with fifty colleagues from the Kefaya movement. This time, I'm alone, in a cell with eight wronged men, the guilty among them wronged like the innocent.

When they learned I was one of the 'Revolutionary Youth' they started cussing out the revolution for failing to clean up the Ministry of the Interior.[6] I spent the first two days listening to their stories of torture in the custody of an unreformable police force that takes its recent defeat out on the bodies of the poor, both the innocent and the guilty.

From their stories I heard the truth about the triumphant restoration of national security. Two of my cellmates are first-timers, young men without an atom of violence in them. Their charge? Organized crime! Yes, Abu Malek is an armed gang of one. Now I understand what the Interior Ministry means when it regales us every day with news of armed gangs it has arrested. We can congratulate ourselves on the return of security.

In the few hours when the sun comes into our dark cell we read what a past cellmate wrote in beautiful Arabic script on the walls; four walls covered from floor to ceiling with Qur'anic verses, prayers and reflections. And what reads like a powerful desire to repent.

The next day we discover in a corner the date of execution of our cellmate and our tears conquer us.

The guilty make plans for repentance. But what can the innocent do?

My thoughts wander. I hear the General's speech on the radio as he inaugurates the tallest flagpole in the world—how it breaks every record. I wonder: does naming Mina Daniel as an

---

6   The Ministry of the Interior is shorthand for the police—from riot police to secret police. In Arabic, the word used is simply *al-dakhleyya*, the Interior.

'instigator' in my casefile break the records for shamelessness?
They don't just kill the man and walk in his funeral procession
but they spit on his body and accuse it of a crime. Does this cell
break the record for cockroach density? Abu Malek interrupts
my thoughts: 'I swear to God if this revolution doesn't get the
wronged their rights, it will sink without a trace.'

Written in Cell No 19, Appeals Prison,
Bab el-Khalq, Cairo
Published on 2 November 2011
in *al-Shorouk* and the *Guardian*

THE HOSTAGE STATE

During Erdoğan's visit to Egypt, a joke made the rounds on the internet. Islamists, secularists and the military all aspire to 'the Turkish model'—which proves, goes the joke, that none of them know a thing about Turkey.

Today, many of us aspire to 'the Tunisian model', particularly since their successful election of a Constituent Assembly[7]—but I worry it might also mean that nobody really understands what's happened in Tunisia.

We know for certain that the military and their disciples are no fans of the Tunisian model. Not because Tunisia is producing a constitution first, nor because of the major electoral victory the Islamists won—these are minor details—but because an elected authority will assume full powers to initiate a genuine period of transition.

In the early days, Tunisia saw a debate over the Constituent Assembly's powers, through which the people and political forces managed to make the Assembly a proper legislative body, rather than a committee tasked only with writing the new constitution. Although the primary function of the Constituent Assembly *is* to draft the constitution, most of the lists put the candidates' and parties' legislative and executive programmes at the centre of their campaigning. That's how Tunisia solved the thorny problem of the revolution that has not seized power—a problem we're still grappling with.

The debate next turned to the Executive and, just before the elections, it was decided that the Assembly would elect an

---

7   On 23 October 2011, the Constituent Assembly of Tunisia was elected, consisting of 217 lawmakers tasked with writing a new constitution.

interim president tasked with forming a government. All of which is to say, Tunisians will only write their constitution *after* the representatives of the people have assumed full powers.

For us, the Selmi document is proof of just how serious the crisis over the handover of power has become.[8] Discussion has been particularly intense over articles nine and ten, and what they reveal about the military's intentions. But far more dangerous is the article annexed to the document which allows the SCAF to object to the draft constitution, and which allows them to form an alternative committee if the parliamentary committee fails to agree upon a constitution within six months.

This means that the Egyptian state is held hostage.

Unless parliament does as it's told and comes up with a constitution (regardless of circumstance, differences of opinion, interference from the military and ex-regime figures) and unless the electorate do what they're told and vote to approve that constitution (no matter what its shortcomings) the military will not set the state free.

In fact, I suspect that if we dare to vote against the Constitution when it is put to referendum, the SCAF may well punish us by suspending parliament on the grounds that a rejection constitutes a vote of no confidence—and at that point we will see an outright military coup. The SCAF has a history of interpreting referenda as votes of confidence.

The issue of the hostage state doesn't end with the Selmi document. Even if it's withdrawn, we'll be in the same predicament. Experience has shown how easy it is to push our elites and political parties into extreme polarization—and the Constitution is their favourite quarrel. In its Constitutional

---

8   What came to be known as the Selmi Document were a set of 'supra-constitutional principals' published by the government on 1 November 2011 that granted the SCAF both autonomy from any oversight and a range of interventionist powers in the ongoing process of electing a new parliament and writing a new constitution.

Declaration,[9] the SCAF gave itself the power to determine when work on the Constitution will begin, even though the referendum granted parliament a grace period of six months. It will use this power to stir up strife and disagreement, which will delay the transfer of legislative power. And we won't be able to object, because the state is being held hostage: if the Constitution is delayed, presidential elections will be delayed, and military rule will continue. But as soon as work on the Constitution begins, the polarization will intensify, parliament and the parties will be entirely preoccupied, and we can forget about legislative reforms or genuine monitoring of the military and government.

Like Tunisia's, our revolution has not seized power, and, as had been the case in Tunisia, the counter-revolution and the old regime have taken the state hostage.

It's time to recognize the ways in which Egypt *is* like Tunisia, and that the revolution, with no central leadership, and containing multiple currents with often profound disagreements and no broad popular bases which would make it easier to resolve these disagreements, can only seize power through elections. Negotiating with the SCAF won't change that fact; nor will attempts to achieve consensus before the elections.

If we accept that Egypt is like Tunisia then we must do as Tunisia did: unite and exert pressure until there is a complete transfer of power to the first elected body, whose legitimacy then supercedes any other.

In Tunisia, a Constituent Assembly was elected to write the Constitution, but also assumed legislative and executive powers. In Egypt we are to elect the lower house of parliament, the People's Assembly. Now we must do as Tunisia has done, and not wait for

---

9   The Constitutional Declaration was announced by the SCAF on 30 March 2011 as intermediate law pending a new constitution. Nine amendments were published in June 2011 further safeguarding various military privileges.

the upper house or the presidential elections, but return to the streets and the squares of the revolution until the state is set free and the People's Assembly assumes full powers upon election.

Think about it carefully. It will not be possible to freely draft the constitution under the overriding control of the SCAF. Even if attempts at interference like the Selmi document are successfully resisted, the mere presence of the SCAF tips the balance of power. For example, the debate over the system of governance, and whether it should be parliamentary or presidential, takes on a profoundly different meaning in the presence or absence of a military council with sweeping powers. Meanwhile, our politicians have shown by their scandalous endorsement of the Anan Document[10] that they are hardly equipped for hostage negotiations.

We must postpone our disagreements over the Constitution, join ranks, and—immediately following the parliamentary elections—form a government of national salvation, with a new Minister of Defence. The SCAF's role must end there, giving way to a second transitional period led by the elected representatives of the people. And then we can argue over the Constitution all we like.

Written in Torah Prison.
Published on 11 November 2011 in *al-Shorouk*

---

10 A meeting was convened by Army Chief of Staff, Sami Anan, bringing together various members of the SCAF and the heads of thirteen political parties. All but the head of the Social Democratic Party, Mohamed Abu el-Ghar, signed on to the resulting 'Anan Document' that laid out an overly slow roadmap towards a transition of power (convening parliament, drafting a new constitution, holding presidential elections), reserved privileges for the army, was vague about key issues, agreed to developing supra-constitutional principles and pledged full support and appreciation of the SCAF.

HALF AN HOUR WITH KHALED

*While Alaa is in prison a major street battle breaks out between
revolutionaries and security forces that lasts several days. It was
fought along Mohamed Mahmoud Street, which runs from
Tahrir Square towards the Ministry of the Interior, began on 19
November 2011. On 23 November, the SCAF, in a concession to the
street, announced the transfer of the Maspero investigation to the
civilian Public Prosecutor. At least sixty people died in the battle of
Mohamed Mahmoud and several thousand were injured.*

*Five days later, on 28 November, Alaa was brought before
State Security Prosecution, which added more charges to his case
file, including 'murder, with the intent to commit an act of terrorism'. State Security Prosecution is a special branch of the Public
Prosecution responsible for investigating national security threats
that operates as an exceptional branch of the judicial system and is
often used to persecute political opponents.*

*Two weeks after that, on 12 December, the Public Prosecutor
pulled Alaa's case from State Security, and assigned it to an investigative judge within the Public Prosecution Authority.*

It seems it is my destiny that my imprisonments should be tied
to the judiciary. I was imprisoned in 2006 with fifty comrades
from the Kefaya Movement and untold hundreds of Muslim
Brotherhood members for our stand in solidarity with the
judiciary's intifada against Mubarak and his regime. We staged a
sit-in for the independence of the judiciary and their complete
oversight of the elections—so we were imprisoned by the State
Security Prosecutor for a month and half.

And now, in the Era of the Revolution, the Military

Prosecutor has imprisoned me as a punishment for insisting on appearing before a civilian judge, and perhaps also for my role in the events of Maspero—also tied to the civil judiciary—in which we took a stand in the Coptic Hospital to ensure a real investigation by the Public Prosecutor and precise autopsy. That stand is the reason my name appears in the case files of the police and the Military Intelligence.

We snatched a victory in the Maspero case for Tahrir's new martyrs—but it was a victory with a Ganzouri taste,[11] because even though the case was referred to a civilian court, I find myself once again faced with the State Security Prosecutor.

In the Era of the Deposed, we used to refuse questioning by State Security Prosecution because it was extraordinary justice, but in the Era of Ganzouri we're agreeing to it because extraordinary civilian justice is better than extraordinary military justice. So I didn't celebrate the Ganzouri victory, quite the opposite in fact. I was returned from the prosecutor in a miserable state and spent my most difficult week in prison. Until then the struggle had been against military trials of civilians, and struggle inspires patience and makes resilience easy. But what's the point of my imprisonment if the case has now been transferred? What's the aim of my resilience?

The lawyers assured me that my appeal against this imprisonment on remand would be heard by a civilian judge. At last I would appear in front of the Judiciary for which we were imprisoned and tortured for defending its position and prestige and independent authority.

All I could think about was getting out in time to be there at the birth of my first child, Khaled. Our doctor had advised an early C-section was best for Manal's health, so with the renewal of

---

11   Kamal al-Ganzouri served as prime minister under Mubarak from 1996 to 1999, and had just been appointed again to the position by the SCAF. Hardly a revolutionary appointee, but also not the worst-case scenario.

my detention we were taking a risk postponing the birth, hoping I could be there. And Khaled was acting in solidarity, went on strike and wouldn't come out even after nine months, holding out for our final hope: the appeal in front of the civilian judge.

Our hopes were high, because there was no reason to keep me imprisoned: I'm innocent until proven guilty, I returned from abroad to appear at my summons so I'm no flight risk, the charges against me are clearly fabricated, the investigation is not serious and the testimonies of the false witnesses don't match up. We put our own evidence forward and witnesses who would prove I was not even at Maspero at the time of the massacre. The truth was evident.

Khaled did his bit and waited for the judge, the lawyers made their arguments, Manal asked the judge for me to be released on bail to be with her at the birth. But I knew from the look that my 'regular' judge gave her that he would bring me no justice.

My morale collapsed completely. I was drowning in fear and worry for Khaled and his mother. For the first time, I felt sorry for myself. My imprisonment had become absurd, and my mind, my heart, couldn't bear absurdity. I understand being jailed by a State Security prosecutor. But a civil judge? Where's our enmity? And what will happen now? Will I become one of the thousands of miserable creatures in Torah Prison? Waiting for months—years sometimes—for judgements that never come, from judges for whom the law declares us innocent until proven guilty, for whom the constitution decrees that our freedoms and rights must not be infringed on without court sentencing—and yet. Will our imprisonment continue, our cases never end, forgotten by the world outside the prison walls? Everyone in the prison is pale and miserable, even the cats, their movements slow, their eyes spent and broken.

I fell asleep convinced of my fate: six months at least before my case will be heard, then months more of postponements before being found innocent. How would I bear it?

Then came Khaled! The next day I got a message saying he and Manal were healthy and well—and a photo. Love at first sight, love at first photograph. The prison and its walls and its cats all vanished, everything vanished except my love for Khaled and my joy at his arrival. I slept content.

On his third day, Khaled visited me. It was a surprise. I assumed the doctor wouldn't let him visit for at least a week. Khaled was with me for half an hour. I held him in my arms for ten minutes.

My God! How come he's so beautiful? Love at first touch! In half an hour he gave me joy enough to fill the prison for a week. In half an hour I gave him love I hoped would surround him for a week. In half an hour I changed and the universe changed around me. Now I understand why I'm in prison: they want to deprive me of joy. Now I understand why I will resist: prison will not stop my love, my happiness is resistance, holding Khaled is continuing the struggle.

I'm never alone in my resistance; there are always people in solidarity. And so I wasn't alone in the joy of Khaled, but was flooded with the joy of comrades. I'd get telegrams, tweets, congratulations for Eid, for my birthday, congratulations for the revolution's return to Tahrir. But Khaled was something else. Masses of telegrams, most from people I don't know and may never have the honour of meeting; writing to express their joy at Khaled's arrival and their love for him, writing to introduce themselves, the names of the members of their families, their addresses, their jobs, their cities, writing to say that Khaled has uncles and aunts in hundreds of homes everywhere in Egypt.

Sadly I wasn't allowed to keep these messages; I was shown them once, then hurriedly they vanished. I will not be able to speak the names of every aunt and every uncle to Khaled, but their love has reached him. Half an hour inspires me with happiness that I survive on for a week. Just the news of his arrival inspires people who don't know us with a joy that makes them send telegrams to an imprisoned father.

Half an hour in which I did nothing except look at him. What about half an hour in which I change him? Or half an hour in which I feed him? Or half an hour in which I play with him? What about half an hour for him to tell me about school? Half an hour for him and I to talk about his dreams? Half an hour to argue about whether he should go down to a protest? Half an hour for him to give me an impassioned speech about the revolution and how it will free us all? About bread and freedom and dignity and justice? Half an hour for me to feel proud that my son is a brave man carrying the responsibility of a country before he's of age to be responsible for himself?

How much happiness in half an hour like that? Is it like the last hour the father of the martyr spent with his son?

Prison robs me of Khaled, but for half an hour. I'm patient because we will spend the rest of our half hours together. How can the martyr's father be patient?

The martyr is immortal, in our hearts immortal, in our minds immortal, in history immortal and in paradise immortal.[12] But what happiness does immortality bring the father? His heart will burst with love for the remaining half hours of his life. Will he empty what's in his heart in the arms of history? I wait for my release and I'm resilient. What does the father of the martyr wait for? That he follow the immortal to heaven?

We thought the judge would do us justice. In 2006, we chanted for the judges to free us from tyranny, then my regular judge jailed me to rob me of Khaled. The father of the martyr thought that the regular soldier would do right by him, when in February we chanted that the army and the people are one hand, then the regular soldier ran us over to rob us of Khaled.

---

12   The word khaled means immortal. So this sentence, in Arabic, reads both as 'the martyr is immortal' and 'the martyr is Khaled.' Khaled, Alaa's son, was named after Khaled Said.

Looking for reasons for my imprisonment is pointless. My imprisonment will not restore their state. The death of most of the martyrs is pointless. Perhaps at the beginning they killed the martyrs to stop the revolution, but why did they carry on killing after it was proven time and again that the revolution would continue? The killing even increases as they draw closer to defeat. I remember the snipers appearing on the day of the Battle of the Camel, they came late, after it was clear that the square would hold. It was killing for the sake of killing, with no strategic objective: killing simply to deprive us of the immortal.

We need to be vigilant: they do not kill us to restore their state, but because killing and jailing are normal behaviour in their state. Yes, normal behaviour. It's just that we kid ourselves. It wasn't only their police who wronged us; did the deans of their colleges not share in running over our children?[13] Were we not wronged by the bakeries and the gas depots of their state? By the ferries and ports of their state? Were we not wronged by its wheel of production that lavishes millions on the director and the consultant—even while at a standstill—but cannot spare a crumb for the worker when turning? Were we not wronged by its economy that closes down the textile factories while the cotton is piled high in the farmer's home but keeps the fertilizer plant pouring poison into our water? Were we not wronged by its football clubs that let security brutalize the fans for cheering too noisily but intervene to shield players when they raise arms? We are wronged by all its institutions and every leader in it and tomorrow we will be wronged by its parliament and its president.

---

13   15 October 2011: In Mansoura University, during elections for . . . the University President, the deans of the faculties of Arts and Veterinary Medicine drove into the university gates to the site of the ballot. Students surrounded their car, shouting that they were corrupt, should be barred from participation, and that their positions as deans were illegitimate. The car eventually drove through the crowd, injuring fifteen students.

I could never have imagined that my heart carried all the love that burst out with the birth of Khaled, how could I fathom the sorrow in the heart of the martyr's father? Lord, how can it be so cruel? To bury your son, rather than he bury his father—is there a greater wrong? A worse imbalance? We kid ourselves and pretend it's exceptional, that it's possible to reform the state—but the evidence shows us its regularity, and that there's no hope but for the fall of that state.

Yes, their state must fall. We're afraid to face up to it, afraid for the country should the state fall. If the square topples the state—what's left for us? Egypt is not the square!

It's true that *Egypt is not the square*. But we've not understood the square. What do we do in the square? Well, we meet, we eat, we sleep, we talk, we pray, we chant, we sing, we expend energy and ideas in order to sustain ourselves, we cheer at a wedding and weep in a funeral, we express our ideas, our dreams, our identities, we quarrel sometimes, sometimes we're at a loss and confused, searching for the future, we spend each day as it comes, not knowing what the future hides for us.

Is this not what we do outside the square? Nothing is exceptional in the square except our togetherness. Out of the square, we're happy at a wedding because we know the bride and groom, in the square we rejoiced at the happiness of strangers. Out of the square, we grieve at a funeral because we know the deceased, in the square we prayed for strangers. Nothing is new in the square except that we surround ourselves with the love of strangers. But the love of strangers is not unique to the square— hundreds sent me messages of love for Khaled from outside the square, even some self-described members of the Sofa Party.[14] Millions grieved for the martyr in every home in Egypt.

We rejoice at a wedding because it is a marriage. We grieve

14   A sarcastic term referring to what is sometimes also called 'the silent majority'. The Sofa Party are those whose political opinions are formed through their televisions.

at a funeral because it is death. We love the newborn because he's human and because he's Egyptian. Our hearts break for the martyr because he's human and because he's Egyptian. We go to the square to discover that we love life outside it, and to discover that our love for life is resistance. We race towards the bullets because we love life, and we walk into prison because we love freedom.

The country is what we love and what we live for; what we celebrate and what we mourn. If the state falls, more than just the square will remain—there will be the love of strangers, there will be everything that drove us to the square, and everything we learned in the square.

Love is Khaled and sorrow is Khaled and the square is Khaled and the martyr is Khaled and the country is Khaled. As for their state, it is for an hour. Just for an hour.[15]

Abu Khaled
Friday, 9 December 2011
Cell 6/1, Ward 4, Torah Investigative Prison
Published on 19 December 2011 in *al-Shorouk*

---

15   This echoes a saying attributed to Ali ibn Abi Talib: 'The state of injustice is but for an hour, the state of righteousness is until the hour of judgement.'

NOTHING TO CELEBRATE

Popular pressure over the Maspero massacre has been multiplied by the major battles of Mohamed Mahmoud Street (19-24 November) and the Cabinet Building (16-20 December) and on 25 December 2011 Alaa is ordered released from prison. A throng of supporters and journliats wait for him outside the Cairo Security Directorate. When he eventually walks out, he stops to speak.

Yes, we have to bring down military rule. We have to bring down military rule, and now the case—all of the Maspero accused are out—and it looks like the case is falling apart. But the real trial still hasn't begun. We are still not trying the ones who did the killing. We can't celebrate that I'm getting out innocent, we always knew it wasn't me that killed the people—but the killers are still out there. We got a regular judge and an investigating judge and I don't know what else but will this judge—and he's a fair judge, he released me—is this judge able to get General Hamdy Badeen as the accused in this case or not? That's the question. And the revolution, this revolution, will have succeeded when General Hamdy Badeen is in cuffs in the courtroom picking his nose and a cylinder of cooking gas costs five pounds.

Delivered on 25 December 2011
outside the Cairo Security Directorate

2012

WHY ARE THE YOUNG PEOPLE AT THE MINISTRY OF THE INTERIOR?

On 1 February 2012, 74 al-Ahly football fans were killed in Port Said stadium after violence broke out after a match. Tensions had been rising between the SCAF and the Ahly ultras, a large, organized group of football fans that had been visibly present and effective fighters in most of the street confrontations since 25 January 2011. In Ahly's previous match, four days earlier, thousands of fans had chanted 'Down with Military Rule'.

In the days immediately following the Port Said massacre, protests erupted in several cities. In Cairo, the protests converged around Mohamed Mahmoud Street and Mansour Street, which leads to the Ministry of the Interior. Security forces responded with live ammunition, birdshot, and teargas. Five days of clashes left fifteen dead and several thousand wounded.

What follows is a fictional interview posted on Facebook.

3 February 2012

Q: What are those young people doing at the Interior Ministry?

A: They're furious at the gratuitous killing.

Q: Yeah but what are they planning to do?

A: Nobody knows. They themselves don't know. They only know rage and death.

Q: So why don't you tell them to go to Tahrir?

A: Because Tahrir has failed to bring justice for the martyrs again and again.

Q: Well, why don't you tell them to . . .

A: What on earth can I tell them? Do any one of you have an actual solution? You think they can be duped with catchy slogans?

Q: We just don't want more blood.

A: These killers aren't just lying in wait at the Ministry, they abduct us off the street and kill us at football matches—so what difference does it make?

Q: So what is it that they want?

A: They want 'bread, freedom, social justice, and human dignity'. They want justice for the martyrs. They want to understand why the old are planning for the future while children are writing their wills.

Q: But what do they want right now?

A: I have no idea. This isn't an organized protest with specific demands. They're chanting against Field Marshal [Tantawi]. Can you bring him to them?

Q: Why did we leave Tahrir? Tahrir is pretty spacious . . .

A: No, Tahrir is too cramped and is all problems and fights and is full of informants and people screaming from the soapboxes and torturing opponents and taxing the hawkers or beating the hawkers and Brotherhood making demands that go against the people's demands and non-Brotherhood coming to fight with Brotherhood instead of the people that are actually killing us—how can you not see all this?

Q: OK, but please make them leave, we've had enough blood!

A: I swear to God I can't make them leave, nobody can.

Q: If you don't know why they're there, or what they want, and you can't control them, why are you standing with them?

A: Because I learned in the revolution to always stand with those who stand up to the bullets, with those who defy authority, those who seem weak but are strong, I learned that what hurts most are not bullet wounds but knives in the back and betrayals from the soapboxes and satellite channels, learned that if I'm not somewhere I could be injured, killed or arrested while others are being injured, killed or arrested, then I'm doing something wrong. If you don't understand this, I don't know how to make you understand.

Q: So what should I do now?

A: Don't insult those standing up to the bullets, even if you don't understand them. Don't theorize. Don't talk about thugs and infiltrators. Don't talk about sheep[16] being herded and manipulated. The young have nothing left but their will. They've been robbed of their life, dreams, brothers, friends, eyes, limbs, spirit, football club, their square and their revolution. Everything and anything. They have nothing left but their will, that one decides what to do and nobody controls him—and the epitome of one's will is choosing how to die, and how to live.

Q: OK, but I want to do something positive.

A: Go down and join them. You don't need to get into the clashes, but go smell the gas, get an idea about birdshot and buckshot, volunteer in a civilian field hospital, hand out vinegar for people's eyes or food . . .

Q: I don't like confrontation. I don't want to go down there.

A: So go and protest in front of the Ministry of Defence, or in Tahrir Square, or join the marches demanding the handover of power, or take a stand in front of Maspero, or organize a Kazeboon street screening,[17] or participate in the Hakemouhom[18] campaign, or work against military trials for civilians, or join one of the revolution's human chains, or join a neighbourhood committee. The point is: do something.

Q: And how long is this going to go on?

A: Until the fall of the regime.

---

16 *Al-kherfan,* the sheep, was a common insult directed at members of the Muslim Brotherhood.

17 *Kazeboon,* 'They're Liars', was an umbrella name given to street screenings that took place in protests around the country that showed footage of—primarily—military violence against protestors (which the military denied ever took place).

18 *Hakemouhom:* 'Put them on trial'.

GAZA: ON BEING PRISONER TO YOUR OWN VICTORY

So we went to Palestine. A life's dream that had taken on almost mythical dimensions but came true with a bus journey and some bureaucracy.

We went in search of hills and valleys, zaatar and olive trees, stone houses, mosques and churches, oranges and guns, keffiyehs and the wreckage of war.

SURPRISE NO. 1: GAZA IS NORMAL

A coastal city that resembles Egyptian cities in most details, as if I'm in Agami Abu Talat. Even the people looked, dressed, and talked like people in Egypt.

We searched for the siege like curious tourists, though we said we came as comrade siege-breakers. On the surface, the blockade was over, the markets are bustling and the supermarkets are fully stocked—the tunnels take care of whatever was missing. The whole way from Palestinian Rafah to Gaza City, huge lorries are transporting tunnel goods. We philosophize and theorize: so Gaza isn't going hungry; this constant talk of starvation must be to someone's benefit.

The first signs of the siege appear at our hotel. The electricity comes and goes, because there's a fuel crisis, and water supplies are limited and the desalination plants aren't working at capacity.

Of course, water and energy problems afflict our Egyptian cities—I'm just not used to encountering them in an expensive hotel in a fancy neighbourhood. We philosophize and theorize: does the siege flatten class distinctions, then?

Another thing we looked for, with tourists' eyes, was the

wreckage of war. Where are the bombed-out buildings and schools? Apart from the Andalus tower, the traces of war are negligible: bullet marks on a few buildings. How strange: why didn't they leave rubble to weep over? We philosophize and theorize: the lack of rubble and debris surely explains the absence of brilliant poetry. The next Mahmoud Darwish won't come out of Gaza.

SURPRISE NO. 2: GAZA IS DYSTOPIAN

Our hotel is on the seafront; the sea is the same as ours, no surprise that it looks the same. But night falls, and the sea is fenced in by floodlights. To make sure the siege is absolute, the enemy has caged the sea itself.

Usually, it isn't possible to engage with any geographical unit larger than a neighbourhood, or maybe a village, as a material entity that we can grasp with our senses. Cities, regions, and nations are essentially symbolic entities. To see Egypt as a whole, you have to look at a map, you have to engage with ideas about history, a nation, and other symbols: the Nile or the Pyramids or, maybe, Tahrir Square.

The Zionists have succeeded in treating the Gaza Strip as a physical body, that can be caged and walled in—even its sea. This 'achievement' in itself is legendary, and beyond my ability to comprehend.

The vocabulary and the details of the siege seem like they're out of a science-fiction novel set in humanity's dark future: an entire society behind bars, the sea fenced in, hovering robots that can kill you at any moment, aeroplanes roaring through the sound barrier at all hours, an economy of underground tunnels, and a mighty hidden enemy whose agents are concrete, iron and fire. You never see it but it is always present.

In *Terminator* the computer Skynet achieves self-awareness in August 1997—and then world domination. In 2029, human resistance inflicts major losses on Skynet, which starts to send killer cyborgs back in time to stamp out the resistance in its cradle.

In current human consciousness the siege of Gaza cannot be permitted. Human society doesn't countenance killer robots; we still talk about war in the language of knights, where you meet the enemy face to face, and courage and strength are more important than equipment. What's happening in Gaza—and some of it is happening in other places around the world—is out of context, like it's been sent back in time from some grim future we haven't arrived at yet.

We don't philosophize or theorize: we shy away from thinking about it.

SURPRISE NO. 3: GAZA IS FREE

Gaza looks like Egypt, but something's different. Every wall, every building, every street corner is inscribed with the names of the martyrs, every family proudly declares its fallen. The traces of war are few but its stories are plenty, and on everyone's tongues. Behind an everyday scene is a history of persistent, determined struggle; I knew that, of course, but I hadn't realized that it was struggle on every corner.

I was confused, and thought that the Zionists withdrew to hold Gaza under a tight siege. But a visit shows you that they withdrew because it was impossible to sustain their presence there, facing such struggle and resistance.

The distinction is familiar: Gaza no longer looks like Agami Abu Talaat, but Mohamed Mahmoud Street. Every inch of it has been paid for in blood, and every inch remembers its martyrs with graffiti and murals. The occupation wasn't a match for them, so it withdrew and relinquished the land of Gaza. And the Egyptian regime was no match for us, so it withdrew its president and pulled out of Tahrir and Mohamed Mahmoud Street.

Gaza defeated the Occupation, so the Occupation withdrew, leaving the siege in its wake, and Gaza has defeated the siege. Gaza forged its freedom from the blood of its children, and here it's reconstructing its buildings by recycling its rubble. We're not seeing any ruins because the people of Gaza are busy with life, prising out and flattening the rebar from the rubble, grinding up the ruins into new cement and bricks.

The Palestinian is one who struggles to live a normal life under endlessly extraordinary conditions. In Egypt, too, we've been living under extraordinary circumstances for the last year and a half. But while in Egypt some try to flee the extraordinary, in Gaza, every street is Mohamed Mahmoud Street. In Gaza no one flees. In Gaza everyone cherishes the extraordinary conditions as much as they do normal life, but they do not immortalize them.

SURPRISE NO. 4: GAZA IS DIVIDED

The streets are not only decorated with the names and faces of the martyrs, but with the banners of the factions. Each house raises its standard: green for Hamas, yellow for Fatah, red for the Popular Front for the Liberation of Palestine, black for Islamic Jihad. Everyone belongs, everyone talks about their faction, everyone complains about being divided.

Even the pictures of the martyrs are coupled with a tribute to their faction.

It seems as if all representatives of authority and of the state are from Hamas: their appearance and manner testifies to their faction. The two authorities are a subject of constant discussion—anywhere, with anyone, at any time.[19] The lurking anger, I understand: Arab authorities have track records of flouting

---

19   In 2006, elections were held in the West Bank and Gaza from which Hamas emerged the victor. Fatah did not cede power, which resulted in a split in the Palestinian leadership to this day: Hamas controlling Gaza, and Fatah, the West Bank.

the rights of their citizens. What I don't understand is the anger lurking among the representatives of the authority. Where does that come from?

And there are so many representatives of the authority. Things take a funny turn, transforming the science fiction story from a dystopia to a black comedy. Informers are everywhere. It's impossible to move around without bumping into them; despite the siege, the occupation, the fighting and the historical events, they still find the time and energy to enforce gender segregation and the veil. Their excuses are at the ready: Gaza is in a critical situation, this is a military zone, Gaza is targeted, traditions and customs . . .

OK, the similarities are still there. We philosophize and theorize: fear dominates Gaza, no one speaks freely.

I don't understand the Hamas plainclothes' insistence on fighting with us. We're only visitors, in five days we'll be gone. Even Mubarak knew how to play the 'margins of freedom' game. Why are these guys determined to mess with us? We try to ignore the disunity, but everybody is talking about it. We try to ignore the Hamas authority, but one of its arms insists on intimidating us. Everyone says the same thing, the same frustration, the same impotence, the same anger. Nothing is happening. Nothing has meaning. We philosophize and theorize: you need a revolution.

They say that the prisoners' hunger strike has united the people. We try to get away from the feuding by visiting a sit-in held by the prisoners' families. They are on hunger strike in solidarity with their children. But the feuding catches up with us: the sit-in itself is divided by faction, placards declaring the allegiance of each prisoner, a megaphone blasting non-stop partisan speeches, arguments over whether men are allowed to visit women's tents to meet with prisoners' mothers, wives, sisters, daughters, and aunts.

Finally we enter the tent. I don't know how I can talk to a mother who's been kept from seeing her son for seven years. I'm rescued by my own, Khaled, who is with me on the trip, when the mothers ask about him. I want to tell them he was born while I was in prison, to show I understand some of the torment, but am ashamed to compare two months' inside with decades of imprisonment. I make up my mind to speak because what's important is to emphasize the similarity between Egypt's rulers and the Zionists. Even the mothers of the prisoners, struggling for their own liberation, ask about Egypt and hope for a breakthrough in Palestine built on the victory of our revolution. We philosophize and theorize: you have to overcome the factions first.

SURPRISE NO. 5: GAZA IS OCCUPIED

I'm suffocated by moving around as if I were a tourist. I'm anxious about the disunity dominating the scene. It's clear that my son Khaled is the key to more intimate interaction. I split from the group and walk around the city with him.

Al-Shate Camp resembles any low-income neighbourhood in Egypt. The market looks familiar, but here goods coming from Israel dominate. I gather that the poor cannot afford tunnel goods. Gaza may give you the impression that the blockade is over, with its shops filled with all kinds of goods, with its people's resentment of the 'starvation discourse' which verges on begging—but the working poor remain at the mercy of what Israel decides to let in.

The population density is higher in the camp, and so is the density of factional flags. It looks like I'm moving between each factions' neighbourhoods. All are delighted with Khaled but they differ in their analysis of the situation in Egypt. The residents of the camp don't follow what's happening in Egypt minute by minute the way that the Facebook and Twitter generation of young Palestinians do, but they do stay abreast of events. There's no 'Sofa Party' in Gaza: whatever your social background, everyone has an opinion. It's easy for us to brag about transcending partisanship in Egypt, but in Palestine, factional allegiance means a lot more because each faction has a genuine history of struggle, a record of sacrifice, and a popular base.

I'm beginning to understand why the young people we met, who seemed closest to the youth of the Egyptian revolution, raised a banner to 'end the division' rather than 'down with the regime'. Ending the division is a call to radically change the system while maintaining the role and status of the factions. But then why were they repressed by the two authorities, and abandoned by most of the factions? Even though everyone agrees that ending the division is necessary to confront the occupier?

My anxiety swells to a peak. I need to see the hidden enemy. I make my way, with my family, to the Beit Hanoun Crossing (Erez checkpoint), the gateway leading to the rest of the occupied territories. The police don't let us get close. Our friends understand our need to see the enemy, so they take us to a small farm on the outskirts of Beit Hanoun, the closest point to the Zionists' wall we could reach.

And finally, we see the enemy. On the horizon: concrete walls, surveillance towers and jeeps. A friend—who had just been trying to explain to me what it meant to be born a Palestinian refugee on Palestinian land—tells me that the barracks I see on the Israeli side of the crossing had been built on the ruins of his village. At the edge of an orchard he invites me to pick a fruit. I walk around the tree and suddenly they yell 'Careful! The enemy is watching you now.' One step beyond the limit can bring dire consequences.

Finally, here, within range of the enemy's bullets and under the buzz of its drones, my anxiety subsides. We taunt them a little by getting as close as possible, to photograph them. We stroll, taking no notice of their unhidden presence. And, finally, we have our calmest and purest moments in Palestine. We talk about everything: children and land and work; revolution and occupation and division; politics and football and love. At the wall anxiety ends, at the wall the fog dissipates.

At the wall, the impact of war is clear, not in the rubble of destroyed buildings, but in the youth of the trees. One shot sums it all up: everything old was swept away, but we were not defeated, and we planted anew. At the wall I understand the significance of the blockade: they tell me how difficult it is to obtain seeds, fertilizer, and fodder. The tunnel economy isn't a proper economy—it doesn't provide raw materials, or the supplies required for industry and agriculture. Tunnels are only good business for consumer goods.

The occupation expends effort and money, and builds complexes of concrete and technology, mainly to prevent Gaza from having real economic activity. The enemy fences off the sea with its huge battleships just to stop fishermen in tiny boats from reaching their sardines.

The Palestinian is one who struggles to live a normal life under endlessly extraordinary conditions. The successive victories of the people of Gaza forced the occupation to withdraw. So the occupation decided to leave them prisoners to their own victory, to deprive them of the most important tool of struggle: the ability to live a normal life. For no matter how normal life seems on the surface of Gaza, the reality is the opposite as long as the vast majority of its people are unable to work for a living (estimates of unemployment range between 60 per cent and 80 per cent). The influx of money and goods from outside is not an alternative.

They've created a prison in the true sense of the word, then. For in prison, the majority don't work, in prison also there is an underground smuggling economy (the currency is cigarettes). But it's not real life.

I remember my own short experience in confinement,
when they imprisoned fifty people from the Kefaya movement
together, and how the overcrowded cells were too much for us to
handle, how we snapped at each other, bickered and quarrelled,
and even accused each other of treachery. Once we got out, the
tensions all evaporated and we couldn't even remember what
they were about.

I remember Dr Muhammad Habib in Asyut telling us about
his experience of being in prison for years, and how struggle and
ambition shrink until they can fit into the cell; and the definition of
freedom becomes controlling when the door is opened and when it's
closed. That day he told us a joke, that he'd stopped calling his wife
The Government, and started calling her The Warden. After years in
prison, you can no longer imagine any greater power.

He warned us of following in the footsteps of generations
whose horizon had fallen so low it stopped at the prison warden.
Today, in Gaza, I understood that it's not about generational
inheritance: anyone can become so consumed by cellblock conflicts that they can no longer see beyond the warden.

The problem isn't Hamas or Fatah, the problem is in
accepting becoming prisoner to your victory: defeating the
warden, then doing nothing more than taking his place. The
tunnels started as an act of resistance, but today they're a source
of tax revenue for the government and profit for the elite.
Without Gazans choosing this, with every day that goes by, the
Authority adapts to the situation, and those making money
crawl higher up. Today, it's Palestinian police who maintain security at the wall, and try to keep everybody away from it: both the
fighter with his rocket launcher, and the farmer who sees fertile
land being deliberately laid to waste. Evil is not their motive,
surely they are trying to protect people from the brutality of the
occupation, to protect the country from an excuse for large-scale
bombing, but the result is the same: they have become jailers.

The Authority is not implicated on its own. If unemployment affects everyone, and the economy is largely rendered ineffective, how can class inequality persist? Why does the impact of the blockade vary? Class inequality is always objectionable, but in most societies it can be explained by market dynamics. In Gaza, it seems to be partially inherited: before the blockade we were like this, and so we will continue to be so. Young people realize how fake this situation is, so are on the lookout for a discourse and a movement that pushes up against the barriers. They're tired of being prisoners of their own victory.

Sometimes they join the fishermen fishing in spite of the battleships, at other times the farmers harvesting beneath the drones; they demonstrate in support of the Arab revolutions without asking permission from any authority; they raise a slogan that seems conciliatory and logical like 'the people demand an end to division', but, in truth, it's revolutionary because it means demand an end to the role of Warden. Perhaps Gaza won't produce the next Mahmoud Darwish, but it produces angry rap, critical of everybody, poignant in its celebrations. Their fatigue and their anger, as well as their moments of joy, is inventing a new discourse of resistance free of the vocabulary monopolized by the factions.

In Egypt, too, they wanted to imprison us inside our victory. We liberated Tahrir Square and Downtown Cairo, we toppled a warden and his henchmen. They tried to confine us to Tahrir, and in Tahrir we moved from the victor's utopia to the squabbling of cramped cells. That's why all our attempts to recreate the mood of the square, in the square, fail. Our youth set out on a feverish search for a new goal, moving from ministries to embassies, our hearts reassured when met with walls, bullets and blood. Now I understand why Abbaseya and the Ministry of Defence called to us.[20] In Egypt, too, we might end up electing a

---

20 Two protest marches that set out from Tahrir in search of new political targets for sit-ins.

new warden. Now I understand why anxiety soars whenever we approach elections: we have paid for it in blood.

The first group to call for an end to division were the political prisoners. Today the prisoners' hunger strike is leading the struggle of an entire people. And when the authorities and the factions try to take control the prisoners remind them with resolute courtesy that it's shameful for a well-fed free man to negotiate on behalf of a hungry prisoner.

How can we allow ourselves to be overcome with weakness, prisoners to our victory, when prisoners are achieving victory in their confinement?

THE LAST SURPRISE: RETURNING

On the last day I'm determined to buy olive oil—how could I visit Palestine and not bring back olive oil? I also have with me two flowers planted in Palestinian soil. But the day passes by with all its disruptions and I don't find time to buy the oil, and at the crossing on the way back I forget the two flowers and the soil. Fate decided to deprive me of trivializing Palestine into any of its clichéd symbols nested in my imagination.

Do you seek out the words of Mahmoud Darwish and ignore the lyrics of young rappers? Do you look for rubble and destruction and ignore the people you've seen flattening out bomb-twisted steel rebar to build new houses? Do you look for zaatar and olive oil and ignore that you've shared a coffee with someone struggling to grow them? Do you look for the fighter with the gun and the keffiyeh and ignore the fisherman and the farmer and the student who struggle every day to stay alive? Do you search for the land of Palestine, and ignore that your son was blessed for days with the love of its people?

Gaza stands fearlessly, calling out to us: come, for I have the truth, people who love life and desire freedom. Come, for I have the last wall: if it falls, so will every wall and every warden and every jailer in Egypt as in Syria. Look for the walls, the enemy is always behind them and the truth always lies before them.

We arrive home. In a small bag I have some azkadenya fruits. The poets have never sung its praises. Wikipedia says it originated in China, but it's a delicious fruit from Palestine planted in spite of the siege and beside the wall. A friend picked them for us.

Yes, I was, in Palestine. Yes, I returned, and Palestine is with me.

Published on 18 May 2012 in *al-Shorouk*

IMPOSSIBLE SOLUTIONS

BBC News, 14 June: 'Egypt's supreme court has caused widespread alarm by calling for the dissolution of the lower house of parliament and for fresh elections. Two days before Egyptians choose a new president, it has declared last year's parliamentary vote unconstitutional. Muslim Brotherhood presidential candidate Mohamed Morsi said the decision "must be respected". But other political figures have expressed anger amid fears that the military wants to increase its power . . .

In a separate ruling, the supreme court also decided that former Prime Minister Ahmed Shafiq could continue to run for president in the June 16–17 presidential run-off election, rejecting as unconstitutional a law that would have barred him from standing. Under the Political Exclusion Law, passed by parliament, senior officials from former President Hosni Mubarak's regime were banned from standing for office.'

Ever since the recent verdicts issued by the Supreme Constitutional Court, everyone's been racking their brains for solutions. I haven't managed to come up with one that can actually be implemented, so I decided to write down all the unrealistic solutions that came to me.

Because these are unrealistic solutions, I didn't waste any time evaluating them, so don't pick a fight with me if you don't like them because they'll never happen anyway.

SOLUTION #1: THE SQUARE WITHOUT THE MUSLIM BROTHERHOOD

The people stun us as millions take to the streets tomorrow in the first spontaneous, unplanned protest. All the revolutionary groups take part and a new political coalition is formed with clear features and decision-making mechanisms. It represents a front and nucleus for a 'Presidential Council' that contests the power of the SCAF. Revolution anew, and the people do not leave the streets until military rule is put to an end.

SOLUTION #2: THE SQUARE WITH THE MUSLIM BROTHERHOOD

Morsi announces that he's pulling out of the presidential contest. The Muslim Brotherhood declare open opposition to the SCAF. We return to the streets and the squares—unified as in the early days of the revolution—and all agree on a civilian presidential council made up of the presidential candidates, including Morsi. This council would carry the legitimacy of the squares and of 75 per cent of the electorate.

We work to prevent the elections, and if the military insists on holding them then the people shut down the polling stations, and call on the judiciary to pull out of their supervision—if they want to prove that there are true judges in Egypt.

Without elections there is no legitimate authority. All national powers recognize the Presidential Council as the only legitimate authority, and we begin pushing for regional and international recognition. The people do not leave the streets until military rule is put to an end.

SOLUTION #3: PARLIAMENT

The speakers of both houses call emergency sessions. Both houses stay in session: in a challenge to the decision to dissolve parliament members do not leave the building. The members admit their previous failure to perform as befits the revolution, and embark on a legislative marathon to issue the maximum number of revolutionary laws establishing public freedoms, reforming the state, adjusting the balance of powers, and curtailing the powers of the military. Then they formulate revolutionary legislation for purging the state and the removal of military elements and remnants of the old regime.

The elections' legitimacy is restored, and at the first sign of conflict between the military and the parliament, the revolutionary masses spring to the defence of the only elected power, after it has increased its electoral legitimacy with the legitimacy of siding with the people's demands. With the mobilization of the masses, parliament can form a government of national salvation and seek to seize power.

SOLUTION #4: ELECTIONS

Everyone realizes the most imminent danger is a return to military autocracy alongside elections and court rulings that boost the National Democratic Party, the security apparatus, and the old networks of corruption. So we all line up behind Morsi as the only candidate against the regime. All patriotic and revolutionary powers support his campaign and work to prevent any tampering with the ballot boxes.

Morsi wins, despite the military's best efforts, and forms a government of national unity.

ABOUT THE CONSTITUENT ASSEMBLY

In addition to the above suggestions, we could agree to a large Constituent Assembly, no less than 200 members, with a high percentage (half to two-thirds) of its members selected through free and direct elections, and the remainder would be fixed quotas for institutions, with a bias towards institutions with an elected leadership (e.g. universities and trade unions) and fewer from the institutions of power. In the absence of parliament, the Constituent Assembly would temporarily assume the responsibilities of legislation and government oversight, with absolute

power to withdraw confidence from a Minister or the entire government. The Assembly amends the constitutional declaration
to turn it into a suitable temporary constitution for as long as it
takes for a new constitution to be written, and for a serious soci-
ety-wide dialogue to be held about all its sections and articles.

Published on 14 June 2012 on Facebook

CONSTITUTIONAL PROTOCOL

Most revolutionaries know a new constitution is needed and understand that repealing Mubarak's constitution is part of bringing down the regime. They know that the drafting of a new constitution is a fundamental part of correcting the conditions that had taken hold under Mubarak and dealing with their legacies—and that the new constitution should completely diverge from Mubarak's.

But, as usual, what seems obvious to the average revolutionary is a struggle for our leaders and political elites.

The Constituent Assembly has delivered a draft of a new constitution that doesn't go far beyond its predecessor. It have contented itself with mild improvements, and is now trying to sell it to us as the best constitution in the country's history.

With the draft's publication, we moved beyond wrangling over the Assembly's composition, and everyone has started to scrutinize and criticize the text, article by article. A broad agreement has begun to emerge on what must be changed. Yet, I'm afraid that simply proposing modifications—even fundamental ones—while preserving the same methodology, will not yield a constitution significantly different from the one we would have arrived at had we agreed to amend the 1971 constitution rather than repeal it. A proper constitution worthy of the revolution requires—among other things—attention to the following points:

I. TERMINOLOGY

After a quick reading of modern constitutions, even the average reader can tell the difference between a constitution written to be implemented, and one designed to be side-stepped. A constitution that obliges and binds the authorities to guarantee the rights it stipulates, and a constitution that is a decorative placeholder, listing rights without any significant guarantees.

This draft—especially with regards to economic and social rights—uses loose language that rarely includes explicit statements of rights. So, it's full of phrases like 'The State endeavours to . . .', 'The State seeks to . . .', 'The State shall sponsor . . .', and 'The State shall protect . . .'. But rarely an explicit statement that all citizens have the right to X or Y.

Obliging the government to work towards a particular goal is not the same as obliging it to meet that goal. For the former, it's enough to form committees to 'work towards' the goal. For instance, to state that agriculture is a basic component of the economy does not guarantee that farmers will find suitable credit that helps them bear the costs of farming, and does not stop the Agricultural Bank from extorting farmers by getting them locked up for defaults on loan payments. (According to law, human rights accords, and the Shari'a, a person should not be jailed for defaulting on debt. But our prisons are full of farmers imprisoned for debts to a government body founded to implement florid constitutional articles ostensibly written to support this 'fundamental component' of the economy.)

Even the simplest and most fundamental of rights, the 'right to life', is not mentioned explicitly. The Universal Declaration of Human Rights states that every individual has the right to life, liberty, and security of person. Subsequent charters and treaties—including the Arab Charter on Human Rights —stipulate that the right to life is an essential right of every person. But this is not stated explicitly in our proposed constitution.

We know, of course, that failure to mention 'the right to life' does not mean that the State has the right to kill citizens.

Murder is a crime according to this draft. But the difference in explicitly stating the Right is that it places greater responsibility on the State for those losing their right to life due to government negligence or failure to provide healthcare. Also, the explicit statement of the Right opens the door to accountability for security forces when they end any person's life, and makes it more difficult (constitutionally, at least) to justify the killing by claiming that the victim 'resisted arrest', or 'has a criminal record'. Stating 'the right to life' leads us, for instance, to consider the scarcity of infant incubators in hospitals as a crime against the infant as well as the mother and all the other practices that we all know about, that demonstrate the State's lack of concern for the life of the citizen.

In modern constitutions, standard practice is to set out the basic rights explicitly, each in a separate article, and with each basic right list the relevant rights branching from it; followed by restrictions on the State; then, finally, its obligations.

II. THE TIME OF WRITING

Time did not stop in 1971. And the development of human society certainly did not stop—especially with advances in technology. And yet, when the Constituent Assembly decided to introduce a new section in the constitution for Independent Bodies and Regulatory Agencies, it failed to mention newly created institutions, such as the National Telecom Regulatory Authority, which is no less important than the Central Bank.

In its current form, the Constitution permits abolition of the Telecom Authority, and so permits placing power to regulate this sector in the hands of the president, the prime minister, or even the minister of communications, without any oversight or accountability. We had hoped that the committee would be more original and understand that communications, especially the internet, have become more than just a technology or a market, but a basic resource, a critical infrastructure, and a distinct right in itself. Its relation to knowledge is akin to the relationship between the road and transport network on one hand, and freedom of movement and economic development on the other.

The Assembly members' disregard for—or failure to recognize—the ongoing development of human society is reflected in their ignoring new challenges that did not confront those who wrote our previous constitutions. The draft stipulates the State's commitment to development and protection of plant species, which is certainly praiseworthy; but it fails to engage with what farmers face today: a market flooded with gene-modified species where the modifications do not improve the quality of the product but do improve the opportunities for multinational conglomerates to maximize profits. The truth is that these gene-modified species threaten indigenous species with extinction. Similarly, the draft ignores the fact that pre-judicial intellectual property rules are now applied to genes. These rules pose a threat to our agricultural and animal heritage. These challenges are aggravated by the State's inaction on documenting and protecting indigenous species, and funding appropriate research and development. This, for instance, has forced the National Agricultural Research Centre to resort to foreign companies to fund its research on Egyptian agricultural species, and ultimately, the foreign company retains ownership of the research results, and—among them—the exclusive right to produce the new seeds.

Had the Constituent Assembly listened to scientists, farmers, and environmental activists, then they might have designed some unprecedented constitutional articles: criminalizing the manufacture and import of sterile seeds that leave the farmer vulnerable to global corporations; or requiring the establishment of an organization responsible for the study, documentation, protection and

development of indigenous species, allocating it a percentage of
the national budget to guarantee that our scientists don't end up
on the payroll of those same corporations. Or perhaps, rather than
being preoccupied with the Shari'a's position on underage marriage, the committee could have communicated to us the Shari'a's
position on permitting companies to own whole biological species
and enjoy greater rights than farmers have over both their land
and the produce they have sown and harvested.

Even generally established rights require fresh attention and
further development due to advances in technology. The draft
does indeed stipulate respect for the privacy of homes and personal communications, using sufficiently clear language. But
it fails to stipulate the regulation of what is commonly referred
to as 'data retention'. For example, mobile operators maintain
detailed records of subscribers' movements based on the phone's
continuous communication with telecom towers. Through these
records it's possible to pinpoint the geographical location of the
subscriber at any time—reaching several years back—to within
tens of metres. The citizen has no legislative protection in the face
of this worrying capability to track him: there is no regulation of
the information that the company can retain, nor the length of
time it's permitted to retain it. (Does the company have a record
of my movements over the past decade?) There are no regulations
governing who can see this information. Does the company sell it
to marketing and advertising firms, for example? Will it deliver it
to National Security upon request, or will it require a court order?

Development and innovation won't stop after the
Constitution is written, and it's not possible to keep up with
every new advance, but when new issues emerge, and there is
public awareness of them to the level of being discussed in talk
shows and feature films, not to mention studies and research,
then it's natural to expect those issues be reflected in a constitution being written in this moment.

III. THE PLACE OF WRITING

If you read Italy's constitution, written in 1946, you will notice its writers were worried about the possibility of a return of fascism. Likewise, the Constitution of South Africa, written in 1996, is overwhelmingly concerned with addressing the effects of the apartheid system. Modern constitutions are borne of the experiences and struggles of their people. Constitutions written in the wake of revolutions reflect the reasons behind the revolution, and the concerns of the revolutionaries.

So, does it make any sense that a constitution written following the eruption of the Egyptian Revolution doesn't even mention the word 'torture'? The 1971 constitution declared torture an imprescriptible crime (i.e. not time-barred from prosecution). But its writers relegated the definition of the crime of torture to the law. So, the regime's tailors cut and stitched the laws so that most of the Interior Ministry's practices—even fatal ones—are tried as minor abuses, with sentences of 'manslaughter' or 'wrongful death' handed down in cases that should really topple entire security departments. The logical minimum requirement for this revolution's constitution is to set out a definition of torture in compliance with its definition in the International Convention Against Torture, though our people's aspirations go further.

Anyone reading a constitution that was drafted after the Maspero events would expect to see an article criminalizing the deployment of the Army against citizens, that protects soldiers who refuse to carry out criminal orders. Anyone reading a constitution drafted after the trial of the Deposed—where everyone managed to evade punishment except those whose responsibility was explicitly stated in the Constitution—would look for constitutional language to convict the entire chain of command for crimes against citizens: so the sniper is convicted, as well as his commanding officer, his presiding officer, his minister, his

president, and anyone who had the authority to stop the execution of the order but failed to.

Anyone writing a constitution for young Egypt, which rose
up against the Geriatric State, would have paid attention to the
people's suggestions for a constitutional article setting a unified retirement age, and applying it strictly (in which case, the
President would have been spared all that fuss and awkwardness
in getting rid of the Public Prosecutor and his ilk).[21]

How can those writing the Constitution today be taken up by
the issue of underage marriage when the greatest problem facing
the Egyptian family is delay in the age of marriage due to economic hardship?[22] What's the logic of the Constitution's authors
looking to protect the State from citizens exercising freedoms
that might break with tradition, when that State routinely allows
the rape of those citizens in police departments?

IV. PUBLIC OPENNESS & TRANSPARENCY

One of the weirdest things we've encountered in our winding
constitutional path is the quasi-secret nature of the Constituent
Assembly's deliberations. Subcommittee meetings are not
broadcast, minutes of committee meetings are not published.
The citizen attempts—in the absence of any official channel—to
understand what's going on in these committees by watching
members hurl accusations at each other on TV talk shows—
until the Assembly Chairman brings them to order, telling them
to bring their disagreements to him rather than airing them in
the media.

And every time voices are raised in protest at a leaked article,
the response is always to deny that such an article is even under

---

21 A joke, as Morsi had recently performed some constitutional acrobatics to install his
    own Public Prosecutor.
22 In Egypt, a couple cannot usually marry until the groom's family is able to provide an
    apartment to move into.

discussion. Later, the denial is exposed as a sham, so then we're told it was just a proposal. Do we not have the right to know about all proposals; who proposed them and who objected to them? The logic behind the proposal, and the reasons for the objections? Do we not have the right to understand what is happening behind the scenes of the drafting of our constitution, to politically assess the members, their parties, and their groups? Who ignored the people's proposals and who stood up for them? Who is saying, in the Assembly sessions, the opposite of what he says in the media? Do we not have the right to know how we ended up copying the articles of military guardianship from the Selmi document into the draft, despite the fact that the Muslim Brotherhood—who have a majority in the Assembly—had led the demonstrations against the Selmi document?

The obfuscation reached such a level that personal connections became the only channel by which a citizen learned the following: those working for the protection of street children requested the constitution use wording to prohibit one of the main causes of this social phenomenon but our Constituent Assembly ignored them on the grounds that constitutionalizing the protection of minors from the small minority of fathers who repeatedly violate and harm their children, would be an infringement on the Shari'a and on the right of fathers to use beatings as a tool of upbringing.

But secrecy is not just an annoyance for the alert citizen, and its consequences do not end when the work of the Assembly is done. After the Constitution is issued, its interpretation by the legislature and the courts will be based on the preparatory work, which includes Assembly proceedings and minutes of committee meetings that have been kept from us. How can we guarantee that those records will not be manipulated to alter the meaning of constitutional articles post-referendum, unless we can follow up on them as they are being written?

Or is it that the legislator, the judge, the civil servant, and the citizens, all need to convene in the office of the Assembly Chairman whenever we're uncertain about the interpretation of one of those loosely worded phrases?

V. SOCIETY-WIDE PARTICIPATION

Approximately 10,000 citizens came forward to address the Constituent Assembly, through hundreds of public hearings, carrying with them over 30,000 proposals, in addition to 100,000 or more suggestions that reached the Assembly via its internet portal. Also, hundreds of workers and volunteers from civil society organizations—working in development, human rights, and charity—came forward in an attempt to voice the aspirations and grievances of the under-represented groups in society, such as street children and people with disabilities.

A group of volunteers from the revolutionary youth worked on sorting and classifying all of these proposals, and producing comprehensive recommendations based on strict criteria, so that no proposal was sent to the Constituent Assembly unless it was voiced by thousands of citizens and was agreed on by a majority of those who the volunteers communicated with. When there was a division of opinion, full recommendations with alternative proposals were sent, so that the committees could select what they found most appropriate. For instance, two complete proposals were sent to the System of Governance Committee addressing the organization of local government with two different levels of decentralization.

A segment of the populace responded to the invitation to participate in writing the constitution believing it was sincere. They went to the Assembly carrying their hopes and grievances, dreams and pains, in response to an official call. And the Assembly chose to cast them all aside and exploit the public confidence just to boost its own image. We know this because

Dr Sahar Talaat resigned from the Assembly, and said, among the reasons for her resignation, that 'the first complete draft does not live up to the aspirations of the Egyptian people, which were clearly expressed in the proposals they presented, and were ignored.'

The members of the Assembly weren't just ignoring the people's proposals, one member went so far as to claim that the majority of proposals demanded the retention of the Shura Council.[23] This is an outright lie, and everyone knows it's an outright lie, and the Assembly members know that we know it's an outright lie. After all, Egyptians impressed the world by refraining from participation in the Shura Council elections.[24] What's weird is that the present draft contains transitional articles for the President and for the Parliament, but didn't define the fate of the current Consultative Council or how the proposed Senators' Council would be formed. I think there is a clear intention to preserve the present Consultative Council as a security in case the balance of power shifts and the Muslim Brotherhood loses its majority.

Unlike the esteemed members of the Assembly, the citizens who took the initiative and presented their pains and their dreams to the committee were completely preoccupied by the Egypt of the revolution. Here's just one example, an article proposed by volunteers in the Community Communications Committee:

---

23   The Shura Council, established in 1980 by Sadat to act as a parliamentary upper house, never came to be considered an important state institution as it had never been able to function independently of the executive. While parliamentary elections occasionally witnessed vigorous battles, Shura Council ballots were routinely ignored by the public.

24   State media outlets, desperate to confer legitimacy on elections under Mubarak, were known for headlines like 'Egyptians impress the world as millions flock to the polling stations.' Alaa's phrase is a cynical reference to the recent Shura Council's election turnout of 12 per cent (compared to 55 per cent for the parliamentary elections held two months earlier).

The State's General Budget, and its Final Accounting, must include all revenues and expenditures without exception. It is prohibited to maintain any revenue or expenditure for any state institution outside the State's General Budget and its Final Accounting. Special funds and all sources of revenue and expenditure shall be subject to oversight by the appropriate regulatory body.

With this simple article, we would take our first step towards solving two problems that have tormented us for years: the parallel economy of the military establishment, and special-purpose funds. I wonder why the Assembly members chose to ignore it?

Since the outbreak of the revolution we've watched the same scene repeat itself: the gates of history open themselves before our notables and elders, and all that's asked of them—to secure their place in history—is a step, one small step. But they are determined, those whom luck brought to this threshold, to stumble and bring our dreams crashing down. The step is easy. Be humble. Be humble and listen to those who have put their faith in you, and entrusted you with their dreams and pains.

Stumbling is also easy: you just have to convince yourself that disgrace and betrayal are protocol.

Published on 2 November 2012 in *al-Shorouk*

2013

DEAR CUSTOMER,
THANK YOU FOR HOLDING

5 January 2013

Are you one of the privileged few with a bank account?

Well done, mate—and you get about a 9 per cent return, I guess?

But do you know what the bank does with your money to get you that return?

It lends it to the government at 16 per cent. That's pretty much their main activity, or do you believe all that talk about investments?

So if the bank is making 16 per cent on your money, and only giving you 9 per cent, where does the rest go?

Into the pockets of the managers and senior staff at the bank. Or are you going to believe it's all administrative expenses?

OK, then how does the state pay that difference?

From your money, mate. From your taxes, from austerity policies and slashing services and cutting subsidies to the majority—who are not well-off, and do not have bank accounts—or did you think this was all from Suez Canal revenue?

OK so if the country is on the verge of bankruptcy and crisis like they're saying, then what will happen?

Most likely the pound will drop, so the value of your money in the bank will drop, and prices will go up for both you and those who are not well-off and have no money in the bank.

And if we really do get to the point of bankruptcy the bank could close down and all your money would be lost, but that's unlikely.

What's important is that the big guys who have pocketed this rate difference are the ones who pay the least taxes, are the least affected by austerity or slashed subsidies, the least affected by higher prices, and probably don't even keep their money in Egypt overnight.

So the state borrows your money without your permission, to apply policies no one consulted you on, then wastes it on corruption, negligence, and poor planning without any oversight from you, and along the way they make you pay the salaries and benefits of big shots in banks and ministries without having any say in their appointment, promotion or compensation. But if you ask them for a salary, for education, healthcare, kerosene, gas, or electricity, they'll shrug and say how can we provide for you? You're too many. And if you don't stop nagging they'll devalue the handful of piasters you've managed to save.

And that's if you're well-off and have a bank account in the first place.

But don't worry. The state will soon diversify and instead of making you lend them your money that's in the bank, they'll create Shari'a-compliant bonds that will make you lend any investor the land you're walking on and that feeds you.[25]

---

25 The Morsi administration's first major Islamic finance initiative proposed that state bodies be empowered to issue Shari'a government bonds sold through public offering and traded on the stock market. It was met with immediate resistance. Al-Azhar's Grand Sheikh Ahmed El-Tayyeb, for example, said in a press statement: 'We are worried that the draft law could allow foreigners to own key strategic assets; in addition, the way the law was drafted indirectly allows usury.'

ON THE SECOND ANNIVERSARY

25 January 2013
  @Alaa: Pessimism of the intellect, optimism of the will.

NEW CASE: INSULTING THE JUDICIARY

29 January 2013

2.12 p.m.

I'm at the Main Courthouse after being summoned for questioning by Councillor Tharwat Hammad in an unspecified case.

2.16 p.m.

Councillor Tharwat Hammad was the investigating judge for both my Maspero and 'Insulting the Judiciary' cases and who knows what else.

4.04 p.m.

The charge is insulting the judiciary. I refused to cooperate with the investigation because of the skewed priorities of investigating authorities that ignore complaints about torture but investigate what is published on the internet.

4.14 p.m.

In my reasons for refusing to cooperate with the investigation, I made special mention of their disregard for the complaint filed by the revolutionary youth who were accused of assaulting Al-Zend, regarding their torture by members of a judicial authority inside the Judges' Club.

4.23 p.m.

I also submitted an official complaint against Tantawi, SCAF, Morsi, the former Attorney General, and the current Attorney

General, accusing them of insulting the judiciary by interfering in its work and perverting the course of justice.

4.24 p.m.

I've been released, so let's get back to what's relevant: the police are thugs and down with the Supreme Guide's rule.[26]

4.58 p.m.

The 'Insulting the Judiciary' case is based on complaints from 1,064 judges against tens of media figures and activists. When will the same number of judges take a stand against human rights abuses?

6.34 p.m.

I call on all defendants in the 'Insulting the Judiciary' case— and other cases about settling scores and silencing voices—to take a similar position and refuse to cooperate with the investigation, until the justice apparatus fixes its priorities.

---

26   The Muslim Brotherhood is organized in a hierarchical command structure, at the top of which sits the Supreme Guide, Mohamed Badie.

FOUR TWEETS ON STATE VIOLENCE

29 January 2013

11.55 p.m.

When the authorities insist that non-violent actions (road-blocks, institutional disruptions, strikes and rude chants) be treated as violent, it follows that non-violence is abandoned because you're going to get a hard sentence anyway.

11.58 p.m.

And when the authorities put people who were just defending themselves on trial for murder, then it pushes them from defensive to offensive violence since they're going to get a hard sentence anyway.

12.11 a.m.

And when the authorities fail to observe the laws and regulations that *they* designed to protect *their own* interests, it becomes certain that people will completely ignore those laws.

12.11 a.m.

When we turn a blind eye to the violence the state exercises in maintaining itself—home demolitions, economic strangulation, the conscription of the Central Security Forces—then the down-trodden will find refuge in violence until you can't but see it.

SOLIDARITY STRIKES

10 April 2013

A thousand salutes to the metro workers that threatened to strike in solidarity with the train workers and saved us all from militarization as a tool of oppression.[27]

The solidarity strike is the most dangerous thing that the regime faces, when a worker strikes for someone else's demands because he's aware of how their situations are connected, that's the politicization of the labour movement we need, and that scares them. That's the reason they're making all this effort to suppress workers who are demanding a food allowance of a few pounds.

---

27 Train drivers striking for safer conditions were issued (at the request of the Ministry of Transport) with a military command to return to work. Metro workers threatening to join them forced the military to retract.

HISTORY REPEATING ITSELF

Protests have been called for 30 June, the one-year anniversary of Mohamed Morsi's election. A new campaign calling itself Tamarrod [Rebellion] has emerged and is collecting signatures calling for early elections. Tamarrod claims millions have signed the petition and is the subject of intense media coverage. There is little else that anyone is talking about.

17 May 2013

On 4 February 1942, Nahas Basha and his revolutionary party (the Wafd) formed a national government with the blessings of the English tanks which surrounded the king's palace.

They tell you history repeats itself. So he told them: first as tragedy, and then as farce.[28]

---

28 The British forced Egypt's King Farouq to allow the Wafd party to form a cabinet and Nahas Basha agreed to rule through British, rather than popular, mandate because of the threat of fascism coming from Rommel to the west. This caused a schism in the national movement that would never be resolved.

SCHRÖDINGER'S COUP

14 June 2013
Let's call 30 June Schrödinger's Cat's Millioneya.[29]

15 June 2013
A curse on Morsi, the Brotherhood, the government, the police, the judiciary, the military, and all those who have any power in this country.

17 June 2013
The state is the original evil. The Brothers are just an add-on, their danger stems from the danger of the state.

17 June 2013
When the revolution wins, we'll implement a plan to divide Egypt. We'll send the Brotherhood's supporters to a state ruled by the military, and the supporters of the *Feloul*,[30] the military, and stability, to a state ruled by the Brotherhood.

21 June 2013
The Egyptian military has shown that they come in when it becomes clear who the winner is so they can freeze the situation. The military will come in when it's over but we won't have realized that it's over.

21 June 2013
I don't know what will happen on the 30th, but it will be very

---

29 A *millioneya* is a million-person protest.
30 The *Feloul* is a catchall term given to the remnants of the old regime.

big and it will really come down to the Brotherhood, and we will all renounce violence. Anything other than that, your guess is as good as mine.

26 June 2013
The irony of our one and only sure victory being both pyrrhic and compromising.

26 June 2013
The only solution is a revolutionary escalation that takes the issue to a different stage and different methods. But there is no time to prepare. Occupying institutions, for example, would have been useful.

27 June 2013
Life consists of a series of choices between Morsi and Shafiq.[31]

29 June 2013
Everyone reaps what they sow.

The 30 June protests are enormous, with hundreds of thousands taking to the streets against the Muslim Brotherhood. Nobody knew what would happen that day, but most people expected there to be violence. Instead, the police protect the anti-government protestors and military helicopters drop Egyptian flags onto the crowd beneath—indicating that they have sided with the protestors against the Brotherhood.

---

31 Ahmed Shafiq, the establishment's candidate in the 2012 presidential election, was in the final run-off against Mohamed Morsi, leaving voters with a choice between the Army or the Brotherhood.

1 July 2013
The English tanks are at the gate, who's the Nahas Basha of the age?

1 July 2013
Before we talk about the Constitution we need to talk about whether humans' fate is already determined or he has a choice #dejavu

———

3 July: General el-Sisi suspends the Constitution and places President Mohamed Morsi under arrest.

———

4 July 2013
Hey US if calling it a coup will stop aid then it is a coup and a half.[32]

6 July 2013
We now know who the Nahas Basha of this age is, but I wonder if there'll be an arrest for me in the Era of el-Bob,[33] or if the Second Transitional Period is a holiday?

7 July 2013
So the question should be, is the military deposing a

---

32 Egypt has been a major recipient of US military aid since signing the Camp David Accords with Israel in 1978. By the letter of . . . US law, aid cannot be given to governments that came to power through a military coup.

33 El-Bob was a gently humorous popular nickname for Mohamed el-Baradei, the liberal opposition figure and Nobel laureate. El-Baradei was the most prominent of the secular opposition figures to endorse the coup, appearing on stage with el-Sisi, as well as the sheikh of al-Azhar, the Coptic Pope and leaders of the Salafi Nour party.

democratically elected murderer, torturer and thief a coup or not, commence debate.

7 July 2013
Schrödinger's coup is in a state of superposition where it is simultaneously a coup and a revolution. Trying to guess until the box is fully opened is a waste of time folks. [then, in Arabic] In other words, the ball's still in play so take to the streets, revolutionaries.

14 July 2013
Privileged people fearing things statistically unlikely to hit them are the best excuse for maintaining highly probable horrors meted on the unprivileged.

15 July 2013
The Greek epics tell the story of Cassandra, daughter of Priam, the King of Troy. Apollo gave her the powers of prophecy and the ability to predict the future. She could have become the city's seer.
But the gods are fickle and in a fit of rage, Apollo cursed her. He didn't take away the power of prophecy, but damned her never to be believed. She had a vision that Troy would burn and went around the city screaming her warning, and everyone ignored her.
To every Cassandra, there is no prize for being first to make predictions, and there's no use in saying I told you so. Cassandra's tragedy isn't that she was unable to convince others. Her tragedy, as in all Greek drama, was her failure to accept the limits of her condition.

28 July 2013
And I will forever remember this as the time when even a principled position could only contribute to the horror.

———

Supporters of the ousted president had two protest encampments: el-Nahda Square in west Cairo (Giza), and Rabaa el-Adaweya Square in east Cairo (Nasr City). Rabaa, the larger sit-in, was peaceful, with many families and children. The Nahda encampment was smaller, overwhelmingly male, and armed. Within days of the Nahda sit-in's establishment a march of Brotherhood supporters had killed twenty-seven people in the neighbouring Bein al-Sarayat district, and tensions have only increased in the three weeks since then. The police and the army maintain a minimal presence.

The night before, 27 July, Alaa and his mother, Laila Soueif, had been in the area (she is a professor of mathematics at nearby Cairo University) when a clash erupted. Alaa carried an injured man to hospital, where he died. A video journalist grabs him for a comment. Breathless and clearly stressed, he says 'the Nahda sit-in is armed with heavy weapons . . . they've clashed with four residential areas, this can't be solved by the residents, this doesn't have a political solution, it's solution has to be security . . . we were shot at me and my mother and a man got hit . . . We've known from the first day, the first day! There was the clash with Bein al-Sarayat and the residents filmed it and they killed people and we've seen their bodies in the morgue. The sit-in can't go on like this.' Two days later, the coup government started using this video in their build-up for what would come next, saying even Alaa was calling for the sit-ins to be cleared.

ASMAA

14 August 2013

Oh Asmaa, I don't know any more who's an enemy and who's a friend. There's no doubt your killing today was treachery, you were neither armed, nor in power. Asmaa, I don't know which path secures Khaled's future. I don't want him to die like Khaled Said or die like Mina Daniel or die like you. I long for him to live and grow up in safety and freedom.

What can I say to you? Should I say sorry? I'm sure I didn't do wrong or commit any crimes or ever intend any evil, but I've lived with guilt since the day Khaled was born.

Asmaa, your death comforts me that, despite the triumph of madness, death is still sober and chooses the best of us.

Lord save us from this hell that we are living in.

———

Asmaa el-Beltagy, daughter of a prominent Muslim Brother-hood leader, Mohamed Al-Beltagy, was born in 1996. She took part in the January 2011 revolution and, notably, in the battle of Mohamed Mahmoud Street, which the Brotherhood directed its members not to involve themselves in. She was an open and vocal critic of the Brotherhood's performance both in parliament and later in government.

Asmaa el-Beltagy joined the sit-in at Rabaa el-Adaweya after Morsi was removed from power.

Today, 14 August, the police attacked Rabaa with unprecedented force and Asmaa was killed while attending to the wounded.

AFTER THE CHURCHES

The immediate response by some Brotherhood supporters to the violent dispersal of Rabaa el-Adaweya was to attack churches across the country. On 14 August at least forty-two churches were attacked by Islamist mobs in Minya, Asyut, Fayoum, Giza, Sohag, Beni Soueif, Suez and Sinai.

15 August 2013

Egypt's Christians have endured the largest, most violent sectarian assault in our modern history. They endured it with unprecedented nobility and with faith in a better future despite knowing that tomorrow still holds a lot of pain.

The Islamists will not understand—no matter how severe their grievance—the value of what burned today. You, children of Qutb, el-Banna, and Abd el-Wahab, have burned the last opportunity for toleration of the Islamist project. And were it not for the Christians' call to love our enemies, there wouldn't even be a chance for forgiving you as individuals.

You fell today, even if you should triumph over the state. Just as the state fell today, by failing to protect Christians, though it triumphed over you.

ABOVE THE SOUND OF BATTLE[34]

According to the WikiThawra documentation, the number of people killed in the break-up of the Rabaa sit-in has reached 837: https:/tinyurl.com/4f2ax7zz

From now on we will have to live with this, the biggest massacre in our history. In a single engagement, within the space of a few hours, the Egyptian police, with the help of the armed forces and on orders from Sisi, Mohamed Ibrahim and Beblawi,[35] and with the support and encouragement of the public, killed at least 837 souls.

Most of us are in denial, a lot of us are telling ourselves that this was necessary, but the number and the bodies of the martyrs condemn us all. These kinds of numbers might die in a war between two armies over several days, or from aerial bombardments—not in a police operation. Whatever the percentage of armed men [in the dispersed sit-in] or the extent of the security threat, nothing can justify this.

On the 14th, history changed.

Mourid Barghouti tells us not to start the story from the middle. But some events force us to start with them. Whatever came before, whatever we might say about the crimes of Morsi

---

34 'No voice should be raised above the sound of the battle'. A slogan from the early Nasser days. Meaning, at a time of war, people of the same allegiance should maintain a united front. Alaa's use of the slogan here counters the original meaning: he insists on raising his voice, breaking ranks with the old comrades of the Left and the Liberal currents who acquiesce in the crime against the Brotherhood, and he demands that revolutionaries and those allied against a politics of violence should raise their voices too. At the same time, it's the resurgent security forces that seek to flatten difference and debate through the nationalistic trumpet of a proto-civil war.

35 Mohamed Ibrahim, Minister of the Interior. Hazem el-Beblawi, a neoliberal economist installed as Prime Minister of the coup government.

and the Muslim Brotherhood, for those who witnessed the
break-up of Rabaa and who saw death with their own eyes, whatever came before pales in significance. At Mohamed Mahmoud
about sixty people were killed, and for thousands of us that
marked a new beginning in history. In the Port Said massacre sev-
enty-four people were killed and for thousands of us that marked a
new beginning in history. The break-up of Rabaa was many times
more terrible. The break-up of Rabaa was more terrible than anything we have ever experienced. It can only be compared to war.

For those who were not there, for those still opposed to the
project of the Muslim Brotherhood and the other sectors of
the Islamist current, history has also changed: a new starting
point has been imposed on us and everything now follows on
from it. The burning of churches, the battles at police stations,
the massacre of the soldiers in Rafah, the arrest of the Supreme
Guide, all these events predate Rabaa, but their meaning—and
their consequences—changed after Rabaa. We will never be able
to escape Rabaa. For years to come we'll be finding that someone
we knew or were related to was killed in Rabaa, that someone
dear to us lost someone at Rabaa . . .

I have a lot to say about why—though I recognize the massacre and I condemn the murderer, Sisi—I will not change my
allegiance. I have a lot to say that damns the Brotherhood as
an organization and political Islam as an idea despite the massacre, but I refuse to say it in the same breath as though I need
to prove I'm against the Brotherhood or prove my loyalty to the
nation or the revolution. The future is bleak because of all the
blood shed before, during and after Rabaa. All those in power,
and those who sought, seek, or will seek power are guilty. Every
faction found its crowd to cheer it and justify its crimes, but this
does not allow us a way out of the fact that Rabaa is unique.
The fact that there have been lots of crimes committed by many
criminals must never be a smokescreen.

'They said, "We are going to destroy the people of this city, for its people only do wrong."'

At first it was our slain are in heaven and theirs are in hell, then it was our slain and yours are both in the morgue, and now there's no room in the morgue for our slain or yours. Since the massacre we have lived horrors, and tomorrow hides more horror, perhaps tomorrow is hiding something even more terrible than Rabaa.

I don't know how many people there are who are not politically aligned with the Rabaa Camp and whose consciences are hurting—but—and even if they're 'a minority of fifth columnists'—if they don't shout as loud as they can: 'Sisi is a murderer and Rabaa is one of the most terrible massacres in our history,' if we don't insist on documenting the truth of every massacre, condemning every killer, honouring every martyr, and seeking—with or without hope—retribution and justice for all, we will become that city of people who only do wrong.

In that city, all kill all, and the slain find no place in heaven, not just the morgue.

O Lord, deliver us from this city whose people only do wrong
O Lord, deliver us from this city whose people only do wrong
O Lord, deliver us from this city whose people only do wrong

20 August 2013

WHAT HAPPENED AT ABU ZAABAL

After false claims that the prisoners were trying to escape, the truth is finally out about the massacre at Abu Zaabal.

Bureaucracy, incompetence, mismanagement and indifference to the safety of the prisoners meant they tried to transport them in packed trucks in the heat of the day. Inefficient preparations meant they crammed one group into a closed truck which they left them inside for hours.

For those who haven't experienced them before, these police transport trucks are stifling even when they're not packed to the brim. They have an air suction fan but if it's not working you can't breathe. And of course they can't keep the suction fan running for long without the motor running too. The struggle to either turn on the fan or let us off to wait outside is a constant issue during prisoner transports, but because there were so many detainees things clearly went way past what is tolerable.

The group in the truck started to shout and bang on the walls. An officer opened the door to yell at them and they grabbed him, pulled him into the truck and demanded to be let out before they suffocated. Other officers intervened and got their colleague out unharmed.

At this point no one had died, the officer wasn't in danger, there was no large-scale mutiny among the prisoners, and of course there wasn't any attempt to escape or an armed attack— and the truck was within the prison walls anyway, so there was no danger of escape. But still there were prisoners squeezed in a stifling truck at high noon. The prisoners kept banging on the walls, so someone from the transport's guard detail decided to fire a tear gas canister into the truck.

The police will claim it was misjudgement and negligence. True, locking them up for hours in the truck was misjudgement and negligence, but the decision to shoot gas into the truck was a decision to kill. You can't convince me that a Central Security Forces officer who transports his men around in similar trucks isn't well aware what firing tear gas into it would do. You can't convince me that a Central Security Forces officer whose experience and training tells him that gas is fired to disperse demonstrations because you have to run away from it in order to breathe doesn't understand that he is now firing it at people who can't run away.

Firing gas into the truck is murder, and everyone who approved the decision is responsible. All those who did not intervene to save the prisoners after the gas was fired committed the crime of gross negligence, and all those who allowed the situation to develop and get to that point are guilty of negligence.

Published on 20 August 2013 on Facebook

——

37 prisoners were killed in the police truck at Abu Zaabal.

YOU KNOW THAT THE KILLING
WAS RANDOM

You know that the killing was random, and you know that
the arrests ranged from random to indiscriminate. You understand very well that when the police kill, they don't distinguish
between armed and unarmed, and you understand very well
that they arrest anyone they can get their hands on—they don't
distinguish between who's a criminal and who's innocent.

The aim was to break a political opponent, not to confront
criminals within its organization. The method was collective
punishment. There isn't anyone who doesn't know that. But
there are a lot of people who approve of it; and even more
who've decided to turn a blind eye even though they don't
approve because they're afraid; and even more just keeping quiet
because there isn't anything to be done.

But there isn't one single person in Egypt who believes that
all, or even *many*, of those who were killed were armed and
posed a threat to others' lives. And there isn't one single person
in Egypt who believes that all, or even many, of those arrested
had committed crimes and need to be locked up for the protection of lives.

So don't act stupid and be surprised when I say 'down with
military rule'. The essence of military rule is the use of arms to
protect the regime from external attempts to change it. And the
arms that are being pointed at the Muslim Brotherhood today
will be pointed at someone else next time; the military are not
secularists against Islamism, the military are the old régime
against change. The Brotherhood went back and forth between
manipulating the mass desire for change, and attempting to

impose changes that the masses didn't want. But the military are not waging war against the Brotherhood for our sake.

Published on 27 August 2013 on Facebook

NOTES ON THE 'RECLAIMING THE REVOLUTION' NARRATIVE

After the Rabaa massacre some groups from the revolutionary youth have started to join the Islamists' demonstrations. In theory this is supposed to come to a head with today's call [to demonstrate], issued by the Ahrar movement[36] and the Third Way,[37] using vague slogans about restoring the January Revolution, but not Morsi; and about popular legitimacy, but not the legitimacy of the ballot box.

Everyone's free to make their choices, but I'd like friends keen on this 'Reclaiming the Revolution' narrative to take note of some details.

Its advocates are always saying the battle has nothing to do with the Brotherhood—and what they do say about the Brotherhood is limited to condemning their reformist attitude. Which means that the problem with the Brotherhood was that they were not revolutionary enough and did not purge the state agencies: they allowed the criminals of the Mubarak regime and the military to escape accountability. The problem is that this narrative overlooks the policies, practices, and crimes of the Brotherhood when they were in power.

The Brotherhood, while in power, used violence to try and solidify their power and pass policies despite the opposition. They used state violence through the police and the Public

---

36 The *Ahrar* (Freemen) movement was a radical Islamist youth group, which included some football Ultras, that emerged in 2012 after Salafist preacher Hazem Salah Abu Ismail was barred from running in the presidential elections. They were opposed to both the military and the Muslim Brotherhood.

37 The Third Way (or Third Square) was a short-lived movement that emerged in the summer of 2013 to oppose both the military and the Muslim Brotherhood.

Prosecution, and they used their own cadres when state violence was not enough. The violence targeted everyone, from the attack dogs let loose by Saad el-Hosseiny[38] on fishermen, to breaking the Portland Cement workers' strike—also with dogs—to the massacres by the police in Port Said and Suez.

Police, during Morsi's time, suppressed social protests with unprecedented brutality, and there was an increase in death by torture in police stations. The standard answer is that the events of 30 June prove the police were conspiring against the Brotherhood, but this means we have to ignore the Brotherhood's own narrative. Morsi, whenever he talked about the police, would go to pains to stress how wonderful they are, and insisted everything was happening under his orders. In particular, the massacre at Port Said. Morsi emphasized that they were acting on his orders, and the Brotherhood cadres and their online corps celebrated it and talked about how the police had 'shown their credentials', while constantly complaining and inciting against direct actions like roadblocks and strikes.

In addition to state violence, the Brotherhood used their cadres' violence against their opponents, not only at the Presidential Palace and the two clashes in Moqattam,[39] but also against social protests in the governorates. The most famous of these were the assault on a women's sit-in in Mansoura, and an attack on a workers' sit-in in Damietta. The torture houses set up at the Presidential Palace and at Bilal Mosque in Moqattam proved that, for the Brotherhood, torture is a systematic practice, supervised by its leaders, and justified by Shari'a.

Morsi's rule witnessed the longest wave of detentions in parallel with state and Brotherhood violence. Around 5,000 detainees between January and April, most of whom were

---

38   Senior leader in the Brotherhood and member of the organization's powerful Guidance
      Bureau. Appointed Governor of Kafr el-Sheikh by Morsi.
39   The Muslim Brotherhood's headquarters.

tortured. All were imprisoned on orders of the Brotherhood's Public Prosecutor, who was appointed through a series of crooked constitutional manoeuvres. We cannot call these detentions a deep state conspiracy. Not to mention the fact that the Public Prosecutor and his office rigged tens of cases against revolutionaries based on complaints presented by Brotherhood law firms. The same firms flooded the courts with complaints about insulting the president and contempt of religion.

Sycophancy to the military and the Interior Ministry, and violence and oppression and detention, were formal policies of the Brotherhood. For those who want to protest against the military, and have nothing to do with the Brotherhood, you can't just reduce our problem with the Brotherhood to their being conservative and reformists. Maybe you could have said that back in 2012, but not now.

Published on 30 August 2013 on Facebook

WHO REPRESENTS THE BOURGEOISIE?

At least in theory, political liberalism and representative democracy—despite their shortcomings—were invented to solve the problem of how diverse social movements that differ due to cultural, class, or ideological reasons can coexist under the sovereignty of one state, and be subject to the same authorities and laws without constant infighting.

Practically, the recent history of democratic transitions is related to the fact that constant strife is a threat to markets that have achieved a level of development and stability. Capital—as one of the social forces, not just as a clique—along with other interests that are broader and more complex than capital but still related to the market and to production, are impacted by strife, so they sell out the more authoritarian and fascist parties, even if they share a historical relationship, in exchange for a democratic transition that would guarantee market stability and growth.

The market asserts itself as a force impartial to cultures, religions, ethnicities, tribalism, clans and ideologies. Even many of the things traditionally related to economic inequality turn out not to be essential for the market itself; thus it imposes on the highly contested evolving state a new balance that reduces the level of contentiousness.

I'm not an academic so I'm not sure, but it's my gut feeling that this applies to several diverse examples, from South Africa to Turkey to Italy to Brazil.

In countries where markets are not developed enough to have large interests related to the workforce and local resources, the economy develops in directions more akin to the economies of organized crime: quick shady profits; masked feudalism; direct transfer of assets and resources from public to private ownership; import, export, and trading that is closer to smuggling; huge public works contracts that are closer to money laundering, etc. Of course, all markets have some of this, some more than others, but some countries have nothing *but* this gangster economy and the very traditional markets that support the majority of the population. These countries remain stuck in the whirlpools of authoritarian anguish, while there is extensive investment in hindering their development (most African countries are examples).

In Egypt, although the underlying causes of the conflict seem less acute, the conflict itself is getting more so, and although it appears to be a developed market, with production, industry, agriculture, local resources, local labour, and a common infrastructure covering the whole country, the market is not really imposing itself at any stage. It is true that all the above have profound problems, and true that all the large fortunes look like they've been made in the cartel economy (not to mention actual organized crime economy that's involved in smuggling everything and splits it with the military). But, at the end of the day, the market is not all just investment in chaos and thin air. There is a real market, but this market does not express itself in the political conflict.

Our economy is usually categorized into formal and informal. This categorization always carries a certain fallacy, but in Egypt it has become absurd. So Wekalet El-Balah,[40] for example, is treated as an informal market, although it is older than the Republic itself, and has features of stability and institutionalization that you won't find in some formal markets. Perhaps there's an alternative categorization based on the impact of a given economic activity on employment and resources.

The important thing is that, in countries where the market

---

40 A large textiles and clothing market in central Cairo.

has imposed stability and tipped the balance in favour of
liberalism a large part of the stability-seeking interests were
concentrated around certain people and institutions (in South
Africa for example, it was the capitalists in insurance companies and in major banks who first entertained the idea that the
apartheid system could negotiate with the liberation movement,
as opposed to the capitalists in the mining sector who always
favoured investing in racism). In Egypt, the market heavy-
weights all seem to be connected to the gang economy or the
globalized market more than they're connected to the market for
local resources and labour. And of course a large chunk of the
market—in all its varieties—is concentrated in the hands of the
military, so it is unable to see its interests outside the conflict.

OK, so whose interest is served by the market and its stability?
Who wants the 'wheels of production' to really spin? I suppose
most of the real economy—whether formal or informal—is
distributed over small-scale capitalists and medium-sized production and trading firms. And those do not have enough
wealth or connections to be effective players in the current
conflict. Those of course are the bourgeoisie in its very classical
meaning, and of course the bourgeoisie requires reformists to
express its interests and help it achieve the desired stability,
which can only be brought about—in the context of the current
political system—through political liberalism and representative
democracy.

Unless there are people with enough economic power to have
an impact on the authorities, and also share the interests of the
bourgeoisie, then the only alternative is forming coalitions that
bring together sectors of the bourgeoisie to express their interests. In Turkey, for example, this happened when the bazaars
turned into institutions representing the interests of the mer-
chants and the producers, and asserted themselves. The bazaars
were instrumental in preventing the military-Islamist conflict

there from turning into street warfare, and in tipping the balance in favour of the Islamists in the democratic transition, but they also had a role in curbing the Islamization, meaning that they put brakes on all parties, and tipped the balance in favour of reform. But of course the role of the bazaars receded with time, as globalization has no mercy on traditional markets.

Who represents the Egyptian bourgeoisie? Who are the political powers that can lead a coalition of stability-seeking capitalism? We were under the impression that the Muslim Brothers speak for wide sectors of the Egyptian bourgeoisie, but, when put to the test, they turned out to express a much narrower interest.

The Left, in Egypt—for all its weird phases and structural defects—always leaned towards radicalism, and is concerned with representing working classes and social sectors other than the bourgeoisie (so that when addressing the middle class, it addresses the youth and the professionals employed by the government). Regardless of the efficiency of representation, we can state that there *are* people working on advocacy for the interests of labourers, farmers, students, those completely outside the formal market, and even social sectors that are threatened with extinction, such as fishermen—but there's no one to express the interests of owners of medium-sized farms, manufacturers and traders, or owners of modern businesses. I think this should be the role of entities like the Dostour Party or the Egyptian Social Democratic Party,[41] but for some reason I feel they don't even come close.

As a radical who is in theory unconcerned with the destiny of the bourgeoisie and, at base, not content with the prospect of stability under representative democracy, I have to admit that a very wide sector of the bourgeoisie threw their lot in with the

41 Two of the most prominent political parties formed in the wake of the January revolution.

revolution, and it looks like they're seeking—through it—their political representation and the unity that would enable them to assert their worldview. The simplest example of this is our ability to cover the subsistence costs for sit-ins and for detainees, and the cost of medical care and bail for the heroes of the revolution from direct donations. It's true that several thousands come from donations of a few pounds, but the organizational apparatus for collecting donations is not advanced enough to rely completely on small donations. Actually, we rely mainly on medium-sized donations (of a few thousand pounds).

I wonder, is there a political movement interested in unifying and representing the bourgeoisie in a revolutionary context? A movement that would help the traders of Wekalet El-Balah organize themselves and join forces with the residents of Ramlet Bulaq to lobby against the Maspero Triangle project?[42] A movement that would help the owners of small tourism enterprises organize themselves and lobby for solutions to resume tourism and protect them from going bankrupt every time there's a crisis anywhere in the country? A movement that would help farm owners organize themselves to lobby against monopolies in agricultural tools, products, and seeds? A movement that would help owners of small and medium technology companies organize themselves and lobby for the revision of the terms of public tenders, and of tax regulations and various other bureaucratic obstacles?

Published on 21 September 2013 on Facebook

---

42 A major gentrification plan that proposed the displacement of the residents of the Maspero Triangle, a poor but centrally located neighbourhood in Cairo. The Wekalet El-Balah market runs along its northern border and though it fell outside the plan's perimeter would very likely be negatively, perhaps even existentially, impacted. Four years later, The Maspero Triangle was razed and construction began.

THE RIGHTEOUS PATH

23 November 2013
   @Alaa: Do not be turned from the righteous path by the
many corpses strewn upon it.[43]

---

43 This mirrors a saying attributed to Ali ibn Abi Talib: 'Do not be turned from the
    righteous path by the lack of those walking upon it.' Ali ibn Abi Talib was the cousin,
    son-in-law and companion of Prophet Mohammad, the fourth and final of the
    Rashidun Caliphs and is considered among history's most just and eloquent leaders.

MY IMMINENT ARREST

27 November 2013 00.28 a.m.

Deja Vu, I'm about to hand myself in to the authorities again on Saturday. My ever imminent arrest is now a running joke in Egypt.

EMBEDDED POST:

—@Ahdaf Soueif: Alaa Abd el-Fattah's statement in English (my translation)

Statement of my intention to hand myself in to the Prosecutor's Office on Saturday midday:

A Charge I Don't Deny and an Honour I Don't Claim

For the second time the Office of the Public Prosecutor has sent out an arrest warrant through the media—instead of to my address—well-known to them because of their history of fabricating charges against me in the eras of Mubarak, Tantawi and Morsi.

For the second time the office of the Public Prosecutor lets itself be a tool of government propaganda, this time on the orders of the murderer (Minister of Interior) Mohamed Ibrahim, instead of the Morshid (the Supreme Guide of the Muslim Brotherhood). Their reason: that I incited people to demand that trials should be fair and should be the responsibility of an independent civil judiciary. As though it's bad for the Prosecutor's Office to respect itself and be respected by the public, it must prove its subservience to any authority that passes through this country—no difference here between a Prosecutor illegitimately appointed at the instructions of the Morshid, and a Prosecutor correctly appointed—but at the instructions of the Military.

The charge—it appears—is that I participated in inviting people to protest yesterday, in front of the Shura Council building, against placing—for the second time—an article in the Constitution legitimizing the court martial of civilians.

The strange thing is that both the Prosecutor and the Ministry of the Interior knew that I was present for eight hours at First Police Station New Cairo in solidarity with the people arrested yesterday on the same charges. But neither the Prosecutor nor the MOI ordered my arrest at the time or demanded that I be questioned. This probably means that they intend to put on a show where I play the criminal-in-hiding.

So, despite the following facts:

That I do not recognize the anti-protest law that the people have brought down as promptly as they brought down the monument to the military's massacres—

That the legitimacy of the current regime collapsed with the first drop of blood shed in front of the Republican Guards Club—

That any possibility of saving this legitimacy vanished when the ruling four (Sisi, Beblawi, Ibrahim and Mansour) committed war crimes during the break-up of the Rabaa sit-in—

That the Public Prosecutor's Office displayed crass subservience when it provided legal cover for the widest campaign of indiscriminate administrative detention in our modern history, locking up young women, injured people, old people and children, and holding as evidence against them balloons they were carrying and t-shirts they were wearing—

That the clear corruption in the judiciary is to be seen in the overly harsh sentences against students whose crime was their anger at the

murder of their comrades, set against light sentences and acquittals for
the uniformed murderers of those same young people—

Despite all this, I have decided to do what I've always done
and hand myself in to the Public Prosecutor.

I do not deny the charge—even though I cannot claim the
honour of bringing the people onto the street to challenge the
attempts to legitimize the return of the Mubarak state.

And so that I don't allow their rabid dogs any excuse at all, I
have officially informed the Prosecutor's Office by telegram (no.
96/381 dated today), and by letter (delivered by hand to the Public
Prosecutor, registered number 17138 for 2013), as I have informed
the Attorney General for Central Cairo (telegram no. 96/382)
of my intention to hand myself in on Saturday 30 November at
midday to the Prosecution at their Qasr el-Nil office.

The protest's people's voices heard
needs no permit from the guard!

Alaa Abd el-Fattah
Cairo 27 November 2013

1.27 a.m.
@ENN_News: #Egypt_news | Breaking | Security forces
arrest #Alaa_Abd_El-Fattah and #Ahmed_Maher

1.30 a.m.
@Alaa: @ENN_News Guys, I'm sitting here at home

1.44 a.m.
Well since the Interior Ministry has already arrested me I
guess I don't have to hand myself in on Saturday. So the question
is: do I go down to stand in solidarity with myself?

3.28 a.m.

Remember: last time I handed myself in after an arrest warrant was issued the prosecutor wrote in my case file that they found me wandering around the courthouse and so ordered my arrest.

3.54 a.m.

Tomorrow there's a session of the Cabinet Building[44] case too, a case that's been going on for three years. But it's not the army officers who killed people that are on trial, it's civilian revolutionaries.

3.55 a.m.

In the Cabinet Building case, revolutionaries have been on trial in civilian and military courts, have witnessed the successive replacement of four governments and three Public Prosecutors, and have been issued a legal pardon, and yet the case still goes on.

3.56 a.m.

Besides which, the Cabinet Building case has broken the record for the number of accused held in one courtroom cage. There were probably fewer people at the Cabinet Building Sit-In than those standing trial for it.

4.33 a.m.

So, do we like cloudflare? Is it as good as they claim?

6.00 a.m.

I just want to make it clear that even if they purged the Interior Ministry and wrote the most brilliant constitution and elected a truly popular revolutionary government and wrote the best possible protest law, I would still not abide by it.

---

44 A street battle between revolutionists and army soldiers that took place outside the Cabinet Office over several days in December 2011.

2.01 p.m.
They say [the trial] will be held in the Torah Police Institute.
The judiciary has been entirely taken over by the Interior
Ministry.

2.13 p.m.
The judge that recused himself from the Cabinet Building
case today, was he new? Or had he been on the case for a while?
When is this case going to finish?

2.49 p.m.
They took out the word 'civilian' because it's understood that
this is a military state and it's going to remain a military state.

3.49 p.m.
@c********i:
Hi! Will u be available to speak to BBC World Service radio
on the recent development in Egypt and your order arrest

@Alaa:
no sorry, I'm trying to finish as much work as possible in the
possibility I'll be detained

4.05 p.m.
The Ministry of the Interior breaks all those in power.
Amr Moussa[45] and Beblawi went public and announced that
the young people arrested at the Shura Council protests would
be released, so the Ministry of the Interior insisted that most of
them be detained.
Some university administrations refused to allow security
forces into their campuses, now the Ministry of the Interior is

---

45 A prominent diplomat of the Mubarak era, then a candidate for president after the
    revolution, now president of a new Constituent Assembly.

forcing itself upon them—and acting with recklessness just as it does on the campuses run by informers.

The judiciary is now openly and fully subservient to the Ministry of the Interior. We know this because interrogations, reviews of detentions and even some court sessions are now taking place inside police stations, prisons and police training camps. The Minister of the Interior has boasted about giving orders to the Prosecutor General in front of prisoners' families.

Mohamed Ibrahim[46] is in the driving seat now and the most half-witted cop can do whatever he wants and every institution has to fall in line and work out how to justify it.

In my opinion even Sisi, the murderer in chief, is cornered by his ally Mohamed Ibrahim. Sisi's priority is keeping things smooth between the army and the public because the deployment of the army and their attempt to control the street in 2011 was very painful for the institution. And now they have a real battle on their hands in Sinai so the institution really cannot handle being out in front, particularly if there's an escalation of popular anger. Sisi's internal standing in the Army comes from the lower ranks, and clearly there are disagreements with the higher-ups, and it's the lower ranks that are most affected by daily friction with the public.

Meanwhile, the democratic wing is worried that the Ministry of the Interior will pull back and stop working, like it did in 2011 and 2012, and they are worried because they want the police to crack down on the Brotherhood. That's why, up until now, no one from the government or its allies has taken any serious position against Mohamed Ibrahim.

And of course with every new crime these allies, authorities and institutions become more complicit, have more blood on their hands, and turning back becomes harder and harder.

---

46 Minister of the Interior appointed by Morsi who then became one of the major architects of the coup against him.

We already went down this road when Morsi first appointed Mohamed Ibrahim. But back then, the state and the institutions were exhausted from their battles with the street, and the police started refusing orders and striking, demanding more weapons and a free hand to use them. This time, they've got what they wanted, so they won't be exhausted easily.

Last time, this path pushed a lot of young people towards violence, and they started looking around for weapons. This time there are a lot of people ready to help them down that road. That's why it's extremely urgent to stop this in its tracks—and the only solution is a unified position from all so-called 'civil' powers against the Protest Law, against the return of the police to university campuses, against State Security, against repression and over-zealous sentencing. Also there must be a unified, immediate demand for the dismissal of Mohamed Ibrahim, and pressure on all the ministers of this government to resign if he remains in his position.

Just as Khairat el-Shater[47] is the Brotherhood's historic leader who led them to power—regardless of the horrors that came next—so Mohamed Ibrahim is, for the police, the historic leader who returned them to the core of the state. He raised the police above everyone, even the army, and put them in power over the people again. Anyone implicated in this—whether by supporting, justifying, downplaying or whitewashing—will hopefully suffer the same fate as the Brotherhood.

4.55 p.m.
The pig bastards killed a student at Cairo University? Now things will flare up.

5.02 p.m.
Does anyone know the whereabouts of the student who was

---

47   Though not the Supreme Guide of the organization, el-Shater was known to be the most powerful figure within the Muslim Brotherhood.

killed at the Engineering Faculty? What hospital he was taken to?

5.03 p.m.

Is anyone around Cairo University? Is it safe? There are students that want to go home but are afraid.

5.06 p.m.

The police fired gas and shotgun at the civilian security guards of Cairo University, fired at the central building. Their fight is with the existence of any independent institution, not just with the students—the professors need to wake up.

5.28 p.m.

Confirmed by my mother Dr Laila Soueif. Mohamed Reda, student in the Faculty of Engineering, Cairo University, was martyred a short time ago from shotgun wounds to the neck. Eyewitnesses confirm he was inside the university campus and was shot by police from outside the grounds. His colleagues tried to move him quickly to hospital in a private car, the police stopped them and arrested them and left Mohamed's body in the car outside the Saideyya School. His father has gone to him and an ambulance is on the way. There's also news of injuries at Qasr al Aini hospital, at least one is in critical condition.

5.37 p.m.

We've always said that the students know that the police see no difference between Cairo University and al-Azhar University, or between Brotherhood students and Nasserist students. Shame on those who can't understand until they come for their own children.

5.43 p.m.

I heard the judge ordered the boys released but the

Prosecution appealed, I guess they want to give them a chance to be tortured for a couple more days.

5.57 p.m.

What's the name of the judge who sent the tortured boys back to the police for fifteen days, so they can continue to torture them without any distractions?

6.03 p.m.

I tell them my mother is a professor at the university and she's standing now with the body of a student killed by the police, and they say she's standing with the Brotherhood. There are no words to describe your criminality.

6.46 p.m.

Legitimacy in Egypt only lasts for one summer. Doesn't matter if it's ballot-box legitimacy, a popular mandate or rule of necessity, it's one summer and that's it.

6.57 p.m.

Another confirmation: a civilian security guard at Cairo University has been injured by shotgun. So, guess what? The Minister of Higher Education is coming out in defence of the Ministry of the Interior, saying they didn't shoot inside the university. So the security guard was out in an illegal protest beyond the university walls too? The problem is when you sell yourself and accept the logic that it's fine to kill anyone as long as they're outside the university walls, the Ministry of the Interior ups the stakes and kills them *inside* the university—so it's best not to pimp yourself out to begin with, Minister.

7.03 p.m.

A lot of students reporting that the civilian security guards of

Cairo University were brave and tried to protect the students, and they refused to let the Ministry of the Interior through the university gates.

———

Within minutes of this post the police raid Alaa's house, beat him and his wife, blindfold and arrest him.

2014

GRAFFITI FOR TWO

Alaa has been in prison for two months when this piece is released. It's the third anniversary of the revolution, 25 January 2014. Here, he combines his prose with the poetry of another political prisoner, Ahmad Douma. The original coda to the piece read as follows:

'We apologize to readers for any confusion or incoherences in the text—they're due to the circumstances of its writing. It was not easy for those used to instant expression on mobiles and keyboards to get through a two-week process of writing with pencil and paper (mostly) in solitary. And neither of us were ever able to spend time with the complete text.

We apologize also to our colleagues in Ward A, Political, Torah Prison, for what they put up with, as a poet who lived in the first cell in the ward and a blogger who lived in the last tried to cooperate. Both preferred to discuss their text by yelling in the night rather than use up the few hours of exercise in the open air.

We tried in this text to express our gratitude to those who dispelled the loneliness of our cells with their love and their care, and our deep belief in a generation that refused to queue for a place at Authority's table. And it would be remiss not to thank the Authority—were it not for the new 'paint' we would not have found the space to think and draw.

Alaa and Douma'

I.
I know that despair is treason
but the revolutionary in my country
—even if he's a sinless prophet—
who sees the tyrant empowered

at the oppressed's command
amid the rejoicing of the poor
will lose his faith.

They say that despair is treason. I was never comfortable with the slogan. I understand its motivation, but I'm worried the word is used lightly. The denial of a natural feeling scares me.

It reminds me of angry crowds circling the square carrying a bloodied shirt, searching for any traitor who allowed despair to steal into his mind or heart. They ruin the sweetness of the square. We pretend to forget them while we weave the myth of those eighteen shining days[48]—but they are always in my nightmares.

In my nightmares they surround my mother; they want to throw her out of the square. Laila Soueif resists them. Laila Soueif who was born from the womb of defeat and so went into the square in 1972 and never came back. Despair never dared come near her—yet they called her a traitor to exorcize their own doubts and fears.

From my mother I inherited a stone cake[49] and from my father a prison cell.[50] And, in line with our traditions, I was given an inheritance better than my sisters, for they inherited morgues and victims of torture and the embrace of grieving mothers. I'm scared to even ask about their nightmares.

They say that despair is treason. I understood but I wasn't convinced. They also said, 'Brother, behind bars you are free.' And here I am behind bars, stripped of my will and my dream. And I know from experience that part of me will stay behind these bars even when the decision comes to let me go.

---

48   25 January–11 February 2011.

49   Reference to a poem by Amal Donqol about the student uprising of 1972. The 'stone cake' is the base of the monument in the centre of Tahrir Square, a central point for both the students in 1972 and the revolutionaries in 2011.

50   Ahmed Seif, Alaa's father, served a sentence of five years (in the same prison Alaa is in as he writes) for 'plotting to overthrow the government'.

Myths are part of my inheritance. People say, 'Who can—for one hour—imprison Egypt?'[51] They say it even though everyone knows that Generals Tapioca and Alcázar and all the other generals will imprison Egypt for as many hours as their dreams of clocks with green hands dictate.[52]

People say, 'You can't kill an idea.' But they said nothing about the usefulness of immortal ideas unheard in the noise of gunfire.

Why are we afraid to admit weakness? To admit that we are human, that APCs crush us and prisons desolate us and bullets scar our thoughts and our dreams. That we are humans suffering defeats, let down by our bodies, made weak by the whisperings of our selves, burned by our dreams and paralyzed by our nightmares. Humans looking to love for support against despair.

II.
Hope
like the key to paradise
you own it
and you're saved.
But paradise we enter
in our dreams . . .
And after death.

If despair is treason, what is hope? At least despair speaks frankly. Hope is treacherous. Have we seen treason uglier than that committed in hope's name?

The army, the people, one hand. The law-abiding state. The constitution first. The people. The elected institutions. Yesterday's

---

51 A well-loved revolutionary song by Sheikh Imam, its lyrics were written in prison in 1972 by Zein el-Abedeen Fuad.

52 A month earlier, a recording of Sisi was leaked in which he talked about visions of the future that come to him in dreams, namely that he will become president, holding a sword and wearing an Omega watch with a green star.

comrades. The veteran fighters. The judiciary that fears only God. The masses. The guardians of the square. The coalition. The organization. The party. The independent media. The patriotic wing. The national council. The honour of officers . . .

Is there treason worse than hope in some—or all, or any—of the above?

Is there treason worse than hope in the ratification of a new constitution that breaks its own foundational promise—that it would not be completed until every last prisoner was released?

Is there treason worse than hope in a state whose institutions do nothing but kill, torture and betray?

Is there treason worse than hope in elections steeped in a national discourse designed to guarantee least competition and most certainty of results?

Is there treason worse than hope in the 'candidate of necessity'—even though his only qualification is 'necessity'?

Is there treason worse than hope in a civilian candidate afraid to look like he's actually in competition with the General?

Is there treason worse than hope in masses that march under images of murderers and torturers? Or hope in comrades who deny defeat out of pride rather than defiance? Comrades who, when the infection spreads and revolutionaries return to the streets and the prisons and the morgue, are not there with them?

Hope, like despair, is treason. But also, like despair, it's a normal human weakness. Here in my cell I wrestle with my dreams and my nightmares, and I don't know which hurts more. Both despair and hope pull at me—but I am never a traitor.

III.
We are not free
confess
but we
cling to tomorrow.

People's tragedy: they committed
the sin of the wish
with no limit.

On a clear day, after two hunger strikes and a snowstorm, the
sky quietens and in our hearts there's calm.

We drink tea in the courtyard. We've passed the stage of dis-
cussing the use of our resilience, the chances of our release. After a
month of disclosures and revisions all that's left to us is memories.

And while we tell stories of past imprisonments, when the
cells seemed more friendly and comrades more loyal, even
though the revolution was, then, an 'impossible dream', I think
back and find myself there, in the past, in the metro, with a
friend, in my high school uniform, handing out an investigative
report complete with photographs of the torture of an old 'cattle
thief' they set alight with kerosene in Fayoum police station. We
change trains quickly before someone recovers from the shock of
the image and arrests us.

I didn't tell my father I had come into my inheritance that
day. It didn't seem important. We were just trying to get rid of
some of the anger, to get that terrible photograph out of the
house. Hope had no part in this.

There, in the past, I find myself less experienced and wiser. I
write of a generation that fought without despair and without
hope, that won only small victories and wasn't shaken by major
defeats because they were the natural order of things. A generation whose ambitions were humbler than those who came
before, but whose dreams were bigger.

There's a lot wrong with me—but I'm no traitor. I've committed acts of cowardice and selfishness, I was impatient often
and rash sometimes, I was proud and I was lazy, but I was never
a traitor. I will not betray the revolution with despair or with
hope. This is a promise.

IV.
Who said we were
unequalled?
Or that we're
an enchanted generation?
We're human
but
in the dark
we wish for light

Our sin was pride, not treachery. We said, 'We're not like those
who came before us; the young Muslim Brothers are different and
the young Nasserists are different and the young Leftists are different and the young Liberals are different.' The weakness of our
myth was exposed when we came up against the young officers.

Today I see that we are flawed, like those who came before
us, making the same mistakes they made. Despite all our claims
to uniqueness and rebellion we are nothing more than the loyal
children of our families and our motherland, holding on to their
beliefs, their habits and their traditions. Our inheritance. And
we hold on to it for our children.

We'll say to them, 'You're different, you won't repeat our
mistakes,' but forget to tell them this is a hope, not a prophecy.
We'll sing them the songs of Ahmad Fouad Negm and Sheikh
Imam,[53] or the anthems of Sayyed Qutb[54] and Hashim el-Rifae[55]
but forget to tell them that this is heritage, not resistance. They'll

---

53 Negm was a leftist streetwise poet who formed a duo with the musician and singer,
    Sheikh Imam. After the defeat of 1967, they started to write and perform political
    protest songs, and have been icons of the Left since then.
54 Islamist scholar, writer and poet. A leading member of the Muslim Brotherhood in the
    1950s and until his trial and execution in 1966. Considered the founding ideologue of
    Salafi Jihadism.
55 Islamist poet who wrote against the despotism of the Nasser regime. Killed in 1959,
    aged 24.

rebel, and in the end they'll return to their heritage of their own free will. But we'll forget to tell them that this is not fate, but failure.

How can we not forget when we're so preoccupied with the myth of the square that we neglect the revolution, so preoccupied with the myth of our uniqueness that we neglect our dreams? How can we not get lost when we're busy fighting a second wave that drowns us? We spend so long telling them that we're not conspiring against them we forgot that they are all conspiring against *us*. Or was it, maybe, us conspiring against ourselves? I forget, but I'm sure it's happened before.

They claim the first waves were dark and murky, but I have no doubts about them. Their details are clear and transparent and accounted for. But the myth, in its attempt to erase weakness and anxiety, violence, absurdity and the anguish of pain and the fragility of the dream, opens the door to their dark doubts.

They claim it's the second wave that was clear and transparent, but I felt from the start a familiar murkiness, a darkness scattered in my heritage in terse phrases: Black September—Sabra and Shatila—a unified right wing—the Naksa—Khamis and Baqari—the Defresoir—coups and camp wars—Gulf wars . . .[56] words we inherited without details or explanatory songs or even mocking jokes. As though those words were only a small part of the consciousness of those who came before us. They forgot to tell us, and we didn't tell them that, in our ignorance, we had held them responsible. And today we pretend that we're not living similar nightmares. We won't admit that, like them, we are powerless.

---

56 Black September, 1970: the collapse of relations between the PLO and the Jordanian state into a civil war. Sabra and Shatila, 1982: the massacre of many hundreds of Palestinian refugees in Lebanon. The Naksa (the Setback) 1967: the major defeat of Egypt, Syria and Jordan by the Israeli Army. Khamis and Baqari: two workers tried for demanding labour rights and hung in Egypt in 1952. The Defresoir, 1973: the point east of the Suez Canal at which Israeli troops penetrated the Egyptian offensive.

V.
The crowding squares
and the millions
the crowding revolutions
made us forget:
that 'the dream is the square'
and the revolution
lives in the self.

Being an adult has strict rules. It's important not to talk about yourself, not to boast or you'll look conceited and trivial. But in prison you have nothing to talk about except yourself; time stops and your will is restricted to the boundaries of your body.

When you talk about yourself with a freedom born of necessity—that's when you find yourself.

There in the past I find myself hunched over a keyboard, building with my wife a website that collected every Egyptian blog, refusing to be bound by rules or categories or borders. Blogs found refuge with us when they were rejected by the Tunisian aggregator whose admins suspected the patriotism of refugees and activists in exile. I see myself printing out calls for citizen journalism and an alternative media and for years handing them out wherever I went.

We didn't try to form a bloc or claim a unified identity; we just wanted to express ourselves. We never aimed to dispel the mystery of our contemporary history, or to deny its confusion and our naivety; we just wanted to make sure that its mystery couldn't be exploited—despite, or by, us—to deny our experiences or rewrite our stories; to erase things that troubled the authorities, or troubled us.

There, in the past, I find myself with less experience and more wisdom, writing about independent selves resisting their isolation with communal work but refusing to melt into the collective. We cooperated with those who came before us, willing to engage with their projects and their theories so long as we didn't have to believe in or proselytize for them. We didn't have generational wars or claim uniqueness but we insisted— and still do—on our tools.

In the absence of both despair and hope, nothing remains but the self. Our aim is to affirm our will in a country that aims to crush us. Our instinct was to seek the unknown in a country whose instinct was stasis. We fought for a day, for one day that would end without the suffocating certainty that tomorrow would be exactly the same as all the days that had come before. Our ambition was that the authorities would spend the night worried even if that worried everyone—but even so we dreamed of a sleep and an awakening untroubled by the authorities.

VI.
What happens to a dream deferred?
Does it dry up
like a raisin in the sun?
Or fester like a sore—
and then run?
Does it stink like rotten meat?
Or will its blood
make you drunk
fermented
like syrup?
Maybe it just sags
like a heavy load.
Or does it explode?

(after Langston Hughes' 'Harlem')

Four squares seduce us. Four squares fight over us. Four squares
tear us apart between them. Four squares dominate the dreams
and nightmares of their people; each square a siren and a maze
that your soul stays captive inside even if your body leaves.

Four squares fighting, each banishing the others, or denying
they ever existed. All the squares are photoshopped except
yours. Outside the squares a terrified public looks for stability.
Each square sings the praises of the public, raises slogans and
demands—some of which concern the public. But there's no
stability on the horizon, for each denies the other.

The first and original square is ours, the square of Tahrir
and the revolution. We say it with conceit and arrogance: the
square is ours. Not the naive conceit they accuse us of, since we
don't claim to own the square or to have a monopoly on the
revolution, but that the square owned *us* and the revolution
monopolized our dreams. This arrogance doesn't come from
believing that talk about how we lit the fuse for the revolution
or were one of its causes—but because the revolution released
our energies, and we embraced it as our reason to exist. We did
not preach the revolution or foresee it, but we dreamed of it and
waited for it and so the square became ours. We built the myth
of the eighteen sacred days around it, and since then we've not
left.

The second is the square of Holy War. They go there for weeks
or months, to the arenas of jihad against infidels and dissenters.
They move to a community that lives on the lawful gains of
raids, the prescribed division of spoils, that governs with Islamic
law and punishment. They come back but their souls stay there
where life is the life of the Companions of the Prophet. They
dream of whipping history and slaughtering time.

Don't judge them too severely—there's something of us
in them. Did we not dream of martyrdom for Palestine? Did
we not raise the image of the lord of all foreign fighters, Che

Guevara? Did we not threaten the army with chants that we'd turn the place into Libya, into Syria? Didn't some of us try to deal with our nightmares by daydreaming of arms? All revolutionaries go through a phase where they shoot at the hours to kill time.

The third is Rabaa Square. Its people lived for weeks in an idealistic, homogenous world, its residents look varied but there is no dissidence; everyone celebrates the Islamist project, everyone believes in its inevitability and its superiority, Christians and seculars recede and the weak of confused creed or faltering faith have vanished.A world in which the Organization[57] assumes its natural significance and size, its vanguard position, sheds the dirt that clings to it from the deal-making of the past, and recovers from all the wounds of repression.

Their bodies were forced to leave it but their spirits stayed, circling the blood of their brothers, dreaming of a state within a state and a city within a city and a nation within a nation, solid like a building, resisting under a historic leadership and according to a divine plan.

Don't judge them too severely, there's something of us in them. Don't you remember those difficult days after the Battle of the Camel when we would chant 'The people demand' in the square and celebrate our 'harmony despite our diversity', all the while scared to leave the square for fear of our neighbours and our families, and the cruelty of the Popular Committees[58] we thought were revolutionary until we found them working hard to bury the revolution alive and punish 'the Tahrir crowd'? All revolutionaries go through a phase where they're consumed by utopias and lose control, and that's when the torture tents appear in their midst.

---

57 The Brotherhood.
58 Popular Committees were neighbourhood defence organizations that sprung up in the security vacuum of the eighteen days.

The fourth square is Mandate Square.[59] Its people live in a pretty black-and-white film about the old days when the state was fatherly and strict and the institutions good and caring and the officer a handsome young man and Egypt a beautiful country girl and the leader beloved and everybody smiling because the plot was always easy and the ending happy. A film repeated every day without becoming boring and always ending before 5 June 1967,[60] or maybe it ends as you hear the news of the downing of enemy warplanes. How can the General and his fans recover from Mandate Fever when they live by feelings we thought had vanished half a century ago?

The square dispersed but their spirits clung to it. In this square there's no need to find solutions for corruption or torture or murder or impoverishment or oppression, for they are all rumours. Egypt can never be defeated and her leadership doesn't make mistakes.

Don't judge them too severely—there's something of us in them. Don't you remember where the chants 'The People, the Army, One Hand' started? Didn't we stand at the entrances to our square sorting out friend from foe by checking ID cards? Didn't we put the judges on the pedestal of our square and ask them for wisdom? Didn't we raise the Constitution—any constitution—to the level of just retribution? All revolutionaries attempt and fail to return to a time of innocence and childhood, and end up in a state of late adolescence.

VII.
The storm of 'Victory'
cannot choose
everyone will perish

---

59 26 July 2013, in response to a demand by General el-Sisi two days earlier, hundreds of thousands of people took to the streets to give the general the 'mandate' he required to deal with 'terrorism'.

60 The start of the Six-Day War that gave Israel comprehensive victory over Egypt, Jordan and Syria: the Naksa.

. . .

and the revolution like a relay of waves
will pound to dust
but not destroy.

I don't mean to say that their squares and ours are the same. But
I commit a brief heresy only to say that, like us, they are possessed; you can see bits of us in them, and bits
    —both good and bad—of our square in theirs.
    In the second square we saw Popular Committees running life
when the authorities withdrew, and in the third we saw women
centre-stage despite their marginal positions in the Organization
and on the podiums. In the fourth square we saw Muslim and
Christian truly as 'One Hand'.
    Human like us, prisoners of their squares like us, besieged like
us, and if our imprisonment and our siege lengthen, our sins will
multiply like theirs. I don't commit heresy out of tolerance for
them, but for us.
    They loved their squares because they lived their dreams there,
but we love our square because there we loved life, and there we
dreamed of a better life for those we love. We may be similar, but
I'm arrogant enough to say that our dream sets our square apart,
and that their dreams are nightmares.
    In each square a myth is built that imprisons its people, and
myths are built on both dreams and nightmares. They committed great sins in their squares and we committed small ones
in ours, but we forget our dreams and build our myths on our
nightmares. They committed great sins but we worshipped false
gods when we worshipped the square, but not the dream. We
strayed from the straight path of the revolution when we built
shrines to our wounds and our fears. We were locked into our
square because like them we looked for an uncompromising victory; we exchanged our dreams for something easier, something

lesser. We lost our way when we sought people's love for ourselves and our square, instead of working for what we wanted
for people. Our square is the only one built on a dream and on
love, but people want stability, and stability needs decisions, and
decisions need strength, and strength kills love and disfigures
the dream. Total victory is treason. It exchanges the power of
the people with what's inferior: arms or the Organization or the
state. It replaces the dream with a roadmap or arrangements of
power or some crumbs of reform.

VIII.
The dancer needs
the public.
The authority needs
the people.
But the revolutionary
when he rises
cares for nothing but
love

Another night passes as we kill topics with discussion. We shout
so that our voices can reach each other through the peepholes of
our cells and we fill the ward with noise as we talk about leaks
and smear campaigns, about newspapers that berate us for losing
popularity and say we're in prison because we were unable to
be decisive, because the scope of our dreams was too big—as
though that were a crime.

I am so angry that I escape to myself in the past, to a
Wednesday in May 2005 that we thought dark because we had
no idea what darkness was in store for us. It was the day of a
referendum we thought ill of, not realizing that it was an omen
of ills to come. It was a day when I was inspired by the wrath
of women and their refusal to stay home and obey the orders

Mubarak wrote on their bodies with the hands of his thugs. That day I was suffocated by our insistence on spaces we thought were safe—like the steps of the Journalists' Union—even though we'd discovered there was no safety whatsoever in the military state.

I find myself there with my comrades planning to venture out of downtown and into Sayyeda Zeinab where we swept the shrine against our oppressors,[61] and to Zeitoun[62] where we prayed to the Virgin against our rulers. We weren't trying to summon a metaphysical force to help us, we were mocking our weakness and acknowledging helplessness—but neither our weakness nor our helplessness held us back.

I find myself with my comrades back then inciting people to regular protests in Imbaba and Shubra and Nahia. It wasn't an attempt to summon the power of the people: we were just trying to tell them that we too had tasted part of their oppression and their hurt, that we were trying to heal ourselves by being with them, and inciting them to be loud in their complaints.

I find myself there with my comrades defying the heart of our fears at the heart of their power, in Lazoghly.[63] It didn't occur to us that it was possible for our small group, hemmed in by oceans of Central Security Forces, to determine anything. We were just letting them know that breaking our bodies would not win them the battle.

There, in the past, I find myself, wiser and less experienced, answering an academic who today contributes to writing the constitution of the 'revolution' when in the past he refused to entertain the possibility of a popular revolution. I answered him by preaching of a revolution that wouldn't need a mobilizing

---

61   Beloved granddaughter of the Prophet, Sayyeda Zeinab and her brother, al-Hussein, are as close as they come to patron saints of Cairo. If you make a wish against someone while sweeping her mosque it is sure to be granted.

62   In April 1968, the Virgin Mary appeared several times above the dome of her church in the district of Zeitoun in Cairo.

63   The headquarters of State Security Police in Cairo.

moment that determined everything in one holy battle, but
would be a continuous process in which the rate of change
quickened and the number of revolutionaries grew.

I find myself back then writing about the selfish nature of
the struggle, about the memorial service as the measure of the
popularity of a fighter, about how we need to defeat our myths
ourselves and not become imprisoned by our rituals.

This is our fate. We have nothing to give people except our
banners, and all we're good at is inciting them to dream. We
have no strength or dominion except love; they love us when
their courage gets the better of them and they discover their
strength, and they hate us when their fears get the better of them
and they're convinced of their weakness and their need for a
strength outside themselves.

IX.
They fight, the residents of
'the centre'
over the title
'the man who renounces'
and 'victory'
for him who betrays with honesty
. . .
all the victors have been defeated
as for us
we chose the margin

In our tradition, we give free reign to a tyrant and will believe
him a just ruler if he meets the moment's needs. One strikes
a deal with us over 'national independence', another swaps it
out for 'prosperity', another might ask us to give up freedom
in return for security and safety, or the protection of minorities. In our tradition dignity is either for the individual or the

nation—you can't have both. And justice is either in the courtrooms or the market, not in both.

They entered the square with us or before us—I don't
remember. The most they wanted was that freedom be auc-
tioned. We said we don't mind sharing your experience but
we bought our freedom with blood and we won't cut deals on
it. They asked, 'So what's your experience?' We said, 'We stay
together and we win both dignities and both justices and all freedoms.' They said, 'You're so great! This is how the young should
be . . . you've dazzled the world with your wisdom . . . beware of
leaving the square.' Then they left the square—and us.

In our tradition free reign is given to whoever meets the
moment's needs. So, has the General met them? Let's see: the
nationalists lined up behind him, praising a Nasserism that lays
siege to allies and avoids engaging the enemy. The leftists lined
up behind him, praising a socialism of debt and budget cuts
and the removal of subsidies. The liberals lined up behind him,
praising the awe-inspiring state and terror-crushing laws.

No dignity of the body or the nation, no justice in bread or
in retribution. The General didn't bargain with them with his
gold or his sword, he offered them nothing except the honour of
appearing in the centre after decades spent in the margins. They
crowded together in his shadow because the centre is narrow
and has room only for the General. They didn't sign contracts or
get paid, they just stood and thanked him for his generosity and
tolerance, then they lamented the good youth who'd lost their way
and returned to the margins, they lamented or mocked or wondered . . . It doesn't matter, in my prison I see them all as equal.

X.
Your palace
is not big enough for my dream
and the cell

is pure absurdity.
Have you ever seen
a cloud
on the move
ask for permission

The prison shuts on Christmas Day and we're each in solitary for
two days during which the door doesn't open. Anger overtakes
me as I read the newspapers that have discovered for the first
time that there are 'Copts' amongst us. At Mass, raised images
of the General outnumber those of the man whose birthday it
is. I look for a familiar face and find none. Where were all these
when we walked into the cathedral carrying the coffins of the
martyrs? Where were they when we stood on its walls protecting
it from teargas and bullets? If the Copts have truly left the margins why is the centre empty of their poor, the comrades of their
martyrs?

The centre is treason because there's room in it only for the
General. My anger takes me back, and there, in the past, I see
myself standing in a protest, ignoring its demands and its slogans
and handing out a statement written by two friends; a statement
written essentially for us rather than the public, inviting us to confess to the wound, to speak of the spread of hate, to resist denial.
A statement insisting that in Egypt there's a deep sectarian crisis.
Despotism hinders us from facing it, but the crisis won't go away
when the despotism ends. We didn't seek that day to break into
the centre or force the issue into it. Our aim was to communicate
with ourselves and to discuss the things that hurt us.

There in the past I find myself less experienced and wiser.
Writing about margins wider than the centre, about a history
made up of many narratives. Margins—as opposed to the
centre—are multiple. I find myself theorizing about the need to
interact with all causes and injustices, however marginal their

people, even if this angers the people of the centre. And to reject
any attempt to impose priorities on freedom, dignity and justice.
    In the square we got lost while we built our myth. We forgot
that the revolution is not a transfer or retreat from the margins
but rather the margins violently breaking into the centre. They
distracted us with talk of 'the main current' and 'the man in
the street' until it seemed that the centre had enough room
for the majority. They traded with us and said it has room for
you if you abandon the youth of the barricades and molotovs,
the street children, the Copts, the people who were killed or
injured outside the square, and the people of Sinai. One after
the other they came to us offering a place in the shadow of the
General on condition that we give up one of our margins—a
part of us.
    The centre is treason and I have never been a traitor. They
think they've pushed us back into the margins. They don't realize
that we never left it, we just got lost for a brief while. Neither the
ballot boxes nor the palaces or the ministries or the prisons or
even the graves are big enough for our dreams. We never sought
the centre because it has no room except for those who abandon
the dream. Even the square was not big enough for us, so most
of the battles of the revolution happened outside it, and most of
the heroes remained outside the frame.

XI.
True I'm touching the ground
but I'm flying in the sky
I dream of living together
in the world itself but
it's our time and there's no parting
your kiss still confuses me
and 'I love you'
from you erases

one of those soldiers
in Baghdad

(after Rayess Bek)

When the dreams of those who came before us rested on the
leader, they were defeated with him. And when they found in
themselves the ability to kill the leader and end his myth they
enjoyed many small victories. We thought we were different; we
don't believe in leaders. We didn't understand that it was they
who freed our tradition from the sway of leaders forever. We're
like them in their strength and their weakness, and we need to
free our dreams as they freed theirs. The square is just a spectacle
to express these dreams; our hearts overflow with it for love of
what appeared in it of our dreams. We made of it a myth that
imprisoned us, blotted out our experience and dissolved ourselves. We got lost inside it and believed it was the aim of the
dream and the heart of the revolution. It's our job to kill our
myth with our own hands as they killed theirs. It's time to pull
down the square so that we may be free, so that we may come
back to ourselves and our revolution.

From my mother I inherited a stone cake and a love that pene-
trates the walls of prisons. And from my father I inherited a prison
cell and a dream not bound by prison walls or surrounded by the
edges of a square or limited by the borders of a homeland. I have
not yet received my complete inheritance; I'm still waiting to learn
how I can spend my life in the square without it taking my soul
prisoner and emptying my dream; how I can stay inside it and still
face the nightmares inside me. I'm still waiting to learn from my
father how I can leave prison without leaving part of myself in the
cell, how I can leave and forgive those who were unjust to me and
those who let me down. How I can transform from a thorn in the
side of injustice to a rock for those treated unjustly.

Until I receive my full inheritance I shall go back to how I was,
without despair and without hope, without a centre or resolution,
dreaming of a revolution not confined to a square, kept company
in the loneliness of my cell by a love unbound by prison.
And finally:
'Congratulations on the new coat of paint.'[64]

XII.
To erase—for the revolution—
a page
is to give us
a chance
to think again
and to write.

Alaa & Ahmad Douma
Ward A, Political, Torah Prison
First published on 24 January 2014
in *Mada Masr* & *al-Masry al-Youm*

---

64 Late at night on 18 September 2012, under the Morsi administration and under
    police protection, municipality workers erased the massive revolutionary graffiti off
    the walls around Tahrir Square. The next morning the walls are graffitied with the
    words 'Congratulations on the new coat of paint,' and shortly after: 'Thank you for
    the new canvas.' The next evening huge crowds flock to the square and graffiti artists
    start repainting the walls under a media spotlight. Meanwhile the government issues a
    statement claiming they had nothing to do with the erasure.

AUTISM

Being in prison robs me of the ability to participate or contribute. I try to make up for it by reading—maybe I'll land a piece of information or wisdom I can pass on to those who visit me, or that will help me the day I'm released.

I read—among other things—about autism. I read and read and remember the ordeals of the revolution and think that autism is a good metaphor for our condition. I start writing texts that match losing—or not having—the ability to speak with a generation gradually losing its ability to chant, or texts that set communication impairment next to our inability to understand those queues of dancers.[65] I try to develop an image where an extreme sensitivity to sound causes us pain when we hear the state's bullets—bullets that those who don't share our disability don't hear. We are upset by the blood of those martyred for reasons other than duty—a sight which does not offend the eyes of those who give mandates. They're weak, the texts and, more importantly, neither scientific nor accurate. Autism is not a psychological illness you get from the shocks of life; it's a known and documented condition connected primarily with learning difficulties and our strategies for dealing with them.

The literature stresses the importance of paying attention to 'the hidden curriculum'.

We might have difficulty learning the school curriculum. We might find some subjects hard, we might find that autism makes it up to us by making others easier. But the heart of the problem is in the hidden curriculum. It's not a secret; it's just the lessons,

---

65 During the recent constitutional referendum (January 2014), the media had made great play of women dancing in the queues to vote.

skills, rules and foundations of human communication. No one's hiding it. Human beings assumed it was intuitive, so nobody wrote it down. Why do we ask 'How are you doing?' when we meet, though we don't want a real answer? What pushes us, sometimes, to fake a love we don't feel and hide the love we do? Why's it important to show varied kinds and degrees of respect to colleagues and bosses? Why does the teacher want to hear a pin drop though there's no pin in her hand? And then there are the complex rules for speech, dress and behaviour which depend on relationships and change with time, place and circumstance.

We all live by a complex and layered system that's always in flux. Most of us learn its details without trying, but most of the people who live with autism stand helpless before it, their isolation only increasing, unless someone makes the effort to teach them the hidden curriculum. It doesn't matter if the details of this curriculum are useful or logical or not; if you don't conform to them society will reject you. Which is easier? To persuade society that a response to 'how are you doing?' with a real report about one's feelings does no harm and might even do good, or that it's OK not to ask how one is doing if it's a quick meeting and doesn't allow for a conversation about one's state of mind . . . ? Or perhaps it's easier to train the 'disabled' minority who are unable to absorb the hidden curriculum to respond with 'fine, thank you' regardless of what they might actually be feeling?

The books warn: don't train for conformity. Our duty is to teach the curriculum and to empower the 'disabled' person to register and grasp what society expects, and then decide of their own free will how they should behave. They might decide to conform, or they might rebel. 'What's easiest?' isn't the only question. Let's look at 'What's richer, what's more beautiful, more compassionate . . . what's better?'

I like the idea of the hidden curriculum. Which one of

us 'normal' people has not been confused or annoyed by the
unspoken rules of behaviour and communication? Which of us
hasn't been gripped by a wish to howl or cry or curse or hug or
kiss at the 'wrong' moment? Practically half the hidden curriculum is about the effects of those moments, how to hide those
feelings. Or, you rebel, and don't.

The arrival of the prisoners breaks my train of thought. I stop
reading. We've been expecting them since the papers printed
leaked stories of their torture, had heard the administration
was expecting new inmates from Abu Zaabal. We had tried to
prepare to receive them, but how do you welcome a friend who
went through the battle with you but went through his experience alone? Will he be comforted if you tell him that this prison,
new to him but old to you, is safe, that his ordeal is over? Will he
be angry? Should I feel guilty or grateful? We must have learned
this in the hidden curriculum; the spectrum of the acuteness of
injustice and the price people pay are nothing new. You've spent
your life within these gradations so why are you confused by the
heat of your new cellmates' anger?

We adopt autism. We receive the new prisoners with a detailed
report about the facts: there's no torture here, but you're probably
here to stay. The law means nothing, the Constitution offers no
hope and the courts are worthless. We will be here until they're
done with their damned road map. They reply with similar
autism: a detailed report about the torture in a steady mechanical
delivery with no embarrassment, no concealment. The books tell
me not to assume the absence of feeling; autism hampers expression and communication, but it doesn't nullify feeling.

Their silence allows in a sweeping anger which we try to avoid
by playing football. But the anger can't be contained, its kicks
are violent and harsh. We try to evade it in a complicit silence.
With the first injury all of *our* anger explodes. We kick back
violently. The game is played by Abu Zaabal rules: everything is

allowed except handball. It ends with a difference in goals but a draw in the number of injuries.

The books say that aggressive behaviour is an attempt to communicate, to express what's hard to express. Were they expressing their anger at us because the torturer chose them and not us? Because the torturer asked them about us? Or are they angry with the torturer? Or with themselves? And what about us? Did we get angry because they made us feel guilty? Or because they told us the details of their experience? Because they seemed stronger than us? Or were we angry because we'd depended on them to set us free?

The rest of the week passes waiting for the football injuries to heal, and the anger recedes. An inner wisdom pushed us to play this match, perhaps the same wisdom that prompted humanity to invent rough group sports. It tells us that violence can be practised in a context other than enmity and oppression, that pain need not touch dignity, that the most trivial reasons can enable our bodies to bear pain, and our spirit can ignore injury and even make fun of it as long as there's a level of safety. Perhaps the match is no more important than the phrases 'I'm fine' or 'God willing'; like other items on the hidden curriculum, it helps you to live and to share life with others.

With the visit of the delegation the anger returns. They could have stopped the jailer and the torturer. If they had threatened resignation with the first bullet, if they'd suspended the Constitution when the Protest Law was first applied, if they'd halted TV broadcasts and newspaper presses with the first lie, if they'd withdrawn their mandate with the first testimony of torture . . . but they insisted on dealing with the killing, the torture and the detention of their party members, of their children's comrades and their colleagues' students and the children of their relatives as slips and mistakes. They exchanged resolute positions and pressure and standing up for what's right for 'advising' and sometimes for begging.

To understand why they warn of the return of the Mubarak State—even though their own state has surpassed it in criminality—you have to learn the hidden curriculum. To understand why they warn against the return of torture when you're sure they know that torture hasn't stopped for one day, you have to understand the hidden curriculum. To understand why they talk about violating a constitution they drew up knowing that the state would not be bound by its articles you need to refer to the hidden curriculum.

The referendum's 'yes' was not to the newly written constitution, but to the hidden constitution that we have long been ruled by and that the state needed to legitimize afresh.

In the hidden constitution there are complex rules that govern torture. They're mainly based on the identity of the victim: torture is a crime if it's committed against certain groups who shouldn't be tortured. It's generally agreed that repressing these groups will be restricted to smear campaigns and imprisonment 'pending trial' in relatively good conditions and for relatively short periods.

The groups whose torture is prohibited are defined by social class, race, a second nationality, party alliance, education, age, and every other detail that can be used to categorize people. Exceptional circumstances can widen the circle of people who may be tortured—on the condition that the abuse happens at the moment of arrest and before the first session with the Prosecution. Torture that continues beyond that is unacceptable.

The hidden constitution follows its own inexplicable logic. No one, for example, demands the use of torture as a deterrent for police personnel who've committed crimes, or to obtain confessions from suspect businessmen, while the torture of terrorists and criminals with a record of violence is practically a popular demand.

Someone born in Sinai may be tortured whatever their

political or class allegiance. The abuse of Beltagy's son is prohibited if his name is Ammar and permitted if his name is Anas.[66]
Killing the man's children is not desirable but is not a crime if
done by the state during the break-up of a sit-in.

This is why those who drew up the Constitution—party
leaders, members of national councils and celebrity commentators—talk about the 'mistakes' of the state only when the torture
reaches Khaled and Nagy[67]. They're not speaking of the systematic and constant violation of the written constitution, but what
they see as an unintentional error in applying the hidden constitution. They speak as though the torturer didn't recognize his
victims, or thought they were Brotherhood. They are certain that
the mistake will be corrected. They insist on the right of the state
to torture people in the correct categories.

They could have prevented what happened or stopped it
spreading if they'd held on to the principles they had written
with their own hand. But after months of supporting murder
and torture and detention and repression and slander their
power to affect things has evaporated. Now, when they've discovered that repression is coming closer to them than they thought,
there's nothing left for them to do except put together miserable delegations to visit prisons or set up farcical conferences to
denounce unintended mistakes.

What they don't understand is that the state has not made
a mistake; the hidden constitution—like any constitution—
defines rights and duties. The state tried hard to remain within
its boundaries and to only torture those whom the accords of
30 June allowed it to, but the revolutionaries refused to adhere

66 Mohammad el-Beltagy: a prominent Brotherhood leader who was arrested two weeks
    after Rabaa, where his daughter, Asmaa, had been killed. His son, Anas, was arrested in
    December 2013 and has been imprisoned since then. His other son, Ammar, was briefly
    arrested a few days after the dispersal but was released the following day.
67 Khaled al-Sayed and Nagy Kamel, two middle-class, non-Islamist, revolutionary youth
    activists whose torture in prison was widely reported.

to the hidden constitution; they challenged it, and so stripped themselves of its protection.

The state produced the Protest Law to use against the Brotherhood, but we insisted on testing it out first with our own bodies. They killed poor Islamist students at Al-Azhar University, so the Cairo University students went out against their shotguns. They started a war on terror which inevitably brought terror to the heart of the capital, but we broke all the rules when we insisted that a bomb at the security headquarters was not enough to erase our memories of the torture we saw inside it.

The state did not make a mistake, it was us who insisted on making deliberate mistakes. Maybe we were raising the stakes, maybe we wanted to expose both the hidden rules of oppression and those who justify them. Maybe we were wise and prescient, because if you don't hold authority to a written constitution then you can't hold it to any constitution; sooner or later you'll join those whose torture is permitted. Perhaps it's a conscience which refuses to abandon those whose fate makes them torturable, or a kind of 'autism' that blinds us to the hidden constitution; a disability that makes us unable to learn it by instinct, an autism that makes us take words literally and so believe, for example, that the revolution really continues and that the people really demand the fall of the regime.

Which is easier? To train the minority unable to conform to the hidden constitution to ignore injustice as long as it falls on others? To avoid challenging authority and to assume its good inten-tions? Or to persuade society that it's absurd to try to live with an authority that allows itself murder and torture and detentions as long as it sticks to hidden rules? The books warn us: don't train for conformity. Our duty is to teach the curriculum and to empower the 'disabled' person to register and grasp what society expects, and then decide of their own free will how they should behave. They might decide to conform, or they might rebel.

'What's easiest' isn't the only question. What's richer, what's more beautiful, what's more compassionate, what's better.

Written in Torah Prison
Published on 4 March 2014 in *Mada Masr* & *al-Shorouk*

EVERYBODY KNOWS

The state insists its prisons are free of political prisoners. But everybody knows that the prisons are full of dissidents held 'temporarily'.

Everybody knows that most prisoners will be released after a few months without having ever gone to trial. Everybody knows most of those that do go to trial will be found innocent. Everybody knows most of the sentences handed down in first hearings will be quashed in later ones and that most of those who are convicted won't be found guilty of serious crimes against lives or security; their convictions will be based on the ill-reputed, ambiguous articles in the widely interpretable law which the Egyptian government has long used to suppress opposition. Or they will be based on the crippling new Protest Law which transforms an administrative irregularity—while practising a constitutional right—into a crime punishable with a prison sentence.

And of course everybody knows that these laws are unconstitutional. Soon we shall be celebrating the hundredth anniversary of the Assembly Law of 1914, issued by the British to suppress the national movement after they declared Egypt a Protectorate. Every subsequent parliament has held on to this law, and every government has exploited it—though it violates every constitution we've had since then.

Everybody knows that the overwhelming majority of prisoners are denied their basic rights, are mistreated on arrest, while being interrogated, and in detention. Everybody knows that—according to the Constitution and the law—imprisonment 'pending trial' is an exceptional measure intended to aid investigations, prevent flight risks, evidence-tampering, witness intimidation or—in the case of major crimes—serious breaches of security. Everybody knows that the above does not apply to the majority of prisoners. And everybody knows that it *does* apply to the policemen accused of corruption, torture and murder, yet the number of cops imprisoned 'pending trial' in the last three years can be counted on one hand.

In fact, when a court ordered two police officers accused of assaulting a judge to be held pending trial their colleagues refused to carry out the order, staged an armed protest without notifying the authorities, and demanded it be made illegal for the police to be detained on remand.

Everybody knows that most members of the Police Department, the Prosecutor's Office and the courts are complicit in imprisoning thousands who will not be found guilty of crimes and are trampling on their rights under orders from their security, military and political bosses for purely political reasons that have nothing to do with justice or laws or constitutions. In other words: open-ended political detention by order of the executive.

And even though everybody knows that everybody knows all this, the state still claims that Egypt has no political prisoners, no torture, no targeting of dissidents or journalists, no random arrests, no oppression.

All attempts to push for the release of prisoners are countered with myths about the independence of the courts and the impossibility of interfering in their affairs. Meanwhile, the police inform us of the prosecutors' decisions before we've even appeared before them.

I don't understand why the authorities need to put on this whole performance, since everybody knows—and clearly the majority don't mind. Nor do I understand why so many public figures, media personalities, party leaders, journalists, writers and presidential candidates still play along.

We've reached a point where every day the newspapers carry appeals to the Public Prosecutor to speed up his investigations so that he may free those who are proven innocent. For the show to go on we have given up on the principle that you're innocent until proven guilty.

So, for the authorities and the elite: they know, but they pretend not to. And some of the general public knows but ignores it, or ignores it in order not to know. We've seen a mother report her son for belonging to the 6 April Youth Movement and taking part in a protest, as if torture were a new tool for the modern parent.

But what about us?

Or rather: what about you? You who are against these injustices and are still on the outside? What will you do? Will you share in the performance, or withdraw silently and wait to be taken from your homes? Will you abandon us? Will you tell yourself it's only temporary? Or that another show, like the elections, is an opening?

We have our own performances: big talk about 'the small prison' and 'the big prison'—Egypt. I'm sorry, but let's be serious: there is no prison except the small prison. In my cell, I control nothing. But you are free to go out and challenge the authorities. It may only be the choice of the time and place of your arrest or injury or death—but that's a choice the prisoner doesn't have.

We get many letters of solidarity full of compliments and praise we don't deserve. 'You're an inspiration and a source of hope.' 'As long as there are people like you, Egypt will be OK.'

In prison we resist despair. Inspiring hope is your job. So please: inspire us. Egypt might 'be OK' if the repression was inspiring more people to resist and brave detention, injury and death.

Perhaps this is why the authorities insist on theatrics even though everybody knows they're fake: doing so normalizes the situation and wastes time on useless strategies of negotiations, advice, legal representations and media campaigns until the default position becomes a belief in the guilt of the accused, a belief that it's the revolutionary's responsibility to avoid being imprisoned or killed, and yesterday's comrades blame you for challenging the show and hold you responsible for the murdered and the lost.

We were defeated the day we made ourselves responsible for the results of oppression. Everybody knows oppression stems from the authorities, and in a not-too-distant past everybody knew that you defeat oppression by destroying the fear of it. And everybody knew that to destroy fear you need to challenge it and mock it; you don't destroy fear by thinking about guarantees of safety and trying to create a suitable environment for protest. Everybody knew that what breaks despair is the constant incitement to direct confrontational revolutionary action, without calculations of profit, loss or popularity.

Everybody knows that this regime offers nothing to most of the country's youth, and everybody knows that most of those in jail are young, and that repression's goal is to subjugate an entire generation to a regime that knows that it is completely divided from them and doesn't want to—and cannot—include them.

Everybody knows there is no hope for us who have gone ahead into prison except through you who will surely follow. So what are you going to do about it?

Written in Torah Prison
Published on 12 March in *Mada Masr*,
al-Masry al Youm & *al-Shorouk*

LYSENKO COUNTRY

Saturday 22 February 2014. Upon the opening of a military medical college, the official Facebook page of the armed forces writes:

'In the presence of [interim President] Adly Mansour, Field Marshal [el-Sisi] and major figures of the state, Egyptian innovations in science and research were today unveiled for the benefit of mankind: the world's first system for the detection and treatment of AIDS and Hepatitis C, at a fraction of the cost of its foreign counterparts, with a 90 per cent success rate.'

The next day, Sunday 23 February, the armed forces organized a press conference for international journalists at the press centre of the military Department for Morale. On stage were the Head of the Armed Forces Engineering Corps, General Taher Abdallah, and General Ibrahim Abdel-Atti, who led the research team working on the new device—and who declared 'we've conquered AIDS, with the grace of God, a hundred per cent . . . I take the AIDS from the patient and I nourish him with AIDS by giving him a skewer of AIDS kofta.'

The device in question was quickly recognized on social media as a novelty golf ball detector sometimes used by Egyptian police and military at vehicle checkpoints, particularly between Sinai and the mainland. It had been in the news a few months earlier, when a British couple were arrested for selling millions of dollars' worth to the Iraqi government, among others, as bomb detectors.

At the beginning of the 1930s, Joseph Stalin's policies resulted in a terrible famine in large areas of the Soviet Union, particularly Ukraine. Millions of people died, most of them, strangely enough, farmers responsible for growing wheat.

Since then there has been a lot of debate around the nature of the famine. Was it exacerbated by natural forces? Was it down to failures in production or distribution? Or was it the inevitable result of agricultural reform policies that were forced on farmers despite their refusal and resistance to them?

Some Ukrainians are even convinced that the famine was a deliberate strategy, a massacre to ensure the total submission of Ukraine.

What is certain is that the policies that led to the famine were strongly opposed at the time, both from within the ruling Communist Party and without, and that the famine came as no surprise to the opposition, which ranged from politicians, to experts, to farmers.

What is also certain is that Stalin at that time was busy eliminating dissidents and his old comrades from the Bolshevik Revolution and any possible future rivals. So the main tools with which the famine was confronted were repression and propaganda.

It was in this context that Trofim Lysenko appeared, the ideal propaganda tool: son of the proletariat, born in rural Ukraine, self-taught in the sciences of biology, agriculture and genetics, free from the academic institutions inherited from the Tsarists and the bourgeoisie. Lysenko was introduced to Soviet society as a hero of the revolution, able to work miracles: to make seeds bear fruit outside season, to double the productivity of the land through the strength of his loyalty to the revolution and to the party.

Stalin was not bothered about minor details like the viability of research or the accuracy of experiments or Lysenko's adherence to scientific methodology. Nor was he put off by the consensus of the scientific community that Lysenko was either supremely ignorant or a criminal fraud. Stalin's problem was political—how to persuade his people to endure the famine and live with want while submitting to his regime? Science would be no use to him, but the Lysenko Myth might.

Under the direct command of the leadership, Lysenko became the most important Soviet scientist. The state established research institutes and scientific journals devoted to Lysenkoism. Lysenko's critics were faced with terror and smear campaigns, deprived of work, jobs and promotions until—at the peak of Lysenko's power—a law was issued that criminalized the critiquing of his theories or conducting any experiments that might disprove them.

With the excuse of confronting the conspiracies of the capitalist West and its Fifth Column among the weak-faithed bourgeois scientists, the most important principle of scientific research was disregarded: that everything is open to doubt and experiment, revision and discussion.

Most Soviet scientists submitted. Some wrote papers supporting Lysenko's theories in order to hold on to their posts; some used the situation to denounce their colleagues and dispose of their rivals; most turned away from research in biology and genetics and concentrated on areas that Lysenko had not invaded and where theory was not subject to absurd ideological conflict.

This situation lasted approximately two decades. Lysenko's authority was not broken until the death of Stalin.

Lysenko appeared in the context of a dictatorship seeking to construct a great state; an empire controlling half the world. His effect was to damage and disrupt science and to entrench authoritarianism to the extent that those who exposed him and destroyed his myth, when it became permissible to do so, *still* ended up in exile and in concentration camps. They had imagined that the lifting of the ban on scientific critiques of Lysenko's nonsense was also license for political critiques of the crimes of Lysenko's bosses.

So what about this new Lysenko who appears at the heart of a miserable military regime, a regime whose ambition is simply to hold on to an impoverished, corrupt, dependent state? Lysenko appears in order to peddle illusions: the valiant Egyptian army is able—with science—to perform a miracle that will put an end to all disease.

In prison, all sources of information are official except the daily papers. I couldn't tune in to the online roasting and I missed all the kofta gags, but I waited patiently for the serious critiques, the professional unmaskings and the scientific disman-tlings I would read in the papers—for our time is not Lysenko's time, and this new Lysenko's feeble press conference fell far short of convincing propaganda.

But the papers came empty of any criticism. Our respected journalists didn't even take the trouble to contact any sources. Lysenko's mystical fabrications were reproduced verbatim. I waited for the comment pages. The next day, Khaled Montaser's column in al-Watan was the only sceptical—although exaggeratedly polite—voice. The following day, Esam Heggi joined him, and declared that the affair was a huge scandal. Even so, his statement was published only in al-Watan and ignored by the rest of the papers. Days passed with no critique, no unmasking, no exposés from anywhere other than Heggi's treason and the insolence of the youth online.

Things changed after Friday (I later understood this was the effect of Bassem Youssef's TV show),[68] but still dissident voices kept within boundaries of courtesy and hesitancy, insisting that the detection machine was viable, but that the treatment machine needed research and that the press conference could have been better produced. Until Bassem Youssef published his article in al-Shorouk no one dared to say that this Lysenko's dis-course was hallucinatory mumbo-jumbo, even though that was obvious to any high school graduate.

---

68   A very popular satirical television show.

Thinking about it, I was struck by how naive I'd been. This is not the first Lysenko to appear at this critical stage in our nation's history. We have, for example, an entire court that was originally concerned with urgent cases in civil litigation that has recently become Lysenkoism's flag-bearer in judicial affairs. It issues pronouncements that bear no relation to any text, agreed interpretation or legal logic but that replace previous 'final' judgements of the State Council. It convicts and imprisons with no reference to the law, it accepts cases outside its competence and rejects cases at the heart of its specialization. The state—with a constitutional judge at its head—bases wide-ranging resolutions on its pronouncements, and the newspapers publish no objection from specialists or experts.

The Lysenko of the Ministry of the Interior announced the end of terrorism. 'Anyone who wants to take us on,' he offered, 'come try it.' And then the Security Directorate in the capital was blown up. At one point, some newspapers timidly criticized him because his officers were not checking the identity of detainees before torturing them, but rarely is anyone bold enough to declare openly that the whole department is run by kofta-wallahs.

One Lysenko insists that there is such a thing as 'clean coal' and another Lysenko insists that there's no such thing as swine flu. Yet another Lysenko claims that a maximum wage policy is being implemented. As for the Grand Ethiopian Renaissance Dam, there's been such an intensity of Lysenkoist statements swarming around it that I've lost all hope of understanding anything about the size of the danger facing us or our plans to confront it.

I imagine that the web is flooded with unmaskings of Lysenkos, so most of you may not notice their absence from the newspapers, but it's worth noting. We do not yet have laws against critiquing Lysenkos, and it's unlikely that writers, journalists and specialists will be harmed if they unmask and expose, if they speak out with a sharpness equal to the enormity of the scandal, instead of oscillating between silence, support, justification and embarrassed advice. These Lysenkos do not have the power to stop every newspaper.

The fear, then, is of the Lysenko in Chief, he whose star is rising despite his failure, who insists on holding forth on subjects well beyond his field, despite his clear ignorance of most things *within* his own field. Yet everybody sings of his genius: the miracle-working son of the establishment, he for whom laws are passed, he who crushes and silences and smears his competition and opposition and doubters of his legend. He who is hysterically promoted to cover the crimes of his bosses.

Don't be distracted by a small Lysenko from the Lysenko in Chief. And don't be distracted even by a Lysenko in Chief from the real power behind him. Authoritarianism in the Soviet Union did not end with the exposure of Lysenko or with the death of Stalin, nor even with the fall of the Soviet Union. Authoritarianism does not reside in an individual, however powerful, but in the structure of the state and its institutions.

Advisors politely say: do proper science, market your products better so your institutions' reputations don't suffer. Meanwhile, they warn us against spreading doubt and mocking Lysenko, against undermining the dignity of their state. And they conveniently forget that Lysenko exists to put a pretty face on power, to hide the ugly truths behind the deceitful myths.

The rise today of a Lysenko from the heart of every sovereign institution[69] is not indicative of some marketing failure from institutions with flawed-but-basically-good fundamentals, but

---

69 A widely used term that refers to state institutions whose power is, in practice, not subject to any popular, parliamentary or legal oversight. Akin to saying 'the powers that be'. There is no formal legal ground for this classification but it is understood to mean institutions such as the presidency, the military, the intelligence servies and the State Security Police.

rather a sign that the fundamentals of these institutions *are* corruption, bankruptcy and failure. Any good reputation they enjoy is a lie. Throughout their long history, these institutions have given us nothing except a long line of Lysenko types trying to cover up their failures, their oppression, their happy dependency, their constant betrayal of the people, their carelessness with lives and their violations of dignity.

Oppressive laws, the inspiration of fear and the promotion of ignorance have succeeded in keeping intact the myth of every Lysenko in Chief, until we have a state that is at one with authoritarianism and its institutions with Lysenkoism. In Russia, Stalin died and Lysenko fell. In Egypt, when the last ambitious tyrant fell, Lysenko took power and spent half a century cloning himself until every official and every spokesperson and every expert became Lysenko. The miracles multiplied and want remained constant.

They're right. Exposing Lysenko destroys respect for the state and ruins the reputation of its institutions because it—simply—exposes their corrupt core. If your mission is to repair the reputation of the institutions and patch up respect for the state, join them and try to produce a modern, stylish Lysenko that's difficult to unmask. If your mission is to reform the heart of the state and the reality of its institutions, don't content yourself with exposing Lysenko: focus on his bosses.

Written in Torah Prison
Published on 23 March 2014 in *Mada Masr* & *al-Shorouk*

INTERVIEW WITH *DEMOCRACY NOW!*

Amy Goodman: Today [31 March 2014], a *Democracy Now!* broadcast exclusive. Egypt's electoral commission announced Sunday the country's presidential elections will be held in late May. At this point, the vote is widely expected to be won by Egypt's former military chief, Abdel Fattah el-Sisi, who announced his resignation from the military last week to run for office. Sisi led the overthrow of President Mohamed Morsi last summer. Since then, some 2,500 people have been killed, and at least 16,000 people arrested.

In our global broadcast exclusive today, we spend the hour with one of Egypt's most prominent dissidents, Alaa Abd el-Fattah, speaking in his first extended interview since his release from prison after nearly four months behind bars. An Open Internet and political activist, Alaa has been at the forefront of the struggle for change in Egypt for many years and has the distinction of having been actively persecuted by the past four successive rulers in Egypt. In 2006, under the Mubarak regime, he was detained at a protest calling for independence of the judiciary and was jailed for forty-five days. In 2011, he emerged as a leading face of the revolution that forced Mubarak out of office. Later that year, under the rule of the military council that replaced Mubarak, he was jailed again, this time for fifty-six days. His son, Khaled, was born while he was behind bars. Then, during the rule of the Muslim Brotherhood's Mohamed Morsi, Alaa was issued an arrest warrant as part of a government crackdown on critical voices.

This past November, after the military's ouster of Morsi and a brutal attack on the Muslim Brotherhood and its supporters, the interim cabinet issued a draconian protest law to further crack down on any opposition. Dozens of people were arrested the next day at a protest near parliament, among them Alaa's sister, Mona, who was eventually released. Despite the 'No to Military Trials' activist group publicly admitting to organizing the protest, prosecutors issued an arrest warrant for Alaa as the organizer of the event. He was jailed in the same prison ward as other leading activists Ahmed Maher and Mohamed Adel of the 6 April Youth Movement, as well as Ahmed Douma, whose health is deteriorating every day.

After 115 days behind bars, Alaa was finally brought before a judge, who released him on bail. His case is still ongoing. He says he expects to be convicted and sent back to prison. In the first interview since his release, Alaa discusses his imprisonment, the wave of repression in Egypt and the state of the revolution. He sat down with *Democracy Now!* correspondent Sharif Abdel Kouddous, who interviewed him in Cairo, Egypt, on Sunday.

SHARIF ABDEL KOUDDOUS: Alaa Abd el-Fattah, welcome to *Democracy Now!*

ALAA ABD EL-FATTAH: Thank you.

SHARIF: Let's start by talking about the night of your arrest. Explain exactly what happened.

ALAA: They broke into my house around 9 p.m. A full special forces squad, they looked like guys coming out of a Hollywood movie, with their faces concealed and with heavy weapons and bulletproof vests and so on. And they just shattered the door and walked into the house, beat me and beat my wife. Fortunately, my son was sleeping, and they did not touch him. And then they started collecting all electronic devices, like mobile phones and

laptops and so on, even though they did not have a search warrant. They only had an arrest warrant. The beating was because
I protested this. And then I was blindfolded and transferred to a
car.

Before they blindfolded me, I—they took me out of the
house, and before they blindfolded me I saw they had the whole
neighbourhood at gunpoint so that nobody would interfere.
It was a massive squad, several cars and tens of people, tens
of heavily armed policemen. And then they blindfolded me
and transferred me—later on, I figured out to Cairo Security
Headquarters—but I didn't know at the time where I was. And
they played tricks with me, like when they moved me from room
to room, they would walk me outside so that it'd feel like I'm
moving from a building to a building. Stuff like that. I spent the
whole night there, thrown on the floor with my hands behind
my back, my eyes blindfolded with a very dirty rag that—I
mean, I actually got an infection in the eye because of it. I was
bleeding. I was beaten with the back of some weapon, I'm not
sure what. But my head was bleeding. And it was quite cold.
And they left me there for twelve hours in that condition. And
then, they kept moving me several times at night.

And then, the next morning, they took me to meet the
prosecutors. Now, the prosecutors are supposed to be part of the
judiciary, and you're—the police are supposed to move you to
them. They're supposed to be independent, and it's very important to set boundaries between them and the police. But what's
been going on for a while is that the prosecutors come to the
prisons, come to the police stations. Even judges. You know,
there are hearings, court hearings, that happen inside prisons.
Actually, most court hearings now are happening inside branches
of the police academy. So the whole justice system now is explicitly, not even in a secret way, but explicitly and overtly controlled
by the police.

So, anyway, I faced the prosecutor and asked for my lawyers. They spent a couple of hours trying to convince me to cooperate without my lawyers, and then they gave in, and my lawyers were brought in. And I was questioned. Turns out I'm not just accused of protesting without permit, but also of armed robbery. And I was transferred to prison. Then, immediately, the treatment, in terms at least of bodily safety and so on, improved. I was placed in a relatively clean and, by Egyptian standards, spacious cell, which means quite small, but at least I had it to myself. I was allowed visits, and I was allowed access to my lawyers and so on, so the very basic rights were allowed immediately after. For the first month, we were placed in solitary. We were not allowed out of our cells except for one hour per day. We were not placed close to each other, so, you know, we couldn't talk and exchange stuff across cells and so on.

SHARIF: Explain what solitary is like. How do you occupy your time?

ALAA: You go crazy [*laughs*]. You sleep a lot. So, you know, it certainly feels like a clinical depression, which it might also be [*laughs*]. But you try to fill your time: so reading, writing.

SHARIF: The Australian al-Jazeera correspondent Peter Greste was also imprisoned in the same wing as you for a month before he was transferred to another wing of the prison complex. What did you discuss, the two of you?

ALAA: Well, there was a lot of explaining. The guy, Peter, is obviously—I mean, he's quite an experienced writer. He worked in many crazy situations, but not this particular kind of crazy [*laughs*]. And he had only spent, I think, two weeks in Cairo before he got arrested. So, we spent a lot of time just trying to give him enough context to understand what's going on, also the legal proceedings that he was involved in and so on. But we also talked about literature, and we talked about Africa. I lived in South Africa. He lived in Kenya. And so, either we discussed the politics of different sub-Saharan African countries or just, you know, imagined being in the savanna somewhere outside of this horrific context and this horrific place.

SHARIF: What is the likelihood of you being convicted and sent back to prison?

ALAA: It's quite likely. First of all: they've created these special terrorism courts. Now, they pretend they're not special courts, they pretend they are regular courts, that it's just that they've formed separate circuits that are completely free and dedicated for their imminent terrorism and protest law charges so that they could speed up the legal process. Criminal procedures in Egypt—well, all legal procedures in Egypt—are very slow. They tend to take months and months, if not years sometimes. It's a big case, even though it's completely ridiculous. It serves no purpose except, you know, serving the regime. There's no sense of justice in it. I already have a suspended sentence, based on a very colourful case that was started by the military prior to Morsi's election and then was dropped. The prosecutor dropped the charge for lack of evidence. And then, when we started complaining about human rights violations committed by the Muslim Brotherhood government, they revived the case again. But the point is, I have a one-year suspended sentence, which means that if I'm accused of even the smallest misdemeanour, I'm going to spend that year plus whatever else I'm getting. So, it's highly likely that I'm going back to prison, or at least that's their plan.

SHARIF: How does that affect you? How does that affect your life, your family, knowing that you will probably be sent back to prison?

ALAA: [*laughs*] It, of course, I mean . . . it's quite horrific, obviously. Yeah, I mean, we have plans to fight this, both in court and out of court. These are not real courtrooms, this is not true justice, so you have to exert political pressure via protesting, via exposing the irregularities in the process and so on. So we are busy doing that. And also we're busy planning a solid defence strategy. But yeah, that's going to be my life for a while, that I'm . . . because even if we get rid of that case, because of the suspended sentence, it remains hanging over my head for three years, at least. And also, it's clear, I mean, I've been arrested before, but it was always clear in the previous times that they never planned to sentence me. It was like they used the pretrial detention as a form of punishment, as a form of executive detention. And so we always knew that it was just about stifling that voice for a while or about exerting punishment that would only last for a few months. But this time it's clear, and it's not just about me. There's been activists in Alexandria who have been sentenced for two years. And the verdict was confirmed in the appeals process. There's been several student groups that have been sentenced, anything from one year to five. These have been common. There's also a couple of cases where students have been given crazy sentences, like fourteen years and seventeen years and eleven years and so on. So, they are on a sentencing frenzy. This is not just about me. And it's almost as if it's a war on a whole generation.

SHARIF: Let me just switch gears and ask you about some of the letters that you wrote from prison. In December, you wrote a letter to your two younger sisters, Mona and Sanaa, which was delivered a month later. And in it, you write, 'What is adding to the oppression that I feel is that I find that this imprisonment is serving no purpose. It is not resistance, and there is no revolution.' Explain what you meant.

ALAA: Well, that was in contrast to the previous times in which I was arrested, in which I was arrested at either at a moment of, like in 2006, it was a moment of peak mobilization for the pro-democracy movement back then, or in 2011, it was immediately before a very strong wave in between two massacres. So it was clear, and in both cases there was a sense of urgency in the fact of my arrest. Like in 2011, the plan wasn't to arrest me; the plan was to prosecute me, and they thought that this would make me—well, the military prosecutors, this was not civilian—they thought that this would, you know, shake me. So, back then, I kind of planned my own arrest, in a way. You know, I felt in control, and it was clearly part of a struggle and there was a strong reaction on the outside that was supportive, and I felt that I was being supportive of this strong reaction, you know, like I had a purpose there.

This time, it was very different. This time, it's a moment of defeat, to be honest. Everything that's been happening since—at least since the end of July 2013, if not a month before that—has been part of a massive counter-revolutionary wave that has compromised a lot of individuals and parties and political groups, deeply compromised them. But also, part of it was that that kind of crackdown, with the massive arrests and so on, it could have been broken if there was a strong enough reaction back then. This was the first case where they used the Protest Law. They've only managed to sentence people via the Protest Law. Basically, if you participate in a protest and there is a single individual in that protest, even if not known to you, who happens to carry a knife, for instance, then you have committed a crime. So if there's a protest, they can arrest you *and* sentence you. They've always been able to arrest you completely arbitrarily, but it's now possible to sentence you very easily, and judges could claim that this is the letter of the law, not, they're not being ordered by the executive or anything like that now. That's not true, but still. So, the reaction back then wasn't . . . it could have been broken then. There was a much bigger window for action then, and it didn't happen. So that's what I was expressing.

SHARIF: Did you take part in the 30 June demonstrations?

ALAA: Very reluctantly so. There was this—now I consider it quite serious—there was this attempt to retain our margin, so we actually did a . . . all the people who were complaining about collusion with the military and with the police and so on were accused of being . . . were accused by our colleagues of being infantile, the Infantile Left—I think that's a Lenin expression, doesn't matter—but anyway, we were supposed to be too stupid to realize the complex politics of it all and so on. So we staged a couple of protests that were under the label and banner of the Infantile Left, where the point of them was to chant against the military and the police and the Muslim Brotherhood, you know, to be confrontational and so on. But it was such a crazy time. The state was basically mobilizing people to go out. And so, any protest that you did was joined by tens of thousands who were out there because the state, practically because the state told them to be out there. And so, even our protests were joined by throngs of people who were saying yes to the military, yes to the police. And you had no space, your voice couldn't be heard. So I participated in *that* [*he laughs*].

SHARIF: Do you feel it was a mistake, given what is happening now?

ALAA: I don't feel it was mistake, because it was already set in stone. I mean, this path was . . . I think we started warning of an imminent coup in December, or at least January, because the way the Muslim Brotherhood started not just depending on the police force for violence, but on their own cadres, and then when they completely adopted a sectarian discourse, inciting against Christians, and then allowing their allies—or allying, aligning themselves with Salafis and jihadis, it just became clear that they're walking a path that's going to lead to the military taking over. And a few of us spent months trying to stop that, either by warning them or by warning those who were supportive of military intervention or by trying desperately to create a more grassroots movement, so that the complications that the Muslim Brotherhood regime was creating could be resolved via a more genuine, popular approach. But the Muslim Brotherhood government was—I mean, they refused to give any concessions in *anything*. Which made politics basically impossible. Like you couldn't win even very localized, you couldn't even reach a compromise in very localized struggles around issues of service delivery in specific small towns. They just baulked. Which made the coup inevitable. By April, the coup was showing its face, right? So, yeah, I was already defeated by April. So, it didn't really, there was hardly anything we could do. I mean, we kept trying, but there was hardly anything we could do. And also, the Muslim Brotherhood kept—I mean, they could not see the real threat. They kept treating us as the threat. Which is not completely illogical, because we *were* a threat to their project. But the more imminent danger was the military, and they could not see it at all. So during these months in which the coup was being planned, Morsi's prosecutor, the one he broke all constitutional rules in order to install, was busy creating cases for me and Ahmed Douma, the *only* cases that he filed were against Bassem Youssef, me, Ahmed Douma, you know, a few people like that.

SHARIF: There is a rich tradition of activism and dissent in your family. Both your sisters are very politically active. Your cousin is very politically active, and so are your parents. Your father was imprisoned several times, one of which your younger sister Mona was born during. This pattern was repeated when Khaled, your son, was born when you were imprisoned in 2011. I want to quote to you something that your father said in early January at a press conference talking about the crackdown on protesters. He said, 'I'm sorry, my son. I'm sorry to your generation. We had dreams and ambitions to bequeath to you a democratic society that preserves human dignity. But you only inherited the prison cells that once confined me.' Any comment on your father's words?

ALAA: Well, I did respond to them in this epic article I smuggled out of prison about what my inheritance is: both my inheritance directly from my parents and also the collective inheritance we all inherited from the previous generations, with its murky . . . This whole military versus the Brotherhood thing is born out of the intra-World War era, and we have to pay its price now, and it's just completely crazy. Most of this country was born after the end of the Cold War, and none of this makes any sense to any of us. But you have these people talking about Nasserism and neo-Nasserism, and you have these people talking about reversing the mistake of dissolving the Ottoman Empire.

But, yeah, I also worry, what is Khaled, my son, going to face? Because it's not just that we . . . we hand over the prison cell; it's also the things that are actually getting worse. The state institutions have lost any semblance of doing their advertised function. If you spend any time in prisons in Egypt, it makes you wonder. I mean: What is the function of the criminal justice system? And it has absolutely nothing to do with security or confronting crime and so on. Most people in prison are there for very petty crimes. A very, very massive number is there for debt. There's hardly anyone in prison that's a danger to society in that sense.

But you could extend that to the public hospitals. Most of them are not functioning at all. The smaller ones are really not functioning at all. They're just empty shells. The ones that do function, it's quite random what you're going to get there. You know, the doctors are trying hard, but there's absolutely no resources, and it's so corrupt. Basically, there's a very high possibility that, you know, the treatment you get there is . . . that you'd be better off not getting it.

Schools, universities . . . and now this year universities have just become not places of learning, but places of conflict and places where the whole discourse from the state, and even from the university staff and so on, is about how youth are a problem that we need to control. So, now al-Azhar University: al-Azhar has a higher percentage of Islamic students. There are more students from al-Azhar in prison than from any other university. More students from Azhar were killed in the dispersal of the Rabaa sit-in than from any other university. So they're just treating al-Azhar as—even the staff that work there—they're just treating the Azhar students as a security threat. And so, now it has massive walls that look like the apartheid wall in Palestine. They have armed anti-riot police present around the university, ready to intervene at any moment. And students have been killed inside their dorms.

I think it was going in decline for a long time, but it has become a completely dysfunctional state with coercion and oppression as its one and only tool, not just its main tool. Even the Mubarak regime was a much more complicated organism. And it's not just terrorism–that they're trying to treat with only, you know–with security measures only. It's everything. It's like housing, they're trying to–you know, people are building informal settlements, because the housing prices are crazy now.

There are many well-documented reasons for why we have
a housing crisis, and there are many proposed solutions, but
they've been doing nothing about it for years and years and
years, and people have been basically just inventing their own
solutions. This usually entails informal settlements that could be
dangerously built, or it could be that they're built on agricultural
land, which means we have less space to grow food and so on.

So they decided to solve this via security measures. They
just go in, storm the place, demolish it and arrest people. And
so everything, I could cite probably six examples of economic
or social problems that are being solved just via security, and
that's it. If this is what Khaled is inheriting, then . . . I think
that's what motivates me, that this is a completely untenable
and unliveable situation, and it's why it's worth fighting against.
We had a couple of years in which we felt that it was possible to
make major victories, that a dignified life is possible, a different
world is possible. And it looks very bleak right now.

Right now I have to tell people that all state institutions are
completely corrupt and need to be dismantled. And this scares
them, because: what do you do after? And obviously there are
other threats that they're scared about. They think, reasonably
so, that the vacuum created by even diminishing the power of
things like the military is quite dangerous. Armed insurrections
by Salafis and jihadis are happening around our borders. People
see Sinai as a threat. Obviously, Sinai is a state-created threat.
It's been—you know, there is a war there now, where the state is,
where the military is using tactics that we've only seen from—
well, I was going to say only from Israelis—but from the Israelis
and the Americans and the British and so on, but, you know,
from an occupying alien force, where they . . . I mean, it's almost
as if they're copying from the Israelis. They actually uproot olive
trees, demolish houses. When an attack against the military happens, they go and demolish the houses of the families that are

related to the people they accuse of the attack. They're fighting this war with Apaches. And things have been like that in Sinai for years and years and years and years and years.

And so, obviously now, where the state only [*inaudible*] via Hellfire missiles, it becomes a space where human trafficking and drug trafficking and arms trafficking, and also terrorism and jihadis and so on, flourish. But then you use that fact to make people live in fear: fear of Sinai, which is a part of the country that we went to war for and people died for. And now it's being treated as an alien threat. And now it's being, it has become I mean, they've mismanaged it until there is a real threat. Yes, there is a real threat. They created it. But now we're stuck with it. And so, people are scared of change.

And I somehow have to find a way to explain to people why we need to dismantle the state and build a different one, and appease their fears, and actually find a way of confronting all the chaos that they are unleashing right now, and all the chaos that they will continue to unleash, and all the chaos that will be unleashed when they collapse. And they are going to collapse. The current military regime is . . . I mean, it could last for years and years. But this current state of emergency is not temporary. I mean: violence is the only thing they have. They're absolutely incapable of producing discourse that young people, even young people who are not revolutionary or radical in any way, even people who would love to believe them: they keep alienating them. They keep alienating them. It was very clear in the referendum when almost all young voters did not show up. The discourse they use is so poor. And you're talking about most of the country if you're saying young people. But even the people who believed them, the people who rallied to Sisi and created the Sisi cult, they were being promised security, stability and food and work and so on. They have an energy crisis, which they're going to solve with coal, which is going to create a massive environmental and health crisis. Healthcare is in collapse. Education is in collapse. We're completely dependent on imports for food staples, which means that we're very dependent on hard currency. And, you know, their plan is to just borrow a lot of money from Saudi Arabia and the Emirates, and that's not going to last.

And when they collapse, it's going to be scary. It's not going to be, you know, when Mubarak collapsed, it was beautiful. And there were months in which the regime was—I mean, they never lost complete control—but the revolution was so strong, and the regime was so weakened. At least in public spaces and on the street people were liberated and could imagine a completely different world.

The moment they collapse, unless we do something about it, the sense that is going to prevail is not a sense of liberation but a sense of fear. And that's going to get the worst reactions out of people. We saw that when Morsi's rule collapsed. Everybody was scared of everybody. Everybody was paranoid. And so, for a couple of months during July and August, there was civilian-on-civilian violence. I think around 200 people were killed in civilian-on-civilian violence that had absolutely no logic and was so chaotic and scary. Even though the police and the military were all over the place. The police completely collapsed in January 2011 and we spent months with no authority on the ground. But they were safe months: people were not killing each other. There wasn't a crime wave. Prisons were open: all the detainees were out in the street, and nothing much happened. While you had these months [July and August] of absolute military control, but people were scared and paranoid, so we had chaos. And I think we're going to get more of that, unless we do something about it.

SHARIF: You've said the word 'defeat' a couple of times. Do you think the revolution is over?

ALAA: No. I mean, I don't know if the revolution is over or not. That's a . . . the revolution is a historical process that you . . . I mean, when we talk about the revolution while living it, we are talking about a dream, a wish, something that we're trying to fulfil, something that we're trying to create. But you can only talk about it being over or not in the distance, when you're looking back. And so, when I say 'defeat', I mean, in the sense of in a battle.

But we'll continue to exist, and since we'll continue to exist, there will continue to be other struggles. It's not like you have a choice. I mean, an individual might have a choice, if they have a way out. But most people don't have a choice. You know, we can't all emigrate, and it's not like migrant labour gets a good deal anywhere in the world. So, I mean, if what you're trying to do is to achieve a life of dignity and safety and prosperity for yourself and for your loved ones, then you have no choice. But even if you're just trying to live, the current situation is so bad that, you know, you'll end up struggling. Like these waves of strikes that are happening right now, they're mostly by people who probably were very supportive of the overthrow of Morsi, but also of Sisi. I'm guessing, obviously, I'm saying it just fits the pattern. But then they have to go on strike because their wages are not good enough. So you have constant flow of unemployed youth. What are they going to do? If the revolution is defeated, they're not going to cease to exist, so they will continue to resist. They might resist by joining the informal economy, which means that they'll have to confront the state constantly, you know, and violently fight for a piece of the street in which they could sell something. They might resist through politics, protest politics, essentially, because party politics is not going to get them anywhere. But they're not just going to disappear.

But for it to be a revolution, you have to have a narrative that brings all the different forms of resistance together, and you have

to have hope. You know, you have to be . . . it has to be that
people are mobilizing, not out of desperation, but out of a clear
sense that something other than this life of despair is possible.
And that, right now, is a tough one, so that's why right now
I talk about defeat. I talk about defeat because I cannot even
express hope any more, but hopefully that's temporary.

Interview broadcast on 31 March 2014
on *Democracy Now!*

GAME OF THRONES

New York Times, *11 June 2014: One of Egypt's most prominent dissidents, the blogger Alaa Abd el-Fattah, was among three men arrested on Wednesday while waiting outside a court in Cairo to stand trial for violating the government's ban on unsanctioned protests.*

According to his sister, the activist Mona Seif, Mr Abd el-Fattah and the two other defendants, Mohamed Noubi and Wael Metwally, were denied entry to the court and abruptly sentenced in absentia to fifteen years in prison. The same sentence was given to twenty-two other defendants who were arrested last November at a rally called by a human rights group founded by Ms Seif, 'No Military Trials for Civilians', which opposes the abuse of Egypt's court-martial system.

Ms Seif, who was among those detained at the protest in November outside the upper house of Parliament, known as the Shura Council, wrote on her Twitter feed that although her brother had attended the protest, the prosecutor's claim that he had organized it was false. The authorities charged Mr Abd el-Fattah with attacking a police officer, taking his radio and helping other protesters escape arrest. His sentence also included a fine of more than $10,000 and a probationary period of five years.

@Alaa: I wanted to keep watching *Game of Thrones.* #downwithmilitaryrule

After Mr Abd el-Fattah's arrest on Wednesday, he posted a puckish tweet from custody, telling his 600,000 Twitter followers that he was sorry not to have finished watching Game of Thrones *and called for the downfall of Egypt's military-backed government.*

I'VE REACHED MY LIMIT

Today, 18 August 2014, at 4 p.m., I celebrated my last meal in prison with my fellow inmates. After seeing my father battling death, trapped in a body that doesn't obey him, I have decided to start an open hunger strike until I am free. The health of my body is of no value as long as it's forced to submit to an unjust power in an open-ended imprisonment that has nothing to do with the law or with justice.

The idea of a hunger strike has crossed my mind before, but I'd put it off because I didn't want to cause my family further suffering, especially as the Ministry of Interior is known to make examples of hunger strikers by clamping down on them. But then I realized that my family is suffering more with every passing day that I'm in prison. The reason my little sister Sanaa has been imprisoned, along with others who were protesting outside the Presidential Palace, is that they were demanding freedom for political prisoners. They imprisoned my sister because she demanded my freedom!

My family's energy has been torn apart by two prisons, and my father's heart has been broken by two trials. My father delayed his vital surgery more than once because of the cursed Shura Council trial.[70] They snatched me from my son Khaled's arms who is still struggling to overcome the psychological impact of my first imprisonment. Then came the Ministry of the Interior's inhumane treatment with their 'humane gesture' (allowing me to visit my father while he is in intensive care), all of which confirmed for me that postponing the decision to

---

70 Also known as the Protest Law trial, in which Alaa has been a defendant since November 2013 and is, at this point, imprisoned for.

go on hunger strike would not help my mother Laila, my sister
Mona, or my wife Manal.

In order to allow me to visit my father, the Cairo Security
Directorate tried to empty the hospital ward of all the patients,
doctors, nurses, and families. More than once, they would
inform us of a time for the visit, only to cancel it afterwards.
And in the end, they grabbed me from my prison cell at dawn,
with the same compassion as when they grabbed me at dawn
from my home.

The commanding officer was so concerned with making
sure I didn't escape, convinced that everything was an elaborate
performance, that no one was actually sick, and that we were all
conspiring to keep him from his time off, that I ended up being
handcuffed to the bars of the police van, the finale coming as
they forced a camera on us, filming against their will a prisoner
held without charge and an ICU patient. That's when I realized
that postponing my hunger strike was not relieving my family of
suffering, but was turning them into prisoners like me: subject to
the diktats and whims of an institution devoid of all humanity
and incapable of mercy.

Every time I've faced trials and prisons, I've welcomed them.
Not only because it's the price you pay for political dissent, but
because it would be an opportunity to fight for the guarantees
and principles of fair trials. Every court hearing, detention
renewal, or trial was a chance to fight against the use of exceptional courts, and a chance to support the judges who were
aligned with justice. We thought they were many. And every
day in prison was a chance to remind society of those unjustly
detained, a chance to put pressure on political groups and the
media to stop the daily miscarriage of justice. But when I finally
stood before a civilian judge, I found less justice than in the
mightiest exceptional courts; a complete lack of procedures,
laws, and standards; and in spite of us exposing the details of

dozens of cases, we've never heard a single judge object to what goes on at the Torah Police Institute[71] while the politicians tell themselves they've done their part by begging for mercy on account of our revolutionary history, with no mention of these flagrant miscarriages of justice.

My time in prison brings us no closer to a state that abides by its own laws, or to courts that are concerned with justice. The only thing that prison does now is increasingly fill me with hate.

Since the start of the bloody fight between the regime and the Islamists, I've spoken more than once about how we shouldn't get involved. When the conservative forces, who are traditionally entrusted with upholding stability, enter into a polarized conflict that has no end until one force subjugates or annihilates the other, then the role of those who are aligned with the revolution—on the whole—is to halt this conflict and stop society from getting involved in it. That's why I expressed several times that not only do we have to denounce the crimes committed by both sides, side with the victims regardless of who they are, but also have to completely distance ourselves from this fight by only raising demands based on the right to life, bodily dignity, and individual freedom. Right now the very foundations of life are under threat.

I'm not alone in the fight to save the foundations of life. My comrades are many, even though their voices have been drowned out by the noise of this conflict. But my closest comrades in the fight for the right to life, bodily dignity and individual freedom, have always been my family: Mona organizes volunteers to stop trials in exceptional courts; my mother is in contact with victims of torture and her mere presence on the ground is protection for the youth and provides an irrefutable eyewitness. Sanaa provides support and provisions for those held unjustly in prison, while

---

71 The Torah Police Institute is part of the Torah Prison Complex and has within it a courthouse where political cases were being held at that time.

my father defends them and all of us in court, overturning laws by exposing their unconstitutionality, and gaining freedom for those unjustly detained by miraculously winning them innocent verdicts. And sometimes he convicts one of the torturers, with verdicts rarer than miracles. Manal works alongside me in supporting and empowering victims and activists with the technical support and expertise needed to organize campaigns and document violations. My repeated imprisonment is a chapter in my family's history of struggle. Together, we build on the work and struggle of the thousands who never give up, and the millions who sometimes rise up.

Today the chain is broken. Sanaa is in prison and needs someone to look after her, instead of her looking after me; Manal struggles alone to protect Khaled from the consequences of my imprisonment and the lack of income; Mona and my mother take turns to care for my father, who is unable to defend me in court. So I ask for your permission to fight today not only for my freedom, but for my family's right to life. Starting from today, I will deny my body food until I'm allowed to stay the night by my father's side, as his body fights to hold on. There's no dignity for a body that's deprived of the embrace of its loved ones.

I ask for your prayers. I ask for your solidarity. I ask you to continue where I have stopped, to fight, to dream, to hope.

Alaa Abd el-Fattah
Liman Torah Prison
18 August 2014, day 1 of the strike
Published in *Mada Masr*

—

Ahmad Seif el-Islam Abdel-Fattah, Alaa's father, passed away on

Wednesday, 27 August 2014, in the ICU at the public Qasr al-Ainy hospital, six weeks after undergoing open heart surgery. Alaa was in prison.

On 15 September, Alaa was released on bail.

YOUR LEGACY

Prison has only increased the hatred in me, for hate is the jailer's legacy.

Your death has only increased the forgiveness in me, for forgiveness is your legacy.

I've come to hate prisons and courts so much, baba, that I would not wish them even on those I hold responsible for your death.

Has prison ever deterred a criminal? Is there any proof of their use? Or has a majority opinion just settled on them?

I swear, I've never met a single cop who admits that killing Khaled Said was a crime, so what do we gain by locking them up? I've never met a single person whose convictions were changed by prison, so what do they gain by locking up their opponents?

A long time ago, we used to talk about the value of truth. I remember your words and imagine courts in an ideal world, a remote, but possible world, that uphold the truth. Courts that uncover and explain the flaw, how the criminal did it, why we let him.

But I can't see any way how prisons help us stop it happening again. Without you, how will I ever explain to people that we *can* dream of a world without prisons. We're down to not even being able to dream of a world where the criminals are locked up, not the victims.

Published on 16 September 2014 on Facebook

MEMORIAL SERVICE FOR ALAA'S FATHER, AHMED SEIF EL-ISLAM

Hundreds of people gathered at the American University in Cairo's largest lecture hall for a memorial service for Alaa's father, the universally respected human rights lawyer, Ahmed Seif el-Islam.

Alaa is sitting on the stage, wearing an off-white shirt, his hair cut short from prison, microphone in hand. To his right is Amr Shalakany, head of the AUC Law & Society Research Unit, and to his left is rights lawyer and former presidential candidate Khaled Ali.

On my way here I received two messages, with a request that I relay them to you, about prisoners, whose voices are being kept from reaching you otherwise.

One is about Omar Abdel-Maqsoud.[72] Omar and a group with him were ordered released on bail, which they posted. Then they disappeared. Today it was discovered they're facing fresh charges of protesting committed during the time they were held—kidnapped, really—by the state. They've been charged as if they were actually released and immediately joined a protest. My father had a lot of cases like this when dealing with the emergency law[73] and administrative detention. Islamist detainees

---

72 Omar Abdel-Maqsoud is a photojournalist who was arrested multiple times in 2014, and eventually held and charged with belonging to the Muslim Brotherhood. He was tortured in detention.

73 Emergency law grants exceptional powers to the president and security forces, which include restricting public gatherings, censorship of the media, surveillance, broad powers of arrest and detention, and the ability to refer civilians to State Security Emergency Courts whose verdicts cannot be appealed. A state of emergency has been in force in Egypt for much of the past four decades: from 1981 to May 2012; then again for ninety days from August 2013. Later, in April 2017, a state of emergency was declared across the country and has been renewed every three months since.

would be moved from detention facilities to State Security, and then be charged in new cases as though they had actually been released and gone and done new things. Or, it wasn't exactly 'new cases' because administrative detention didn't require cases to actually be brought. Today, with the Protest Law, it's not much different.

The second message is from Mohamed Fahmy of the al-Jazeera English[74] group, the case that's shamelessly called 'the Marriott Cell'. It's a long message in which he expressed his condolences for my father's passing, but the most important point is his comment on an interview Sisi did with AP, in which he said that if he'd been in power during their case, he'd have just deported them. Mohamed Fahmy is responding to Sisi, telling him: we're seven Egyptians and just one foreigner, and although I hold Canadian citizenship, I'm from Port Said and I assert my Egyptian nationality and I'm not asking for anything except to expedite our appeal to the Court of Cassation, so we get a chance to present our defence.

Both messages convey a sense of panic at the absence of my father. Both reflect the moment that's causing many of us to panic at his absence. It is a very dark moment for human rights and that's meant for me that since the news of his death I've been dealing with the loss of Ahmed Seif the lawyer rather than the loss of my father.

I wish I could have come here to tell you about my father, who won't be able to tell stories to Khaled, my son. I think a lot of people in this hall listened to him tell stories, and know Seif the human being, who is inseparable from Seif the citizen and Seif the lawyer, and so on, and know how he used to take fables

---

74 Three al-Jazeera English journalists were arrested in December 2013 after Egyptian authorities banned the broadcaster, part of the new regime's political enmity with Qatar. In June 2014, the journalists Mohamed Fahmy, Peter Greste, and Baher Mohamed were sentenced to seven years on charges of aiding terrorism.

and words invented by children, and turn them into very rich stories, weaving into them anything that happens to be around, a story on TV, or a Mickey Mouse comic.

I wish I could have come here to tell you about my father, who I was—until recently—always fighting with over who gets to read Mickey first . . . But I'm not ready for that, and this isn't the right place.

I wish I could tell the youth of the revolution . . . [*He pauses for a breath*] . . . who are consumed with anger and despair, about Ahmad Seif who was part of an armed communist group, and it wasn't a false charge, because—like them—he lived through a mighty moment like January '77[75] and the uprisings that preceded it. To be honest I never understood his old history because I only knew him after his imprisonment, and he is the most tolerant person I've ever known, so I really can't imagine how he ever thought violence was a solution . . . Maybe it was fashionable in those days . . .

But what I want to say is that he was like us, he wasn't supernatural—

[*His voice breaks. He swallows, holds back tears.*]

He was like us . . .

[*He sits up straighter, his voice steadies.*]

A student activist, coming from the countryside, who chose his university based on what would take him furthest away from his family, and then spent the rest of his life trying to get closer to them. Looking for pathways for his anger, looking for a way to understand what's happening in the world, looking for a way to connect with the wider struggle, so he travelled to southern Lebanon to train with the Palestinian resistance.

He lost everything, except his family, who supported him. I think many of you heard about how he hid out after his sentence

---

75   In January 1977 widespread protests and riots erupted in response to the removal of subsidies on bread. Arrests of communists and other opponents of the regime followed.

and waited until Mama was pregnant with Mona, and then turned himself in. You've heard about his bitter experience of torture[76] and so on . . . A lot has been written about all this, and I'm not even able to tell you those stories . . . I'm telling them as they're told in the newspapers.

I'm not able to tell you about this person who would come up with adventure stories, about a truck on a mountain pass in south Lebanon, or stories about driving a taxi to support me when he and my mum were still students, or about the publishing house he started with my uncle, where many of the most important writers—and novels that were made into important films—were first published, whose office was just downstairs from our apartment, where I'm living now, and where I spent my whole childhood surrounded by piles of books, all wrapped in plastic, and I'd use them like large Lego bricks, arranging them on top of each other to build castles, not understanding that they're part of this person's history. I don't know how to tell you, because I myself never fully understood. His stories were really just stories to me.

I'd like to tell you about when he would line us up, thirteen kids—his very extended family, children of his colleagues and his comrades and his neighbours—and take us on a trip because he had a court session in Fayoum, and he was responsible for us, so he'd fit us all into the Fiat 128 and take us with him. On our way back—and now I wonder if this was because of the experience of prison—he'd ask us, the little kids: 'Don't you want to get lost?' And we'd say yes, so he'd take a sudden turn and we'd discover some place in Egypt we'd never seen before. He'd pass by someone waving him down on the road, so he'd stop, and send two or three more of the thirteen kids to the back to let the guy in, and he'd listen to his life story, and start helping him . . .

---

76 Seif and sixteen others were convicted of joining a communist movement in 1983. Seif served a five-year prison sentence and was severely tortured.

These are pieces that became the person we're missing today for his public role.

[*He takes a breath.*]

Or shall I tell you about him as my lawyer . . . ? Of course his students are many, and my cases are still ongoing, and I'm reassured as long as they're the ones representing me. But with him there was something different, he didn't talk to us just about the case, he would talk to us about our political choices through the case, he would talk to us about how to continue our struggle through the court. He used to hold the court in high regard, to give it value. He would stand before the military court and talk about the law in a way that would eventually convince the military judge—who is not a real judge at all—to respect this invention called the law, called justice, without romanticizing it.

He would talk to us, too, about the history of the law, he would talk to us, just kids, teenagers taking our first steps in protest movements. And it was important for him to talk to us, even if we weren't going to specialize in law, important that we understood how the law was developed, and what the law could be like, what justice could be like. Most people who came in frequent contact with him, whether they were family or defendants, or activists on the street or in student movements who invited him to talk at their events—they all developed a certain sensitivity and understanding of the Constitution and the law that allowed them, later, to form groups to assist lawyers and relieve them of some of the burden of their work, and to engage with the processes of legislation.

He wasn't a regular lawyer, but maybe more importantly on the professional side, or the side of him that I got closer to, is how he used to think: as an activist, as a politician, and as someone taking part in organizing the rights movement and developing it towards engagement with the political movement, the movement for democracy, the movement for freedom, and the movement for human dignity. Of course he did none of this alone, it was all done jointly with the Hisham Mubarak Centre[77] and with the rest of the rights movement.

Perhaps when we say 'his students', the word is not quite accurate; he studied law and got his diploma in prison so he started working as a lawyer a bit late, and when he came out of prison some people were already working to establish the rights movement. Some were of his generation, some were younger, some were older. He came out of prison and joined them, and learned from them; he treated Hisham Mubarak as his mentor, although they were peers, and Hisham was actually younger. And I think this was his relationship with *all* his students, a relationship of true mentorship.

And there were organizational innovations, not just legal innovations. For example, through the Hisham Mubarak Centre he held a series of workshops for regular lawyers, on how to utilize human rights charters and constitutional appeals in their regular casework. This network not only transformed and expanded the acceptance of a human rights discourse in the country, but also, when Mahalla happened, and the people at the Hisham Mubarak Centre realized there was going to be a terrible security onslaught and that they'd need a lot of volunteers, the 'Front to Defend Egyptian Protesters' was formed. The largest role was played by Khaled Ali and many young volunteers with him, and it continued until the revolution, relying on volunteer lawyers, many of whom hadn't done human rights work before, though there was this network that had been built through the syndicate and through those workshops.

New mechanisms were developed to manage the provision of subsistence—to detainees, to workers on strike—at the Hisham Mubarak Centre. Maybe it wasn't my father who invented

---

77 Hisham Mubarak was a human rights lawyer (1963–1998). Seif founded The Hisham Mubarak Law Centre in 2008.

them, but he was the one who insisted that rights centres must play a larger role than the service they provide, or at least that it might be possible that they play that role. That role is totally a political role, but never deviates from human rights standards. They become open spaces where people can assemble and organize themselves through these centres, with the help of their resources, with their legal support. So, we had experiences—maybe some gentlemen here will talk about them in detail—like hosting the Popular Campaign for Solidarity with the Palestinian Intifada, hosting the Coordinating Committee for Labour Rights and Freedoms, the Social Security and Pensions, the Right to Health . . . All those initiatives and groups worked on specific issues—the Right to Medicines, even AGEG (the Egyptian Anti-Globalization Group), when the movement against the global predominance of capital and arms took the form that was later labelled the Anti-Globalization Movement, some groups in Egypt were interested in developing that intellectual framework locally, and were hosted at Hisham Mubarak. The 6 April Youth Movement, at some point, were hosted in a flat that was shared between Hisham Mubarak and the Egyptian Centre for Economic & Social Rights.

It became an incubator for lawyers, researchers, and rights centres.

When someone left, rather than thinking of it as someone gaining experience and knowledge and leaving—which could lead to crises and arguments—mechanisms were developed to make that departure part of the role and the mission of my father, and of the Hisham Mubarak Centre: so it spun off several rights centres, that are now playing very important roles, with continued support, encouragement, and cooperation. They'd realized that there were only a few rights centres that took a strong radical position in favour of democracy and were ready to engage politically without compromising human

rights standards, and those were the organizations taking up
the difficult cases. At first, torture cases were some of the most
difficult, meaning that we couldn't talk about them. But other
types of cases are still difficult, those deviating from what society
considers—or what the regime insists that society considers—to
be proper, whether in freedom of belief, in personal freedom, in
sexual orientation, or whatever. He was defending those labelled
as terrorists, defending those labelled as infidels, defending those
labelled as thugs, defending those labelled as queers and so on.
But each of these centres was small, and possibly fragile on its
own, so they developed mechanisms to issue joint statements
and take joint positions. Perhaps, in the militarization phase
that followed the mandate,[78] it was this group of centres who
were able to take joint positions, they were the ones who broke
the silence at the very beginning. They broke it even before the
massacres, and warned of the massacres, said there would be
massacres and the reaction would be sectarian violence, that
there would be civil strife, that we will pay the price dearly. They
were the first to take these positions, and supported the youth
who went down and demonstrated against all the traitors, only
to be quashed on the streets. Those centres utilized the mechanisms that had been developed—and that my father held on to
so they could work in unity. These organizational innovations
are not exclusive to the human rights movement. These are
organizational innovations that—maybe we don't even realize to
what extent—have seeped into and become part of our organizational thinking.
   To finish . . .
   [*He pauses, looks down for a moment before continuing.*]
   I'm sorry I wasn't able to tell you much about the human . . .

---

78   When Sisi asked the public for what he called a popular mandate to fight against
     terrorism, huge crowds took to the streets in positive response on 26 July 2013. The
     Rabaa el-Adaweya massacre followed nineteen days later.

except in fragments, as if I'm piling them up, because I'm not able to yet.

But what I hold on to is that, on a personal level, I can feel the loss and the panic, and I'm overpowered by the thought that he won't tell Khaled any stories. But on a public level . . . [*He shakes his head, waves his free hand as if to say 'no'*] . . . we don't need to feel loss, because he left us the key to his way and his work. He left us all we need in order to continue his journey, and most importantly the belief that you don't have to be extraordinary. He never spoke about himself as having any exceptional abilities. He insisted on speaking about the difficulty of the experience of torture. He insisted on speaking about the difficulty of the prison experience. He insisted on speaking about his weaknesses, and his mistakes. And I don't think this was modesty, I think this was a much larger and more important message . . . [*His voice catches, he draws a breath, is crying.*] All that's asked of us is that we fight for what's right. We don't have to be winning while we fight for what's right, we don't have to be strong while we fight for what's right, we don't have to be prepared while we fight for what's right, or to have a good plan, or be well organized. All that's asked of us is that we don't stop fighting for what's right.[79]

23 September 2014 at the
American University in Cairo

---

79   Alaa says '*nantaser lelhaq*'. The two words carry multiple meanings conjugated to a specificity that is difficult to translate fully into one succinct English phrase. *Nantaser* comes from *intisar*, which means 'victory'. Here, used as a verb, it means 'to champion, to fight for, to defend'. *Al-haq* means both truth and justice. But 'all that's asked of us is to champion justice' does not carry the elegance or the true power of the Arabic phrasing, which comes in part from transforming *nasr* (victory) from the statist, high-power context in which it's normally used, into the verb *intisar* (to defend, to champion). Here it becomes an action that even the most defeated can still take and this phrase remains widely associated with Alaa.

ON THE SAKHAROV PRIZE

It was with joy that I received the news of my nomination for the Sakharov Prize for Freedom of Thought, the same joy any act of solidarity inspires.

Since my release from prison in Egypt on bail, with my fate still bound to the Special Terrorism Courts and the draconian Protest Law, I've been facing constant harassment from official and unofficial representatives of the regime. New trumped-up criminal charges pop up every few days. A horde of political talk show hosts on supposedly independent TV stations discuss old and out-of-context tweets, twisting my words and assigning sinister implications to them. There's a relentless smear campaign meant to prepare the general public for my eventual return to prison. Needless to say, I'm banned from appearing on local TV stations, and from travel outside Egypt.

So it is solidarity such as that of European United Left/Nordic Green Left (GUE/NGL) that creates the pressure to keep me out of jail and out of harm. It was also a comfort to find comrades in unexpected places; GUE/NGL's stance against neoliberal policies and against the distortion of European democracy seemed in line with the aspirations of persecuted revolutionaries in Egypt and the broader Arab context.

I was proud to be nominated along with the Tunisian rapper, Ala Yaacoubi, and the Moroccan rapper, Mouad Belghouate, both imprisoned for insulting the police in their popular songs. I was relieved that the European Parliament members (MEP) who nominated us understood the point of doing symbolic violence to the image of the powerful who commit systemic *actual* violence to the bodies, souls and livelihood of the powerless;

relieved that the MEPs understood the meaning of questioning the humanity of those who derive their power from dehumanizing their opponents.

I was not surprised when a new smear campaign was launched in reaction against my nomination. My family has faced such campaigns before by supporters of the Israeli occupation and Israeli apartheid. The latest when my sister, Mona Seif, was shortlisted for the Martin Ennals Award. But I was surprised when the president of the GUE/NGL decided to withdraw my nomination based on a two-year-old tweet taken out of context. And I was surprised that this was done without an attempt to contact me for clarification, and without any regard for how such public condemnation affects my safety and liberty. The president of the GUE/NGL has now sent a clear message to the Egyptian authorities that whatever international solidarity and support I have is fragile—easily destroyed with a single tweet.

The GUE/NGL are of course free to form their opinion based on whatever sources of information they choose—including well-known neocons writing for the *Wall Street Journal* about an out-of-context tweet. However, since they made the nomination and made it publicly, it was their responsibility to ascertain how the manner of retreating from it would affect my safety. Other options were available to them; they could have asked me to withdraw, or they could have quietly dropped my name from the shortlist.

The GUE/NGL's president's statement claims that I 'called for the murder of a critical number of Israelis'. For what it's worth, here is what I would have said if anyone from GUE/NGL or any other MEPs had asked me to clarify.

The tweet in question is certainly shocking if taken out of context, but even then it cannot be framed as 'a call' for anything. It was a 'mention' to two friends, part of a private conversation—a thread spanning multiple tweets—that took place

over a public medium (limited to 140 characters) on the first
night of Israel's 2012 attack on Gaza. A conversation between
friends who already knew enough about each others' views to
make it unnecessary to clarify and elaborate, for instance, the
distinction between civilians and combatants—as one would if
one were making a public statement. As this was not a public
statement, only those who follow all three of us on Twitter
would have had this tweet appear on their timeline at 2 a.m. on
15 November 2012. And even after the smear campaign, it has
only been retweeted four times.

To pretend that you can interpret this tweet two years later
without consulting the people involved in the conversation, and
to claim that it constitutes a call to action, is simply ridiculous.
That I should now feel the need to explain and clarify what
wasn't intended for a general public in the first place, and to be
condemned for my thoughts, rather than my actions, in such a
manner is clearly an attack on my personal liberty. The chilling
effect of having to adapt to such harassment and condemnation
should be perfectly clear for those honouring Andrei Sakharov's
legacy.

The conversation relating to the war on Gaza started with
a friend expressing her doubt that the conflict would ever be
resolved by local actors. The other friend in the conversation
and I replied, insisting that like most such conflicts, it would
be resolved locally. The tweet stated what seems to be the basic
strategy of most national liberation movements, especially those
that opt for armed resistance:to make the price of occupation/
colonization/apartheid too expensive for the society that supports it. The strategy of the Palestinians is exactly that—via both
violent and nonviolent means (boycott, divestments and sanctions, and armed resistance, for example). Since this was during
a time of war, I had armed resistance in mind. Think of Vietnam
or Algeria; many would say this is exactly what happened: after

a critical number of casualties in asymmetric wars, the civilian population supporting the occupier refused to continue its support—despite the fact that the casualties suffered by the society resisting colonization were massively higher.

My tweet was not a call for anything; it was not even a statement of opinion. It was a statement of one of the facts of the conflict. If GUE/NGL had asked me about my views I would have directed them to my March 2012 debate on Deutsche Welle.

It should perhaps be remembered that the first laureate of the Sakharov Prize was Nelson Mandela back in 1988, when he and the African National Congress (ANC) were considered terrorists by many democratic governments. At the time, his views on the necessity of violence for resisting apartheid must have required and inspired complex debates on appropriate tactics and strategies, the rules of engagement, the moral, political and social limitations that should be put on revolutionary violence, etc. There would have been plenty of statements attributable to him or his comrades—including the famous Rivonia Trial speech in which he admits to planning sabotage—that would have looked pretty scary out of context.

Finally, I hardly ever call for any solution or action on my own. As an individual, I have always expressed my opinions and positions in the clearest and strongest language. But as an activist, I have always worked for any given cause with and through the largest united front possible. When it comes to calls for solutions or actions, and for the sake of consensus, I would make the very compromises I refuse to make when speaking only for myself.

More importantly, I do not call for anything when it is not a cause that I'm directly engaged with. I stand in solidarity with the Palestinian people, but I never presume to tell them what to do.

If my views on violence—specifically against civilians—are what is in question, the answers can be found in my actions and my published views in my local context and my own struggle in Egypt.

Published on 7 October 2014 in *Mada Masr* & *Jadaliyya*

FIVE POSTS FROM OCTOBER 2014

9 October 2014

Whatever became of those plans to restore the churches burned by the Brotherhood at the Army's expense? Oh yeah, not one brick has been laid, and they arrested the people who tried to restore them at their own expense.[80]

13 October 2014

Anyone who tells you that the solution is to apply the law is bullshitting you.

The solution is to apply the law to the strong *before* the weak, to the rich before the poor, to Sisi before the doorman.

And that's on condition that the law is consented to by society, particularly by those most affected by it, and has been formulated through a democratic process.

And on condition that the law doesn't infringe on the basic rights and freedoms of the individual.

And on condition that the law is logical, comprehensible, accessible to people, and known to them before its application— not an ambush that's set for them.

And on condition that whoever the law is applied to has access to a fair, unbiased trial that's not rigged, rushed, or repeatedly delayed.

And on condition that whoever is subject to the law has the opportunity to change the law, and can challenge it on the basis of whether or not it meets standards of public consent and protection of basic rights. And these must be *real* opportunities.

---

80 Today is the anniversary of the Maspero massacre.

And on condition that the agents of the law are subject to oversight and held accountable, and are accepted by those most affected by the law.

There are many conditions before 'applying the law' is a solution to anything. But it would be enough to start by applying it to Sisi before the students.[81]

16 October 2014

Prison never changed an idea. Oppression never held back tomorrow.[82]

It's true that the future won't be held back by prison. Time for the prisoner stops, but outside the prison walls it races ahead. Your kids grow up and need school fees that you've got no idea how to provide while you're locked up. Your mother or your father get sick and could die. Your work is disrupted and delayed, and people won't hold your job for you for too long.

And just as oppression wastes tomorrow rather than holding it back, so prison impedes the development of ideas, rather than changing them.

Do you really think that captives whose basic rights have been ignored and whose children's blood has been shed, will re-evaluate their ideas, their choices, their leaders? That they'll reconsider their discourse, however sectarian and catastrophic? Why? What good would it do them while they're ossified in prison? And where are they supposed to get new ideas when they're denied access to all media, in solitary confinement, and sometimes denied visits?

---

81 At the start of the academic year, a few days earlier, student demonstrations erupted at several universities across the country to protest new security measures, including the use of a private security company on campuses, infringements on academic freedom, and the prolonged detentions of fellow students arrested during previous demonstrations. Security forces cracked down on the protests, arresting dozens of students, including many from their homes in pre-dawn raids.

82 A famous protest chant.

19 October 2014
The death of a state is an ugly thing. God only knows if society can survive it.

26 October 2014
Keep sitting silently watching us be imprisoned one by one and the students getting killed one by one until the disaster comes knocking on your front door.

New York Times, *27 October 2014: Alaa Abd el-Fattah, an influential Egyptian blogger, was arrested in court on Monday in Cairo as he appealed a fifteen-year sentence for violating Egypt's ban on attending unsanctioned protests.*

Mr Abd el-Fattah, who had been free on bail, was jailed along with nineteen other defendants also accused of participating in a demonstration in Cairo late last year.

The ruling comes the day after Mr Abd el-Fattah's younger sister, Sanaa Seif, and 22 other activists were sentenced to three years in prison for attending a street protest in June calling for the release of the first group of demonstrators.

Mr. Abd el-Fattah, known to his hundreds of thousands of Twitter followers as @Alaa, was bizarrely sentenced in absentia in June as he waited outside to be allowed into the courtroom. To ensure that the authorities could not say that he skipped Monday's hearing, he posted a photograph of himself waiting outside the court on Twitter.

2016

THE ONLY WORDS I CAN WRITE

Five years ago, on what would turn out to be the last normal day of my life, I sat down at my desk in a small IT firm in Pretoria and pretended to be working while I was actually writing a short article for the *Guardian*. It was about why the Egyptian revolution should be taken seriously. Or at least that's how I remember it. I can't get back to that article now; it's been more than a year since I had access to the internet. In Egypt, prisoners aren't even allowed a phone call. But I shouldn't complain: at least I get to see my family two or three times a month. Other political prisoners (mostly Islamists) are not allowed visits at all.

On that day, five years ago, I first engaged in the battle over the narrative of the revolution, a battle that would consume me completely for four years. But on that day I wasn't even sure a revolution was happening in Egypt—I feared it would fizzle out even as I wrote about a new form of youthful pan-Arabism.

It would take me another day to fully accept that it was for real and three more before I could fly back to Cairo and join Tahrir. I moved from doubting the depth of the uprising to worrying about arriving too late and missing out on all the action.

After the fall of Mubarak, the battle over narrative grew in importance. The state was forced to compromise with the revolution while trying to contain it by appropriating its story. We articulated why we continued to protest and indeed why we ever protested at all. Are the kids who threw stones at the police revolutionaries or saboteurs? Should the prisoners who died in prison riots be counted among the martyrs of the revolution or not? What's the role of the military in the Mubarak regime? Should education continue to be free in public universities? Do we need a new constitution? If so, who should write it? And so on. I wrote and wrote and wrote, mostly in Arabic, mostly on social media but sometimes for a national daily. I was mostly talking to fellow revolutionaries and my voice became increasingly cautionary: how fragile the revolutionary moment was, and how precarious our situation was, were my main themes. And yet I couldn't shake off the sheer sense of hope and possibility—despite setbacks, our dreams continued to soar.

People talk of a barrier of fear but to me it always felt like a barrier of despair and, once removed, even fear, massacres and prisons couldn't bring it back. I did all the silly things over-optimistic revolutionaries do: I moved back to Egypt permanently, had a child, founded a startup, engaged in a series of progressive initiatives aiming at more popular, decentralized and participatory democracy, broke every draconian law and outdated taboo, walked into prison smiling and walked out of it triumphant.

In 2013, we started to lose the battle for narrative to a poisonous polarization between a rabidly militarized pseudo-secular statism and a viciously sectarian-paranoid form of Islamism. All I remember about 2013 is how shrill I sounded screaming 'A plague on both your houses,' how whiny and melodramatic it felt to complain about the curse of Cassandra warning of an all-consuming fire when no one would listen. As the streets were taken over by rallies that raised the photos of policemen instead of their victims, sit-ins were filled with chants against the Shia, and Coptic conspiracies flourished, my words lost any power and yet they continued to pour out of me. I still had a voice, even if only a handful would listen.

But then the state decided to end the conflict by committing the first crime against humanity in the history of the republic. The barriers of fear and despair would return after the Rabaa el-Adaweya massacre. Another battle over narrative would start:

getting non-Islamists to accept that a massacre had happened at all, to reject the violence committed in their name.

Three months after the massacre I was back in prison, and my prose took on a strange new role: to call on revolutionaries to admit defeat. To give up the optimism that had become dangerous in its encouragement to choose sides: a military triumphalism or an unpopular and impractical insistence on complete regime change. What we needed was all the strength we could muster to maintain some basic defence of human rights.

I narrated defeat because the very language of revolution was lost to us, replaced by a dangerous cocktail of nationalist, nativist, collectivist and post-colonialist language, appropriated by both sides of the conflict and used to spin convoluted conspiracy theories and spread paranoia.

In early 2014, it was still controversial to ask revolutionaries to engage in a human rights campaign limited to revoking the protest law and the release of political prisoners. Most still believed the revolution was winning (defining winning as either the demise or the triumph of the Muslim Brotherhood). The idea that the state of emergency was the new normal was rejected by most.

Today it seems like we won that final battle for narrative. While the state still has its supporters, their numbers are shrinking rapidly, especially among the youth. Most people are no longer debating the nature of the events of summer 2013. The coup versus revolution debate is passé. Even Sisi supporters don't really believe that prosperity is coming soon. It's harder to gauge the sentiment among supporters of the Islamists: sympathy with their plight is certainly increasing, but faith in their ability to organize an effective unified front against the regime is probably negligible. Despair prevails.

I spent most of 2014 in prison yet I still had lots of words.

My audience was much diminished, my message not one of hope, and yet it felt important to remind people that even after admitting defeat we can still resist; that going back to the margins we fought from during Mubarak's time was acceptable as long as we continued to fight for basic human rights. But by early 2015, as I heard my sentence, I had nothing left to say to any public. I could only write personal letters. The revolution and, indeed Egypt itself, would slowly fade out even from those letters, and by autumn 2015, even my own, personal words dried up. It's been months since I wrote a letter and more than a year since I've written an article. I have nothing to say: no hopes, no dreams, no fears, no warnings, no insights, nothing, absolutely nothing. Like a child showing signs of autism, I am regressing and losing my words, my ability to imagine an audience and mentally model the impact of my words on them.

I try to remember what I wrote for the *Guardian* five years ago on the last normal day of my life. I try to imagine who read that article and what impact it had on them, I try to remember what it was like when tomorrow seemed so full of possibility and my words seemed to have the power to influence (if only slightly) what that tomorrow would look like.

I can't really remember that. Now tomorrow will be exactly like today and yesterday and all the days preceding and all the days following. I have no influence over anything.

But one thing I do remember, one thing I know, is that the sense of possibility was real. It may have been naive to believe our dream could come true, but it was not foolish to believe that another world was possible. It really was. Or at least that's how I remember it.

Written in Torah Prison
Published on 24 January 2016
in the *Guardian* & *Mada Masr*

THE BIRTH OF A BRAVE NEW WORLD 1:
BETWEEN UBER AND THE LUDDITES

Britain, dawn of the industrial revolution: angry crowds of weavers and skilled craftspeople storm the new mills and set about smashing the steam-powered machinery and mechanized looms that threaten their livelihood. For a brief moment, society keenly follows the progress of the Luddite movement (as it's known, supposedly in reference to one of its leaders), until it is decisively defeated and reduced to the stuff of proverb. 'Luddite' becomes an insult used to denigrate those who attempt to slow the march of progress and modernization, or to stop it altogether—a reminder of the absurdity of challenging science and technology. Only Luddites resist change. How stupid of them!

Paris, dawn of the fourth technological revolution: in demonstrations which turn violent, taxi drivers attack Uber drivers and sabotage their cars as a protest to threats to their livelihood. Only Luddites try to hold back history. How stupid of them!

Cairo, dawn of the fourth technological revolution: rowdy demonstrations by drivers of white taxis see Uber drivers ambushed and handed over to the police. Only Luddites try to hold back history. How stupid of them!

California, dawn of the fourth technological revolution: Uber drivers file a class action lawsuit against the company demanding to be recognized as waged employees entitled to the usual labour rights and protections afforded by any employment contract. In the company's detailed and convoluted defence, it claims that the drivers are in fact users of the company's services who enter into contracts on a per-ride basis, and as such cannot legally be considered employees. Inside the courtroom, discussions cover details like to what extent the company is responsible for training drivers or providing equipment, while outside the courtroom, the company's message is more blunt: these are Luddites, even if they have embraced modern technology. Luddites because they refuse to acknowledge that the age of employment contracts which bestow rights, protections, insurance, holidays and fixed salaries is over, for these things have no place in the coming economic and technological reality. Luddites who refuse progress and modernization, and stand in the way of science and technology. Only Luddites try to hold back history. How stupid of them!

INVOLUNTARY LUDDITE

This article is necessarily full of mistakes. I write based solely on memory and imagination. What choice do I have? In the first year of my detention, the Prison Authority allowed me books, magazines and periodicals in Arabic and English without restriction. After some negotiation they also allowed my family to bring in articles printed out from the internet, after they'd been checked by prison security. I was allowed to subscribe to various local and Arab newspapers. But with progress along the transitional roadmap, the stabilization of constitutional life, and the successive victories of the army, police, judiciary and media over terrorism, State Security—inevitably—had to intervene, and ban everything that was previously allowed, save for national newspapers, and, after prolonged negotiation, Mickey Mouse comic books and one novel per month.

Vainly, I try to understand the logic behind these proscriptions. I don't question their legal grounds, of course; I'm not stupid enough to assume that the constitution, the law, or prison regulations are matters that concern the heroic men of the Ministry of the Interior. I do wonder, though, about the security imperatives which dictate that a prisoner—who is incapable of any action—be deprived of reading material that is available to those at liberty. What is the potential threat to public order or to the regime—even the prison regime—that might ensue if I were allowed to subscribe to the London-based newspaper *al-Hayat*, for example, or consult a page on Wikipedia?

But the faults of this article are not confined to factual mistakes made for want of references. The problem is that I myself have become an involuntary Luddite. Here in my cell, time doesn't pass and history doesn't move. I don't hear about new developments in the outside world, and if I do, I don't understand them; if I understand them, I can't observe their effects on people or witness the reactions they provoke. So here I am, a genuine Luddite, attempting to engage with a complex issue that is subject to wide debate, despite being incapable of following or understanding that debate. Forgive me, then, if I assume that I have something to add, and then my words turn out to be redundant, and already refuted.

In all cases, I'm not too concerned about the future of taxis, white or otherwise. For at least three years (perhaps longer if the state's justice intervenes, or shorter if divine justice does), my only ride will be a prisoner transport van—a mode of transportation that has undergone no developments since the demonstrations of 1986. What I am concerned about is the future of the labour market, to which I hope to return at some point. I'm also concerned about my precarious position as an IT specialist kept out of the field for several years, and therefore unable to keep pace with its changes.

The conflict between Uber and the white taxis is only the opening battle in what is to be a long war waged over the concept of labour as it emerged in the wake of the industrial revolution. Anyone who thinks their job or livelihood is safe today may well find themselves, with no advance warning, amongst the ranks of the Luddites tomorrow. Even Uber drivers themselves are not safe: soon, self-driving cars will be the norm, and Uber might dispense altogether with the human element and the errors and problems it brings. At that point, those who have opposed their colleagues' struggles for permanent contracts will realize the value of these contracts in protecting against arbitrary dismissal and guaranteeing severance pay. Who can compete with robots when it comes to cleanliness and observance of traffic rules? It would put paid to the sexual harassment issue, too.

Are you confident that your job couldn't be done by an army of workers on casual contracts? Are you ready to compete with robots? Or are you, perhaps, joining the disciples of Ludd? And then there's the ever-increasing likelihood you'll be made an involuntary Luddite. Only robots are capable of satisfying our rulers.

LABOUR PAINS

Let's return to the original Luddites. However we try to understand their motives, the historical fact remains that the industrial revolution brought with it jobs, comfort and prosperity, and unprecedented stability and security that far outweighed what it destroyed. It is logical, then, for 'Luddite' to have become a derogatory term synonymous with backwardness and conservatism.

Based on that experience, theories have emerged which explain the history of societies with reference to the development of disruptive technologies, i.e. new types of knowledge and technology which fundamentally alter the form and nature of production, labour relations, and property. Their appearance is inevitable, their spread spontaneous—which is necessarily positive. Those who stand to lose out are always minorities looking to deprive the majority of the fruits of progress. And whatever the resulting harms are, they are temporary—the inevitable labour pains of the birth of a brave new world.

The advocates of disruptive technologies claim they, and the upsets they cause, are akin to natural phenomena. They may be the result of research and experiments by individuals and corporations, but they are inevitable. Nothing can stand in their way or change their course; if a technology is suppressed in one country, it will simply pop up in another, and in the end, its effects will encompass the entire planet.

Where these theories were once tools for analysing the past, they have become ideological tools for shaping the present and moulding the future, a doctrine that dominates entire markets, where investors compete in a frenzy to find the next disruptive technology or idea and be the first to finance, exploit—and ideally monopolize—it. They also race to push the current disruptive technology out into new markets and fields. For example, it was the success of the idea of the sharing economy in the market for alternatives to hotels (i.e. Couchsurfing and Airbnb) that encouraged investors to fund the application of the same technologies to the transportation market (Uber and Lyft), and companies to expand geographically into new cities and markets, and so on.

When a given doctrine comes to dominate the largest interests in markets, its sphere of influence tends to expand to the point that it becomes hegemonic, controlling states, governments and all institutions: either by establishing facts on the ground, and then applying pressure to write them into law; by mounting battles in court; by lobbying decision-makers and courting them with campaign donations; by shaping public opinion through promotion and advertising; by recruiting elites through research funding and conferences . . . and so on. In this case, all available means are marshalled to propagate the narrative that disruptive technologies are an unmitigated good, that they are inevitable and that any attempt to stand in their way or hesitation to embrace them, any attempt to manage them or their effects, is inherently harmful and will inevitably fail.

Seeing as I stand accused of casting doubt on official narratives, and being an inveterate offender when it comes to challenging hegemonic ideas, I find myself instinctively doubting this account of disruptive technologies. This is despite my usual enthusiasm for modernization, advancement and technology—information technology most of all—and despite the many benefits these services, networks and technologies have brought me.

It is true that the industrial revolution brought widespread prosperity, but the labour pains that accompanied it were not quick to subside, and it was generations before things settled. Neither the Luddites nor their children, nor even their grandchildren, reaped the fruits of the industrial revolution. And what relative prosperity it brought was not a result of technology alone, but of the interplay between technological innovation and political arrangements, such as the regularization of working hours, the prohibition of child labour, the establishment of standards for industrial safety, the introduction of a minimum wage, the negotiation of wages through collective bargaining, the introduction of regular statutory holidays, and an acceptance of the idea of health and education as rights to be granted in the form of public services funded, via taxation, from the profits of the industrial revolution's beneficiaries—along with many other arrangements for the rights of wage laborers as we know them today. It is these rights that the fourth industrial revolution is threatening.

If industrialized societies had continued to allow factory owners to employ children for long hours in inhuman conditions, or failed to introduce progressive taxation based on profit—as was the case early on in the industrial revolution—it would not be possible today to consider Luddite a synonym for stupidity and backwardness.

Most importantly, the process of transformation was a path of bitter conflicts between different classes and interests. The labour rights mentioned above were wrested by force from states, governments, and factory owners after decades of protest, struggle and revolution. Yes, the Luddites were defeated, but in their place came working-class fighters and activists who did not reject progress but sought to influence its terms and the course it would take. Elites and ruling classes treated them with the same violence and derision meted out to the Luddites, but the resistance continued. Sometimes protests were so heated that workers sabotaged machinery—the difference, of course, being that where the Luddites' sole design was to sabotage machinery, the workers saw sabotage as a means to exert pressure, which society rapidly replaced with unionization and legalization of industrial action as alternatives to violence and counter-violence.

Reducing the historical process accompanying the industrial revolution to temporary labour pains preceding prosperity not only obscures the details of class conflict within the major industrial nations, but also obscures nations' differing experiences of these transitional pains. The industrial revolution brought about colonial expansion, and increasing colonial violence, as industrialized nations opened new markets and sought new raw materials. Savage competition between industrialized nations over the fruits of modernization resulted in the outbreak of world wars.

In short, the discovery and invention of new technologies may be inevitable, but their deployment and dissemination, and the structure of the markets and power relations which are based upon them, are far from it: they are the results of policies, which in turn are the outcome of conflicts within society.

Studying technological innovations, analysing their effects and questioning the propagandistic narratives which accompany them, is vital. Engaging with and against these technologies and the interests behind them—with the aim of influencing their course, limiting the pains that come with their growth, maximizing the benefits of their adoption, expanding the base of their beneficiaries, and compensating the aggrieved, are also vital.

The only people more stupid than those who stand in the way of history are those who prostrate themselves before it. Those leave no trace or memory at all, not even as a cautionary tale like the Luddites.

Written in Torah Prison
Published on 16 June 2016 in *Mada Masr*

THE BIRTH OF A BRAVE NEW WORLD 2:
ATOMS & BITS

Advocates of the 'Fourth Technological Revolution' narrative insist on drawing dubious parallels with the Industrial Revolution. And yet they claim that modern technologies like the sharing economy, artificial intelligence, deep learning, 3D printing etc are primarily concerned with informational space, rather than material space, thus implying that this technological revolution is geographically neutral—and downplaying the severity of its collateral violence. The implication being a stark contrast with the Industrial Revolution, which provoked fierce competition over raw materials, energy sources and global trade routes.

Certainly the prospect of the sharing economy giving rise to a world war is unlikely, but that's not to say that it doesn't involve any violence or repression, because this idea of a clear separation from the material world is a myth. Uber could never have flourished were smartphones not already widely available. Smartphones are produced in large numbers at relatively low cost, with a substantial profit margin for Apple and the like. The model relies on enormous Chinese factories where workers suffer appalling working conditions: sometimes labourers are detained at their workstations in what basically amounts to forced labour. Apple has faced repeated scandals over working conditions, most notably the high suicide rate among workers. Those factories also rely on rare minerals, which are extracted in primitive mines in Africa where child labour is rife, health and environmental conditions are dire, and profits fuel vicious conflicts between militias and armed gangs.

Even in the United States, potential violence is not absent from the equation. With the development of its economy, primary manufacture has largely given way to the production and consumption of software, design and services. And despite the drop in unemployment rates, many attribute the rise of the far right (Donald Trump, Ted Cruz and their ilk), to the fragile position of the working class in this new 'flexible' labour market. A new, aggressive discourse has surfaced, with mass mobilizations and calls for solutions from the past as a reaction to the political, economic, media and academic elite's insistence that labour rights and protections need to be rolled back.

But more dangerous than the flawed parallels between the Industrial Revolution and its alleged technological counterpart is the assumption that the unequal distribution of benefit from adopting new technologies is down to resource distribution. The accumulation of capital gains was never purely a result of technology and markets, but first and foremost of state policies. Brazil, for example, accumulated social institutions and services, as it invested the profits from exporting raw materials into health and education, while the DR Congo only accumulated weapons and militias. China accumulated infrastructure and scientific and engineering expertise from the profits of its manufactured exports, while Bangladesh accumulated the corpses of impoverished workers in crumbling factories.

In fact, by comparison with the Industrial Revolution, the intangible nature of the technological revolution might mean that fewer gains are created overall, but that accumulation is more concentrated. The Industrial Revolution transformed the production process itself, then the nature of the goods produced, and changes in the labour market happened as a result. But the sharing economy offers no new means of producing goods or services. The scope of its transformation is the labour market itself—not what the labour does.

Uber, for example, has not altered transportation technology. Uber's answer to the question 'How will I get from home to work?' is the same answer offered by a taxi, i.e. that you'll hire a car and a driver for a single journey at a price proportional to the time and distance. What has changed is the mechanism of contracting a driver, the distribution of profit earned, and the ownership structure of the service.

The sharing economy model depends fundamentally on the fact that the cost of the service to new users—the cost of downloading an app and creating an account—is tiny, while the cost of entering new markets is low, so it is unlikely that any new accumulation of capital, assets, infrastructure, expertise, knowledge or services will take place.

Uber Egypt's office is probably small, the number of employees actually needed to manage the market is small, and the nature of their work will not result in any knowledge transfer. And, of course, the company will not own or develop assets or equipment, and will not invest in infrastructure. The driver provides the car, and the state provides the roads and the dollar-subsidized fuel. And when the company makes profits in Egyptian pounds, it will transfer them out of the country in dollars. So the only accumulation is happening in California: the profits are there, as are the investments and top jobs (management, design, programming, planning etc.). And since Uber defines itself as a software company, rather than a transport company, don't expect it to pay significant taxes, neither here nor there. Most major Silicon Valley companies register their headquarters in tax havens, and claim that they make most of their profits in those headquarters, to benefit from double taxation prevention agreements. The US has serious difficulties in recovering taxes from the world's richest corporations, like Google, Apple, and Facebook—so much so that Obama became personally involved in negotiations with each of these companies, and still came away with little more than crumbs.

As for Egypt's track record in benefiting from the fruits of the

Industrial Revolution, that's a sorry tale, despite our early integration into its markets—the current dollar crisis being a case in point. And our track record in collecting taxes is no better: just listen to the stories about the state's inability to collect income tax from some of its own employees, because they happen to be judges.

There is no reason to assume we will perform any better in the present technological revolution. The only proven fact is that Uber offers a better service to the consumer. Anything else is just rosy dreams and fairy tales, and maybe some good intentions. But good intentions, as our inspired president famously said, do not build a state.

Written in Torah Prison
Published on 17 June 2016 in *Mada Masr*

THE BIRTH OF A BRAVE NEW WORLD 3:
WHO CAN COMPETE WITH UBER?

There's no question that Uber delivers a top-quality service. And it's not just cosmetics like the car model and cheerful driver, or perks like air conditioning, but serious issues like passenger safety and effective mechanisms to prevent sexual harassment. But Uber's superiority and dominance are not only down to quality; they rely on structural factors in the markets in which it operates.

I'm concerned by the relentless attempts to impose the technologies of the sharing economy on sectors like education or healthcare. I'm bracing myself for the day when some new technology appears to disrupt my own field. That's why I'm interested in the white taxis' seeming inability to compete, an inability inseparable from Cairo, just as Uber's own success is inseparable from California.

Egyptian taxi operators, and potential investors in taxi services, are deliberately prevented from developing the service. For example, prior to the launch of 'Taxi el-asima' (City Cab),[83] there was an attempt to establish a company that would manage a fleet of taxis through a central control room with shortwave wireless radio. But the proposal was refused permission by the security agencies and key ruling authorities. A second attempt replaced radio with mobile phones and GPS monitoring of the fleet: it was also refused. The security agencies didn't just reject the idea of a central control room, they went so far as to ban GPS technology and obstruct the development of geographic information

---

83   Taxi al-Asima was the first taxi-fleet project in Cairo to be approved (2006), with a central control room operated by Cairo Governorate.

systems, in some cases by making them illegal, and in others by refusing to make state-held cartographic data available at a reasonable cost until the ubiquity of iPhones and Google Maps forced a change of policy. The leverage Californian corporations have over our authorities is enormous; doors of ministries, and even the presidency, open for their reps while local companies are left to deal with labyrinthine bureaucracy and nightmarish security constraints.

Technical developments aside, there have been conventional initiatives to provide forms of public transport more humane than microbuses but cheaper than taxis. In most countries public transport is subsidized, so it's not an attractive prospect for investors looking for high margins. So these initiatives tried to establish public transport cooperatives, with a wide ownership base where drivers and a sector of passengers are represented— but came up against legislative shortcomings that effectively do not allow for the establishment of cooperatives .

As for the white taxi, its drivers and owners—like all Egyptians—are denied the right to organize freely. So they have not been able to participate in shaping the development of their service by raising meter tariffs in line with the rising costs of fuel, spare parts, or even basic goods, or by instituting flexible pricing to differentiate between peak hours and calm periods, or between daytime and late-night service, or between in-city journeys and highways. Taxi drivers in most developed countries have these rights, and so the price reflects the varying levels of risk, strain, and vehicle wear.

By contrast, the state has adopted development policies that create an ideal environment for Uber. It has developed and expanded new cities and neighbourhoods with no investment in public transport, despite the relatively low cost of laying railways in the flat desert. Fast roads are never given designated bus lanes. And instead of facilitating and incentivizing private sector investment in public transportation, the state offers credit incentives for the purchase of private cars and continues to subsidize their petrol, even after we've become a massive importer of fuel.

These development policies not only reflect incompetence, short-sightedness and the extreme centralization of decision-making, but, above all, they reflect a bias towards the interests of a sector of society that made their fortune investing in real estate, and designed cities and neighbourhoods based on their own worldview, their own cultural values, and their own vision of modernity and luxury, embodied in gated communities and private cars that drive huge distances between places of residence, study, work and leisure.

This value system is not separate from the Californian influence. The economy of California is almost the only modern economy in which public transportation does not play a significant role, even compared to other American states like New York. It's also no coincidence that one of Cairo's earliest suburban gated communities is named Beverly Hills.

MEASURING THE DISTANCE BETWEEN
CAIRO AND CALIFORNIA

Fans of disruptive technologies and the 'Fourth Technological Revolution' fervently deny that there is any ideological or cultural content to these technologies, attributing imbalances in geographical distribution to historical precedence. In their view, all an entrepreneur needs—anywhere on the planet—is an idea. Everyone enjoys the same opportunity to transform their idea into a viable business at low cost. This ignores the fact that designing new software and applications requires decades of capital accumulation, and for companies like Apple, Google, Orange and Vodafone to provide infrastructure and remove bureaucratic obstacles. In theory, the only difference between Uber and an Egyptian company is who got there first—as long

as the Egyptian company has an idea that successfully solves a
real problem.

It's not hard to see where these myths break down. If all it
takes is an idea then Uber would never have dominated. Uber
didn't invent the mechanisms of the sharing economy, nor was
it the first to apply them to private cars as an alternative to taxis.
Uber came up with almost no new solutions, ideas or unique
features that weren't provided by their competitors and predecessors, other than strategies for flooding the market and crowding
out competition using methods of questionable legality.

Even the prerequisite that the idea must provide a solution
to a *real problem* is just a myth. Cities like Paris and New York
enjoy functional, punctual high-quality public transport systems
with good geographic coverage, and their taxi services were never
the object of widespread dissatisfaction as those in Egypt were.
So: there was no problem in need of a solution. Nevertheless,
Uber has attacked those markets with such ferocity that it
threatens the livelihood of taxi drivers, and tempts governments
to abandon the maintenance of public transport systems—especially since public transport workers' unions enjoy a powerful
negotiating position thanks to the transport sector's potential
impact on other sectors of the economy.

If opportunities were truly equal, we would have seen globally
successful apps and services emerging from countries that have
contributed significantly to the development of information
and communications technology. Yet neither Western Europe's
leadership in developing the Web, nor Scandinavia's leadership
in developing mobile phones, South Korea's leadership in developing networks, or Japan's leadership in developing electronics,
are reflected in lists of the most-used apps. Even competition
from American states other than California is rare.

The California and Silicon Valley model is built on a glut
of available financing that changes the rules of the market,

exempting companies from the need to make a profit provided they achieve steady and rapid growth on the premise that
expanding the customer base and increasing its dependence
on the service represents value that can later be converted into
profit. In this model, the investor doesn't benefit from dividend
payments, but rather from the proceeds of selling the company,
at many times the original investment, to a larger company,
which takes on the task of transforming it into a profitable
enterprise, or even offsetting continuing losses against tax deduc-
tions (as with the sale of Instagram to Facebook, for example).
Alternatively, the investor may make their profit after the company is listed on the stock market, the share value having risen
to reflect the company's market share, rate of growth and value
added, regardless of the operating costs or difficulty of making
profits.

The secret behind Uber's success is quite simply vast financing
that allows the company, year after year, to swallow massive
losses. Uber currently does not make a profit, nor does it need
to make a profit in the short or even medium term. Its financing
allows it to flood any market where it encounters competition
or resistance, for example by awarding extra bonuses to tempt
drivers away from competitors, or by extravagant spending on
marketing and PR campaigns that have wide-ranging impact,
including on decision-makers; most importantly, it allows
rapid expansion into new markets without the need for lengthy
deliberation over profit or loss projections. Most worrying of all
is Uber's ability to bear the cost of legal challenges from competitors, drivers, customers, local governments and civil society, and
to prolong litigation processes so as to exhaust their rivals, then
finally settle out of court before any verdicts are reached that
might set binding precedents.

At a certain stage, this rapid growth turns into a monopoly. This
is due to the 'network effect': new drivers will choose Uber over

its competitors, because it has the larger user base—and the same goes for customers. The reciprocal customer-driver rating system becomes more efficient as the number of users and rides increases.

Weathering losses at the launch stage, or when attempting to gain a foothold in a new market, is normal behaviour for any capitalist enterprise. But shouldering vast losses for an extended period of time in order to achieve market dominance is usually called 'flooding the market'. Pumping so much capital into a sector that it doesn't need to be profitable is usually called a 'hidden subsidy,' and expanding this practice is generally understood to damage competition and distort markets. If an Egyptian company dealing in material products (a food manufacturer, say) used a similar strategy to enter a European market—flooding it with subsidized goods in order to crush competition and achieve a monopoly—it would be barred immediately. But Silicon Valley companies continue to cover the cost of their losses, even after their customer base has grown to hundreds of millions of users.

Economies far more advanced than ours are finding it difficult to reproduce or compete with this California model, despite the widespread popularity of policies to encourage entrepreneurs and startups, so can you imagine how our country is doing?

Germany, for example, is attempting to compete by encouraging banks to fund the software and app market, by facilitating credit for startups, and accepting the risk that many companies will fail, hoping that a single success story will compensate for tens of losses.

In Egypt, on the other hand, whatever the finance or credit terms are, it usually requires personally signing cheques or trust receipts—which means that risk-taking and experimentation leads to prison and ruin.

China might be the only country which has succeeded in shielding its economy from Silicon Valley's attempts at disruption, and in supporting local companies that offer alternative services. Using the same mechanisms with which it drove its industrialization, China has implemented protectionist policies and strict constraints on which foreign companies are allowed to enter the Chinese market and in what sectors, imposing a long list of prerequisites (Mark Zuckerberg spends much of his time in China attempting to convince authorities to allow Facebook to operate). This strategy reflects the import substitution policies adopted by post-colonial nations during periods of state-sponsored industrialization. To which must be added, in the case of the information sector, the authoritarian drive for total control, and the strict restriction of freedom of opinion and expression.

Given that we probably have no intention of reforming our development policies, or upgrading our infrastructure, or improving our education, or encouraging our personal initiatives, or unlocking our public freedoms, or even substituting our imports, and given that we probably won't copy anything from China except the authoritarian tendency, it's best if you and I stop worrying and learn to love Uber.

And tomorrow will be a happy day, when Uber replaces drivers with self-driving cars, making the trip to university cheaper; and the day after will be even happier when they abolish the university, so you're spared the trip and can study at Khan Academy from the comfort of your own home. And the day after will be even happier still when they do away with your trip to work and have you doing piecework from home in a flexible, sharing-based labour market, and the day after will be happier and happier when they send you off for early retirement because you've been replaced by a robot.

Don't forget to turn on the AC. Fuel is subsidized, and the subsidies must reach their deserving beneficiaries.

Written in Torah Prison
Published on 18 June 2016 in *Mada Masr*

2017

A PORTRAIT OF THE ACTIVIST OUTSIDE
HIS PRISON

We came of age with the second intifada. Took our first real steps out into the world as bombs fell on Baghdad. All around us, fellow Arabs cried, 'Over our dead bodies!', Northern allies chanted 'Not in our name!', Southern comrades sang 'Another world is possible.' We understood then that the world we'd inherited was dying, and that we were not alone.

We strove to understand. Company brochures, press releases from NGOs, officials' statements—it was never enough. We read everything there was, got involved with translating some things, had arguments about them. Then we set off in every direction: initiatives in the market, civil society initiatives, initiatives in any space where we found a little freedom. Intellectual projects and economic ones, development projects and charitable ones. We criticized authorities, chanted against rulers, cooperated, when possible, with institutions (unions, universities, sometimes even ministries). We sought out our predecessors, learned from them, taught them. For the most part, we refused their legacy but respected their experiences.

We understood that information technology was the key to shaping the new world and realized how exposed we were to global monopolies, so we adopted free and open source software as a condition for the development of society and achieving independence, and as a crucial tool in modernizing the economy and ending its subjugation. We started to campaign, toured all the universities: students lecturing professors. We organized conferences, and training programmes. We targeted everyone, from middle school IT teachers to engineering students to judges and journalists. We connected our criticism of the negative effects of intellectual property rights in software with its effects on the pharmaceutical industry, and found ourselves engaged with social issues, like the right to healthcare. We connected our criticism of corporate monopolies to criticism of neoliberal globalization, and found common ground with a broad spectrum of activists around the world.

Technology localization became our top priority. We worked on the Arabization of terminology, translated user interfaces, taught computers the Arabic rules for numbers, spelling and grammar. We designed fonts, developed software and built websites. Our interest in localization and language engineering intensified our interest in Arabic language and culture. We connected bloggers across the Arab world, and encouraged artists, writers, researchers and translators to share access to their creative outputs and their archives. Working to support Arabic online content, it wasn't long before we came up against censorship, prosecution, accusations of heresy and the imprisonment of the word. So we joined ranks with the defenders of freedom of opinion, expression, and belief, of press freedom and academic freedom.

As we built online networks and political movements we also set up businesses that offered solutions, services and consultancy for local markets, we worked to convince investors to provide finance, and persuaded institutions to take on innovative projects. We set up IT labs and technology clubs in Cairo's informal neighbourhoods and in the villages of the South. We built wireless networks to extend the internet to Egypt's countryside. Then we were invited to share these experiences in sub-Saharan Africa, and so became engaged with networks that worked to establish online connectivity and local language support as economic, cultural and social rights.

When the world noticed us and our story started to interest

journalists and become material for research centres, we insisted
on our own narratives rather than those being imposed on us.
We studied existing narratives and showed their connections to
interests and biases that were not ours, and so were invited to
speak at conferences in cities south and north.

We engaged with reality, tried to change it, influence it, to
anticipate and shape it. We were of course one of the weaker
parties present, but we were present. At every step we came up
against security restrictions, bureaucratic obstacles, rigid institutions and power imbalances. On every path we walked, our
ambitions were severely restricted and our energy wasted on
absurdities.

We shared this journey with many peers, each in their field.
After a decade of anger and dreams, of working and learning,
of attempts to reform and adapting to being on the margins,
of experiments, demands, and objections, we all arrived at the
same point: that the whole world was in crisis and on its way
to change, and that unless we engage with these challenges, our
societies would be crushed. And from there we all came to the
same inevitable conclusion: that the ruling regime is a fundamental obstacle to society's ability to renew itself and modernise
its institutions to be able to engage with the challenges ahead.
So we were not surprised by the revolution: we had sought it.
And we were not surprised that it inspired protest movements
in Europe and the US—were we not inspired by the protests in
Seattle and Genoa? Did we not protest together against the war
on Iraq? Wasn't our work for change and reform linked to open
debates, shared struggles and virtual communities that brought
together comrades from every continent?

But then we lost, and everything lost its meaning. And since
our defeat, any complex issue raised is immediately trivialized,
so that understanding becomes difficult and action impossible.
So it becomes that the energy shortage is caused by a corrupt

employee paid to switch off the main circuit breakers, or it's because of Gaza. And the dollar crisis is because they appointed Abdel-Hakim Amer's nephew, or because of some Brotherhood-related currency exchange companies.

The authorities have decided: meaning is dangerous, defending it is a crime, and its proponents are enemies. Doing things like communicating with the world in an attempt to understand and influence it, criticizing the status quo and warning against impending crises, engaging in individual or collective action to impact markets or institutions, are nothing but harbingers of 'fourth generation warfare'.

It's over. We have been defeated, and meaning has been defeated with us. And just as we were—in every step—affected by the world and affecting it, so was our defeat both a symptom and a cause of a wider war on meaning, a war on the crime of people searching for a supranational public sphere where they might find intimacy, exchange, communication, even quarrels, that allow a common understanding of reality, and multiple dreams of alternative worlds.

I'm in prison because the regime wants to make an example of us. So let us be an example, but of our own choosing. The war on meaning is not yet over in the rest of the world. Let us be an example, not a warning. Let's communicate with the world again, not to send distress signals nor to cry over ruins or spilled milk, but to draw lessons, summarize experiences, and deepen observations, may it help those struggling in the post-truth era.

For me, I gained nothing from a decade of rage except for some simple lessons. Most importantly, that every step of debate and struggle in society is a chance. A chance to understand, a chance to network, a chance to dream, a chance to plan. Even if things appear simple and indisputable, and we aligned—early on—with one side of a struggle, or abstained early from it altogether, seizing such opportunities to pursue and produce meaning remains a necessity. Without it we will never get past defeat.

I've learned that the ruling regime is just an obstacle. The real challenges are international in nature, so seizing opportunities for debate becomes even more important when the conflict relates to issues that transcend national borders.

Finally, siding with the stronger party is generally not useful. The powerful need nothing from you but to parrot their propaganda. The weak often cause as much trouble as they suffer. Their arguments and discourses are often as brittle as their positions in society and their diminishing chances of safety and survival. Taking their side, therefore, even as an experiment, stimulates deeper reflection, investigation, analysis and imagination.

We *were*, then we were defeated, and meaning was defeated with us. But we have not perished yet, and meaning has not been killed. Perhaps our defeat was inevitable, but the current chaos that is sweeping the world will sooner or later give birth to a new world, a world that will—of course—be ruled and managed by the victors. But nothing will constrain the strong, nor shape the margins of freedom and justice, nor define spaces of beauty and possibilities for a common life except the weak, who clung to their defence of meaning, even after defeat.

Written in Torah Prison
Published on 27 March 2017 in *Mada Masr*

YOU HAVE NOT YET BEEN DEFEATED

RightsCon is the conference Alaa attended in October 2011, between writing his article on Maspero, and returning to face the Military Prosecutor. Every year Access Now, the organizers, honour his work, and this year, 2017, he is able to write a letter to the conference.

To RightsCon,

This week I start my fourth year in prison. I might be released in October, if my appeal is accepted. But then I might not. I might be released in March 2019, when I have served my full sentence. But then I might not. They have other pending cases against me. If released, I might be able to attend this conference, but then I might not: my sentence comes with five years of parole to follow, and who knows if you'll be able to find a conference venue in a country that gives visas to people like me by the time I am allowed to travel.

I don't mean to be too pessimistic; the best-case scenario is as probable as the worst. The real problem is there's very little you can do to influence which will come to pass.

But that's not really what worries me. We live in hugely reactionary times. My defeat was inevitable.

What worries me is that by the time I manage to make it to this conference, or another like it, I will be a total embarrassment to organizers and attendees. In my isolation I can only build a fragmented picture of what the world outside looks like. And when it comes to tech that picture is solely based on which views and actions of governments and giant tech companies manage to filter through state-controlled media. Not what people and communities are doing and saying.

You wouldn't enjoy watching a Luddite ramble on about a terrifying dystopia in which labour rights are trampled by startups that don't even plan to make a profit (or pay taxes) but are somehow able to raise enough capital to flood markets, overwhelm regulators, influence policy, litigate perpetually and still have enough left to spend on PR that spins all this as the glorious disruptive effect of the gig economy. A dystopia in which free debate in a shared public sphere, rooted in a commonly experienced very decentralized reality, is replaced with a newsfeed, selected by an obscure algorithm based on one's circle of friends and choice of celebrities.

I can see you rolling your eyes already while I fret over the bot that will determine which news is not fake, the bot that will determine which policy is better, or the question of who owns the data, who controls the cloud and how did it come to pass that we replaced the mystical notion that we are born with all the knowledge of the universe already within us to the no less mystical notion that the only learning we need is Bayesian and that the only abstraction we need is MapReduce?

Lest you think me too pessimistic, I will admit that this dystopia is as probable as the utopian vision that insists the killer drones will turn out to be like the good terminators, that Facebook will defeat fake news with a truthbot and its human companions who are happily employed in glorious state-of-the-art call centres as content moderators. That Elon Musk will solve the world energy problem, Bill Gates will end hunger, Google will find a cure for cancer and Uber or Foxconn's effect on labour rights is irrelevant because we'll all be paid a basic universal income, have unlimited credit lines, or run our own Bitcoin mining operation. The counter-revolution never happened, the naive dreams of early internet communities and the free software movement are not lost they have just been updated, cleaned up and stripped of any hint of ideology to make them more universal. And no, the fact that nobody pays tax any more is not a threat to democracy because they all give so much to charity. Yes this utopia is probable too, as probable as the vision of a coalition between Trump, Sisi, Duterte, Orban, Modi, Erdogan, Putin, Bin Salman, and who knows maybe even Le Pen, leading the civilized world into a new age of prosperity and security and stability and sustainable growth. Yes it could happen. Millions upon millions believe it and they can't all be wrong, right?

However, you do have a chance to influence where in the broad spectrum between these equally unlikely (or likely) scenarios the future lies.

Yes, on the simple question of how to finally retire the hashtag #FreeAlaa you have little, if any, agency, but on the question of whether the internet is a space in which we come together to enjoy, assert, practise and defend universal rights and freedoms you have a lot of agency.

Unlike me, you have not yet been defeated.

I don't have much to say by way of advice. I am, after all, out of touch and slightly outdated. The best I can do is repeat themes I used to touch upon when participating in conferences like these in the past (the last time was 2011 I think):

Fix your own democracy: This has always been my answer to the question 'How can we help?' I still believe it's the only possible answer. Not only is where you live, work, vote, pay tax and organize the place where you have more influence, but a setback for human rights in a place where democracy has deep roots is certain to be used as an excuse for even worse violations in societies where rights are more fragile. I trust recent events made it evident that there is much that needs fixing. I look forward to being inspired by how you go about it.

Don't play the game of nations: We lose much when you allow your work to be used as an instrument of foreign policy, no matter how benign your current ruling coalition is. We risk much when human rights advocacy becomes a weapon in a cold war (just as the Arab revolutions were lost when revolutionaries found themselves unwitting and unwilling recruits in proxy wars between regional powers). We reach out to you not in search of powerful allies but because we confront the same global problems, and share universal values, and with a firm belief in the power of solidarity.

Defend complexity and diversity: No change to the structure of, or organization of, the internet can make my life safer. My online speech is often used against me in the courts and in smear campaigns, but it isn't the reason why I'm prosecuted: my offline activity is. My late father served a similar term for his activism before there was a web. What the internet has truly changed is not political dissent, but rather social dissent. We must protect it as a safe space where people can experiment with gender and sexual identities, explore what it means to be gay or a single mom or an atheist or a Christian in the Middle East, but also what it means to be black and angry in the US, to be Muslim and ostracized in Europe, or to be a coal miner in a world that must cut back on greenhouse gases. The internet is the only space where all different modes of being Palestinian can meet. If I express this precariousness in symbolic violence, will you hear me out? Will you protect me from both prosecution by the establishment and exploitation by the well-funded fringe extremists?

Assert your right to be a creator not a consumer: We love tech because it allows us to be the performers in our own spectacle, the storytellers in our own narrative and the philosophers of our own discourse. Not an eyeball for advertisers or a demographic for pollsters. Keep it that way please. Keep it that way.

Written in Torah Prison
Delivered on 13 April 2017

2019

THE GHOST OF SPRING

On 30 March 2019, Alaa is released. He has been in prison for five years.

3.26 p.m.
    I am the poison, I am the remedy
    I am the medicine, I am the cause
    I'm the ghost of spring past

ON PROBATION

The next morning, 31 March, Alaa emerges from his first night of 'probation'. Having served five years in prison, he is now sentenced to spend every night in his local police station for the next five years.

8.38 a.m.
  Freedom for Ahmed Douma.

8.41 a.m.
  I miss you, but I can't miss the probation.

10.07 a.m.
  Overwhelmed by electronic communication after going cold turkey for 5 years.

4.34 p.m.
  I'm sure you're keen to know my opinion about the state of things. Sorry, but I'm busy, I've got probation.

5.27 p.m.
  In general, when it comes to the constitutional amendments, I'm in favour. On one condition. That they bring back exile as a punishment.

1 APRIL 2019

8.31 a.m.
  I don't know how to express the beauty of the feeling of watching Khaled's swimming practice for the first time,

Or how to express the cruelty of having to leave him halfway through to make it back for probation.

10.35 a.m.
Overwhelmed.

3.41 p.m.
Your happiness with my release from prison makes me happy but unfortunately I'm not free. Not even in the sense of the imperfect freedom common in our country.

I hand myself in every day to an insult and humiliation called probation. Logically, I should spend it in conditions better than in prison, not worse. Legally, I should spend it at home. Sixty months of prison should be a sufficient price and more for a protest that lasted a quarter of an hour—even in a repressive state. If we talk about justice . . . but we'd better not because the subject of justice upsets them.

5.25 p.m.
Freedom for Ahmed Douma. Or, let's be reasonable and realistic. Probation for Ahmed Douma.

4 APRIL 2019

12.51 p.m.
Prison is an assault on the self. From the insistence on a uniform to the absolute control of details like hair and beard to assuming that the default is the prohibition of everything and anything extra to the official is a big concession.

But the political prisoner is different. And this difference is both a curse and a blessing. For prison of course fails to erase the political self. And how easy it is for the comrades to persuade you that this is a victory.

But what am I to do with a political self torn from its ordinary physical and human context? How do I live as a symbol however iconic it may be (literal: however high a status it may have)

Like a ghost I appear but do not become corporeal. I move in your time but I'm suspended in the past.

I used to be Alaa Seif, Alaa Abd el-Fattah was a role I played in the public sphere. Now . . . I don't know

12.56 p.m.

When did it become OK for adults to communicate mostly in emojis and gifs?!

10 APRIL 2019

6.51 a.m.

I'm in danger.

Last night state security officers came to Doqqi police station, woke me up, and threatened to throw me back in jail if I don't stop exposing the unfair & illegal conditions of my parole.

This is the second threat I receive during my nightly solitary confinement. Officers refused to identify themselves.

They also threatened to remove my books, iPod and hold me in worse conditions, completely ignoring any talk of the law.

1.40 p.m.

Since every person who has ruled or will rule this country is intent on ruling for life, and since every person who has ruled or will rule this country is intent on imprisoning their opponents, we're all at risk of being imprisoned. That's why the fight to improve prison conditions and oversight is the most useful thing that can be done.

17 APRIL 2019

On Monday 15 April I went to the National Council for Human Rights to file a complaint regarding the state's persistent use of probation orders. I met with Mr Mohamed Fayek, President of the Council, and members of the council, George Ishaq and Ragia Omran.

The complaint begins:

After five years of life without privacy, of life with bed bugs and cockroaches, do I not have the right to sleep in my own bed, in a clean room with a door that I choose to keep open or closed? Am I not entitled to a clean, private bathroom?

After five years of being cut off from my son, is it not our right to spend long hours together on any day of the week? For him to fall asleep in my arms like a regular child?

After five years of forced unemployment, of information blackout, cut off from communication with the world, is it not my right to use my own time to rebuild my skills and knowledge and catch up with changes in my field?

After five years of total dependence on my family, who have carried the labour and the costs of looking after a prisoner in a country that doesn't provide even the minimum requirements for its inmates' health, is it not my right to work and now provide for my family without arbitrary restrictions?

The police probation system at work now in Egypt robs me of the right to reconnect with my family, my right to knowledge, my right to work and forces me to sleep every night in terrible conditions that are unsanitary and unsafe and—as if that weren't enough—under constant threat of re-arrest.

INTERVIEW WITH *MADA MASR*

MOHAMMED HAMAMA: How did you write the articles about Uber?

ALAA ABD EL-FATTAH: With a pen and paper.

LINA ATTALAH: When I interviewed Laila [Soueif, Alaa's mother], we were a bit astonished at how informed you were while in prison writing that series, seeing as how the various sources of information—the internet, books, research, conversations—were not available to you. Still, you were very aware of what was going on. So the question: how do you create knowledge while in prison?

ALAA: That article in particular coincided with a loosening of restrictions over the books and magazines allowed in. It happened suddenly, and came after a period in which I was being smuggled in books. Publications were being reviewed by the National Security Agency and only novels or comics were allowed in. I avoided making trouble. Not to make it easy for them, but because I was tired of fighting. Then, all of a sudden, they decided to let current magazines in—mostly mainstream publications that I don't usually read, including foreign ones, like *Wired* or *Time*. They weren't publications about language or criticism, or anything about capitalism, or what the powers that be are up to. Even so, it was something new that I hadn't been exposed to for a long time.

That same year, the debate over artificial intelligence was everywhere. I would read the Egyptian papers—I was allowed *al-Ahram, al-Akhbar,* and *al-Masry al-Youm.* All the Egyptian papers tried to cover the subject, in ways that ranged from total ignorance to transcribing corporate press releases. There are a few voices at *al-Masry al-Youm* that are ostensibly respectable—important and informed opinion writers like Abdel Moneim Said. But all they do is look at Apple's latest press release for a new product and write an article from it, heralding a new, marvellous age. Even outlets that are tools of capitalism—like *Newsweek, Wired,* or *Time*—were more critical than the Egyptian press. So I really felt this vacuum. The subject wasn't new to me in the sense that I had no opinion—I was reformulating things I had thought about before going to prison.

For the Uber series in particular, what happened was that it was clear there was a debate happening on social media in Egypt. My sisters would tell me about it during visits. They were torn. Given the family's traditional leftist leanings, they were worried about the impact on taxi drivers; but because they are women, there was also the safe space offered by Uber. So they had questions, and we spent two visits talking about it. It was fun. So the article grew out of those two things.

HAMAMA: You said what was allowed inside changed every so often. How so?

ALAA: There was no rule. There was never an explicit ban when it came to books, but things would be set aside for months for 'review', and after a while I would forget about them. With every visit I'd be brought new things and some would be let in and some wouldn't. Yesterday I remembered that *The Catcher in the Rye* never made it in. It got stuck with them. I don't think they rejected it for censorship reasons. I think they have one officer there who understands English and was in the security directorate or something and it just fell through the cracks in the system. The ban was clearer with magazines and newspapers.

Foreign publications made them very nervous. Part of it is that the state every so often picks a fight with the *Economist*, or BBC, or Reuters. So they would know there's a dispute with various foreign media.

LINA: Speaking of books, we wanted to ask you if some discovery, something extremely informative, stayed with you over the years of prison, a discovery from things you read that you had no knowledge of before prison. I understand, for example, that you discovered Walter Benjamin in prison.

ALAA: I did, in the early period, before my initial release. I also re-read Edward Said. I had read him when I was very young and I imagined that I knew what he was writing about, but I didn't really. I had a project to re-read things from the last century or before that I felt were really pressing for us now, but when I was sent back to prison, to that oppressive atmosphere, I didn't keep it up. I was in a different state from the one my father was in when he was in prison. When I invest psychologically and emotionally in something, it makes me feel vulnerable—because at any moment they can come and take it from me and then I'd have to wage a battle over something I care about. It was easier for me to deal with everything on a more superficial level and just try to do the time. So I didn't have a study project exactly.

Another problem was letters. If I was sitting, waiting for a response to something and they were delaying it, and it might or might not be allowed in, and my response might or might not be allowed out—that would put me in a bad mental state.

My reading was extremely random and based more on entertainment than any specific intellectual project. Only towards the end, my cousin started bringing me materials about what was going on in Europe in those days, like Yanis Varoufakis's memoirs about managing the debt crisis in Greece, or some recent theorizing about the crisis in the labour market, or ideas now popular in Europe like universal basic income. I think he's the one who developed a reading project, not me, to help me keep up with what was being said.

I did get a lot of comics. This is my favourite narrative art form, more than cinema or novels. I made some discoveries. A friend sent me Japanese manga translated into English. Of course, manga is a huge category. I knew it existed, but I didn't know where to begin, I had only read the classics. So that opened up some new, nice things. There's a fantastic comic, called *Daytripper* in English, that was really meaningful for me. It's published in the US, but the artist and writer is Brazilian. It's got a magical realist bent, which is really appropriate for prisoners. It's a perfect gift for any prisoner who can read English. Or maybe someone can translate it. I also read some very good science fiction, and I collected stories and narratives about failed revolutions.

HAMAMA: So, our revolution was a failure?

ALAA: No way! How could you say such a thing? Everything is great. We won and saved the soul of the country.

NAIRA: You said your experience of projects in prison was different from your father's?

ALAA: When my dad was imprisoned, he was a graduate of the college of economics and political science. He studied law inside and came out to work as a lawyer, and he did things with prisoners, too. We are very different personalities.

LINA: You didn't think about studying something?

ALAA: I considered it when I was imprisoned alongside friends like Ahmed Maher, who got a diploma in prison. They brought in materials about the available fields, but I got fed up with the formulation, the language, the method, the fonts, everything. I really couldn't deal with it. Before the end, I was thinking about how I was going to make a living on probation and how I could go back to programming after five years of complete interruption. I was convinced that I hadn't lost the skill, but it's about proving that. Convincing people of that is hard. So I thought I'd do a master's degree, a BA isn't enough. I asked my mom to bring me the materials about the master's programmes at the computer and information faculties at Cairo, Helwan, and Ain Shams Universities. But it was an utter disaster, pure misery. It's extremely bureaucratic. The first thirty pages are a description of various procedures and laws. It's incredible, there's nothing to engage the student at all. Then I saw the pages where they outlined the structure of the departments. There's a group of emeritus professors who got their degrees before computers even existed, plus everyone is on secondment or travelling, so the departments are empty anyway. It's utterly haphazard and is the embodiment of the destitution of the Egyptian state. It just stopped caring.

LINA: Did you have a chance to catch up on programming? Was there any source for discussion? Was there a chance to talk about technology from a technical standpoint, specifically programming, over the five years? Or are you coming out now from a completely different place?

ALAA: My family tried to get books to me at a certain point, but now, no one writes books in which it is assumed that you're not sitting in front of the internet. Even the parts about programming, the scientific journals, are filled with barcodes and QR codes. Egyptian papers are unbelievable, they're always talking about what you've read on their website. They're not publishing news, they're publishing comments on news that we all supposedly already know about. We would just sit there holding the newspaper trying to decipher it. There's a subject and people are arguing about it, but I couldn't understand what the subject was because they never prefaced it at any point. Terrorism coverage, for example. The papers cover the funerals, but not the incident itself, so I would have to figure out what was happening from the story about the funeral. If this is the way the papers are, imagine computer stuff.

What I am discovering as I try to return to life generally—I still haven't tried returning to professional life—is that the things that I've lost and I find difficult are the most unexpected things. I get lost in the streets. I get confused when I'm asked to do two things at once. When I try to simultaneously schedule more than one thing, I get exasperated and lose it, not to the point of hysteria, but it's stressful. I imagine that when I return to work, the big things won't be hard, but the small things will. They'll be very disorienting. I spent four and a half years uninterrupted—from late October 2014 to late March 2019—all in the same place, having the same routine every day. It's well-known that prisoners experience post-traumatic stress, but I thought it was because of a painful prison experience. Now it's clear to me that it's because of the jump from the deep freeze back to the world. And Cairo, wow—there's lots of stuff happening at the same time. It's very disorienting.

HAMAMA: This is a good segue into the subject of probation. This transition from an unvarying routine to zero order and zero routine. Anything can happen, it could be a good or a bad day.

ALAA: The first thing you need to understand is that probation isn't twelve hours a day, especially in my situation where there is a perceived threat. Showing up a little late should be normal, but with me, there's no guarantee. I don't want to test it. The problem is that the law doesn't set an exact time—it specifies sunset to sunrise, which leaves it very much up in the air. It could be set by the prayer times which would make it vary. But for them, it's 6 p.m. to 6 a.m. Sunset is not at 6 p.m. and sunrise isn't at 6 a.m., but it doesn't matter, for them, it's six to six. That means starting at 4 p.m. you need to begin moving to a place close to the police station, and at 5 or 5.15 p.m., you need to start heading to the station. There's Cairo traffic of course, and this is during rush hour. And then you need to have a bag with you with a change of clothes, bedding, books to read. So starting at 4 p.m., I'm already on probation. I get out at 6 a.m., but no one is awake then and no one does anything. I've got a list of people divided into two camps: those who are awake at 6 a.m. and those who aren't. I try to meet the people who get up at 6 a.m. and have breakfast with them. So I've got four hours that are supposed to be mine, but they aren't really.

Police stations aren't set up to house people, regardless of whether there are dedicated quarters. The quarters are nightmarish places and totally ad hoc. There are lots of shifts at the station, lots of people, lots of assigned officers. There's no stability. There is a special effort to treat me well, at least as well as the station's capacity allows. They are trying to treat me comfortably, but the arrangements themselves are tiresome, they don't have the capacity.

The problem in my relationship with the authorities is that, for them, the norm is to violate your physical dignity. As long as your body is fine—You've eaten? Had some water? Slept?—everything is fine and they shouldn't hear a peep from you. There's always pressure from the authorities for you to think this way. Or you have feelings of guilt because you know others are in worse conditions. You complain that they won't let in foreign speciality magazines and you know you're spoiled and that others don't get visits at all. Things like that. Of course, this mindset is wrong. It means you're normalizing the violations. There's always someone who's worse off than you. It's the same logic as, 'Look at Syria and Iraq and Libya.' Everyone should fight for their maximum rights and we should all try to support each other.

Even in my confrontations with National Security officers, they insist that they are making exceptions for me. What exceptions? That I'm in a room by myself, it's clean, that they let me listen to music and have books, things like that. There is nothing that allows them to deny me these things during probation. There's nothing that lets them deny me these things in prison. So I don't understand what we're even talking about. But even if we forget all that, the police station isn't equipped. At least in prison there's stability—the more time passes, the more comfortable you feel with it. But in the police station, it's a new scene every day. You turn yourself in each day to start over again from scratch—every single day. It's exhausting and destroys any ability to return to your life.

In practice, I look for someone to have coffee or eat breakfast with, then I go wake up Khaled and drive him to school. So at least I've seen Khaled. There's no work, of course. At 6 a.m. there's nothing going on—it's like a scene from 1945 when people were farmers and civil servants and the streets were lit with gas lamps. Now I've got to perform all biological functions in twelve hours. I try to cling to my right to be able to enter with my phone and laptop so I can work. I work for maybe six hours and sleep for six.

It's so depressing for us to accept that it's just normal for a person to be punished for ten years for a demonstration and then have to argue with them to get them to apply the law, which was issued by royal edict in 1945.

NAIRA: Is Khaled confused to see you outside prison?

ALAA: Fortunately no, but of course I'm not able to be present in his life the way I'd like because of probation. He's not confused exactly, he was prepared for me to get out and spend time with him. He was happy for us to do different things together. In prison I saw him, of course. He came nearly every visit, unless he was travelling. I'd sit with him for maybe ten minutes in the crowded hall and then I had to see everyone else who came to visit. Now, we can spend time and it's his time. This is where I most feel there's been a real change. Without Khaled, probation would be lethal and exhausting. It's a terrible tool and the idea that you just turn yourself in like that is so, so oppressive. When they put me in prison they came and took me; but to participate in one's own imprisonment is extremely troubling. If it weren't for Khaled, I really think I'd be worse off than if I was in prison.

HAMAMA: This idea of normalizing the relationship between the body and authority, that a person normalizes oppression when he says he's better off than others and so starts making more and more concessions . . .

ALAA: I try not to do this. I try to never do it—to make concessions on something that was already agreed upon, but it requires incredible energy. It consumes you. It's much more exhausting than giving in to them, and it requires support. Since the option of submitting isn't really on the table, the only option is to kill things inside you. Like when I decided in prison that I wouldn't care too much about anything. I didn't stop demanding things and fighting for them, but I stopped caring about them.

HAMAMA: There is an apparent contradiction between negotiating and taking a radical stance. How do you resolve this?

ALAA: I'm a student of the South African struggle. They were
awe-inspiring in their ability to work on all levels. When the
apartheid regime finally agreed to negotiate, everyone connected
to the opposition said, 'Talk to Nelson Mandela.' The man had
been buried in prison for nearly a quarter century and he still
came back with something new. He didn't refuse to meet them
but he would say, 'Release us from prison and we'll negotiate.' At
every step, he would say the same thing.

I'm not saying we wasted the chance to negotiate, no one
was convinced of the value of it. All parties thought they were
capable of settling everything on their own. Incredibly, all parties
still think that, even the weakest ones. Egyptians are obsessed
with this idea of a decisive win—that there will be this one battle
we can wage and settle everything once and for all, and all our
foes will disappear and we won't need to fight them ever again.
But the Islamists aren't going anywhere and neither is the army,
nor the people that reject the whole system, nor the people who
want a liberal democracy. It's a fantasy. The very idea of a decisive resolution is annoying.

Egyptians' imaginative space had no room for the idea that we
could sit down together at some point and see what we're going
to do with ourselves and this country and each other. I don't
think the current situation allows for it or there's any space to
think like this.

When we were in the middle of the revolution, we had no
problem using nationalism and identity, thinking we could adapt
these discourses of power to a common, broad-based discourse
that would be ours that we could reproduce and believe in. And
then part of what happened was that the monster was awakened
and hijacked it all using the same nationalist, identity-based

discourses. The same is true of the trap of masculinity, which it's very easy to fall into when you're in a state of confrontation—an actual physical, bodily conflict—but then later you pay the price. It may be more useful to talk about these things, and for this to be the advice we give to people. Whether they listen or not doesn't matter, because the process will at least be useful for us. This is something we need to talk about, but not with the logic of, 'If on this day, we had done that, then this other thing wouldn't have happened.' That's not how it works. It was much bigger than us, the Muslim Brotherhood, or the Army.

The important thing is we abandon the project for a decisive resolution. That we abandon the idea that these things are solvable and there are definitive solutions for everything. Like, what's the solution to traffic? What does that mean? You're in Cairo, there's no solution to traffic. Most of the basic problems facing Egypt—that the state keeps failing to solve and that anyone would fail to solve—are too big to solve. There isn't a solution per se, so we need to sit and talk to each other. There are some things that are not possible to solve without talking with the whole world, global problems. So we need to let this go. This mindset is especially annoying at a time when there is no room for action. For example, when we finally start talking about gender and violence against women, people in the movement start saying that the solution is to stiffen penalties and imprison people. That leads nowhere except to more people in prison. We need to learn how to negotiate with each other. Not to bring the Right and Left together, but within the left.

HAMAMA: There are global problems . . .

ALAA: There's nothing but global problems. We are just playing around looking inward in Egypt, we're wasting time.

HAMAMA: If we want to talk about resistance, local or universal—resistance to what exactly?

ALAA: I've reconsidered many things in a big way. I've come to feel that the word 'resistance' is a trap. The Western Left has spent twenty years cheapening the term. Anything any marginalized person does is called resistance. Palestinians keep on breathing? It's resistance. But people will continue to breathe no matter the conditions. Steadfastness is resistance. Circumventing the regime and getting one over on it is resistance. Anything can be resistance. This battle to define terms is a losing one and we should just abandon it.

My feeling is that the world is in such crisis that it has made us incapable not of action, but of imagination. The generation that's taking over now came up in the 1990s, when there were lots of ideas and lots of theorizing, but no action, so action was the necessary thing. Now we've spent ten years acting and have discovered that we're acting on ideas born out of the Second World War. There is a dire crisis of imagination, and at the same time, people are dying to do something. It's clear that the entire world order is in crisis, and the crises are mounting. Just look at the UK, it's an utter farce.

I feel that we need to go through a phase like the one that gave rise to Dada and the Surrealists. We need to go through a period where absurdity is celebrated and then dismantle everything, and we need to do it thoroughly, because deconstruction through ridicule, mockery, and post-truth has become an assault on meaning itself. You can't distinguish lies from truth when there's no such thing as truth and striving after it is ridiculous. I'm not talking about memes and ridicule and the like. On the contrary, I've come to see these things as destructive of any ability to treat any subject seriously. The idea that satire is resistance has become harmful. We're not going to stop telling jokes, but we need to reconfigure how we think about things without falling into the easy outs of mockery, ridicule, and crying over spilled milk.

People are excited about these ideas that are just old ideas in a new package, and they're very fragile and easily hijacked. Like universal basic income (UBI), which is driving me mad. I mean, anything the libertarians come up with is wrong in principle. The idea that the Left and the rabid Far-Right are in agreement on this means something is wrong. Bringing all the poor into a cash economy means you're taking them and just serving them up to the banks. I'm not sure, because economics is not my strong suit and I haven't read up on it, but I feel there's something wrong with this whole story. It's a trap we're falling into.

There needs to be a global dialogue first before we figure out how to get out of these crises. I'm not up to speed. Are spaces like art or academia doing this? I feel these spaces have been nationalized and homogenized around the world, not just here. This is the impression of a prisoner who read magazines and the like. And the internet has become a strange place, impossible to grasp. No one gets it.

LINA: It's true, it's like the internet when it first started.

ALAA: You remember that article by Hossein Derakhshan? When he wrote that he got out of prison and found the web was dead thanks to chats and social media? Getting out, I feel like we've gone back to the Stone Age. People speak in emojis and sounds—ha ha ho ho—not text. Text and the written word are great. So I'm disturbed. I feel like there has been a regression even in two-way conversation, not just collective, in the ability to deal with complex topics.

Part of the problem with Egyptians' debate over Sudan, in my view, is less the fault of Egyptians than the medium. You're just swallowed up by it. You have passionate discussions with your friends because Facebook is made that way. You have a conversation where you try to theorize what you experienced and try to understand what these people are doing, and you try to reach out to people who are up on the subject and can tell you about Sudan's history, not just about what's happening now. And you're in these circles of people sending gifs and heart emojis. So this is the inevitable product of the conversation. This medium is stifling. It's very strange that the entire world knows that these tools and mediums are defective and they have no faith in them and are suspicious of them, but they just keep using them. There's a need for an alternative imagination. I don't know when it will emerge.

LINA: Postmodernism and deconstruction and the critical schools associated with them are always criticized as all rhetoric and theory and no action. Are you saying we need some theorizing and there's not much space for action?

ALAA: I sent you a good book by Mark Fisher, in which he defends the idea of popular modernism or popular images in modernism. He's originally a music critic enamoured by David Bowie and punk, but adopted Derrida's idea of hauntology. I think we need a space to act similar to that one. It's the defence of a collective project coupled with the deconstruction of discourses of power. Right now, we work on a social or collective project and become captive to questions of identity or nation, or incremental projects, like the socialists' historical imperatives.

We need to grapple with confusion, ambiguity, and absurdity as things that exist in the world but that are largely harmful. We need to stop treating absurdity as something good. That's for when we're living in an extremely well-ordered society. We need to deal and engage with absurdity and try to escape it

by championing meaning. That can only happen in a space
of action, and it won't happen until we sit and theorize with
each other. The action may be extremely simple, especially in
a situation like Egypt where everything is being throttled. But
it doesn't mean that just because I successfully act that means I
am resisting. I'm impressed with the persistence of *Mada Masr*,
for example, and given our circumstances that's an achievement.
It's a space for action, and it would be useful to sit and talk with
each other about what else could happen. How can we not be
excited that this group has stuck with it five or six years?

Clearly, there are some available spaces for action in Sudan and
Algeria. Yes, the military is lying in wait and so are the Islamists.
They will always be there. Where are they going to go? They won't
disappear. But people are still in a moment in which they can act.
The same is true in the Global North. The absurdities taking place
in France, the UK, or Germany are evidence that the world is in
crisis, but there is a space for people to act, to experiment and to
fail. I don't feel like that window has closed, as evidenced by the
emergence of people in the US taking strong stances on Israel
from within the establishment. This is no small thing. It doesn't
mean Palestine is about to be liberated because it will only be
liberated by Palestinians. It's more significant for Americans than
Palestinians. Even the excitement over UBI—I'm worried about
the plan, but the energy behind it is proactive. It's an energy that
uses tools like academia.

So while there is some space for action in the world, in Egypt
it's extremely narrow. We've never seen this level of repression,
but at the same time, it's fragile. The Egyptian state seems unable
to seriously control people's thought. What exists now has a very
limited impact on people's imagination. There doesn't seem to be
any broad popular engagement with it, but no one knows how
to posit alternatives or come up with tools to address people's
imagination. I'm not even sure people still want this.

I have a question for people who have some space, like *Mada Masr*: how comfortable is it for me to keep on shrinking the circle of people I engage with? How long can I be comfortable in that space? It might be a normal thing, I feel it myself right now. This is what makes it so there's no room to act. This might be necessary for us in order to crystallize our thoughts without distraction, or outside interference, or the need to translate our language into something that won't shock other people. This works as long as I'm aware that I'm in a bubble in order to crystallize my thoughts. The bubble is not a space for action, it's a space for thought.

HAMAMA: So the revolution failed?

ALAA: Yes, by any measure. For example, what did the revolution want? Of course, approaching it as an entity with a single will is tricky, but taking the bare minimum, the revolution spoke about the democratic rotation of power—meaning traditional liberalism—and about stopping violations of the body. Those were the minimum goals of the revolution.

But the revolution did break a regime. What exists now is an attempt to build something else, not the same regime. This is not a return to the Mubarak order. What exists now must consume incredible energy in order to govern, and it relies on a major, ongoing regional threat. Without the Syrian, Libyan, and Yemeni nightmare, it would have been extremely difficult for the regime to build any legitimacy. So it's a major error for any opponent of this regime to ignore the magnitude and atrocity of what's happening around us and not revise their calculations accordingly. We can show no tolerance of sectarian discourse. Let's set aside the Islamists. They are oppressed and we must speak about the abuses against them, but their ideology is a disaster and will remain so. We must find a way out.

As a rule, revolutions are defeated. I was always saying we were pretty feeble. I think it's an abject failure that in a moment like 2011–2012, when it had broad popular support, we were unable to articulate a common dream of what we wanted in Egypt. It's fine to be defeated, but at least have a story—what we want to achieve together. I'm not sure we had that.

LINA: Are there any questions we've overlooked?

MOHAMMED EL-RAI: The conventional question: where's Egypt headed?

ALAA: Shouldn't you have asked that before you boarded the plane? I'm fine and happy with this conversation that is strange, like me. Coming out of prison, I feel strange.

18 April 2019

WHEN I LEFT YOU

21 April 2019
  =@Alaa: You know, when I left you in 2014 you were popular.
How have you done this to yourself?

THE WEIGHT OF THE WORLD

Among family, I—half-joking—asked where should I go to rebuild my life when they finally release me. The quick answer was 'avoid islands, they might not be around much longer'. I couldn't work out if the sarcasm was about how long it will be until I am free, or how imminent environmental catastrophe is.

A few days later I made fun of a friend who used the word 'ark' in a phone call. I asked if she expected a repeat of Noah's Flood. She answered with a kind of panicked seriousness that she was terrified of the inevitability of her kids inheriting a planet unrecognizable because of climate change.

Climate change is often imagined as a modern variant of the Flood—like the Night King and the Long Winter in *Game of Thrones*; a moment of truth when the wrath of the heavens descends on humankind as a punishment for ignoring all the evidence and busying ourselves with conflicts and ambitions unworthy of the approaching, existential threat.

These depictions encourage us to think that being aware of the catastrophe is the key to avoiding it. Thousands of scientists and activists have made it their lives' mission to raise awareness of the dangers of greenhouse gas emissions until the perils of climate change are in our nightmares and in our jokes. But what has this increased awareness actually changed?

Imagine if Noah's people had become aware to this degree of the danger of the Flood and its inevitability. Would this aware-ness have led to smarter behaviour than what we read in the holy books? Or would they have fought over the high ground and ship-building timber?

In the battle over limited resources that could determine

who lives and who dies it's likely that the wealthy, the powerful
and the influential will use their privilege to ensure their and
their loved one's survival after the Flood—and will work hard
to retain this privilege in the post-Flood world. As for those
without power or influence they'll try to attach themselves to
Strong Men or organized groups that might provide a path to
safety; or they'll take refuge in extreme religious ideologies that
hold out the hope of a miracle; or perhaps go to another extreme
and try to destroy all the means of escape monopolized by the
few because they are attempts to derail scriptured destiny. Some
people will accept a brief life and live it with no thought for the
future, some will exploit fear to corner the timber trade or to
assume prophethood or claim possession of construction secrets
to build indestructible dams.

Even the most secular commentators insist on a discourse of
the end of civilization and the extinction of the human species.
And yet the biblical parallels remain disjointed and confusing—
out of sync with the popular perception. A few thousand
survivors with a reasonable amount of genetic variation can
repopulate the earth. Civilization isn't that frail; wherever there
are people able to narrate their histories and imagine different
worlds, civilization exists. That's not to say that there's much
cause for optimism; we may not become extinct, but millions of
us will face deadly circumstances. And most of us will not escape
a deterioration in quality of life and a decrease in our ability to
guarantee any level of comfort for future generations.

It's important to understand that even though we all face the
same threat, we will not be equal in the extent or the timing of
the expected degradation or the size and nature of the losses. In
fact we suspect that some of us will benefit from the catastrophe.

This mix of a planetary problem, a globalized consciousness
but a local arena—if any—for action, and a conviction that
inequality will inevitably continue—all this doesn't just lead to

a sense of hopelessness that inspires dark humour and darker nightmares, but pushes us into states of antagonism and polarization. This in itself is a threat closer and more urgent, if not of greater effect, than the dangers of climate change.

For example, after oil-producing states for decades worried about their inability to prepare their economies for a post-petroleum age we discovered that the planet will not withstand the extraction of all the reserves of fossil fuels. Sooner or later oil producers will be forced to cut production and the importance of petrol will recede as coal's did before it. Knowing this will push the big producers to rash actions such as flooding the markets and dropping prices to stall movement towards renewable energy sources, or to grab the biggest possible portion of the market before it shrinks. Add to this the drive to translate accumulated financial surplus into regional power and international influence. These policies interact with geopolitical issues, reigniting old conflicts and sometimes creating new ones. And as is usual with these conflicts they do not restrict themselves to their material motives but cloak themselves in factional impulses like the bickering between Sunni and Shia, or with culturalist discourses like the tension between 'totalitarian' Russia and 'liberal' Europe, etc.

We will probably not run out of oil, but drinking water is a resource that becomes scarcer as the temperature of the planet rises. Fights over water are as old as civilization, but climate change and its effect on rainfall threatens well-established populations and their economic activities. Lately conflicts have sharpened between herdsmen and farmers in lands extending from east to west Africa. Water disputes take on a tribal, factional hue and so are presented to us as a conflict between Muslim nomadic herdsmen and stationary Christian farmers. It's not an accurate picture, but dominant narratives have the ability to reformulate reality, and the longer the conflict lasts the more

we become implicated in details that go beyond the environmental crisis.

From the Mekong and the Indus to the Jordan, the Tigris,
the Euphrates and the Nile, most water conflicts are old; they've
played their part in forming states and informing their foreign
and military policy. Climate change now exacerbates the seriousness and urgency of these conflicts. We see the efforts of
water-poor but cash-rich states as they seek to guarantee their
future water security by acquiring larger shares of the waters of
these rivers and to ensure the presence of cooperative rulers and
political systems that prioritize the export of water even at the
expense of the preparedness of their own people and local economies to withstand the effects of climate change.

Internal conflicts are also sharpened. A clear example is the
rebellion of the Gilets Jaunes in France against a tax policy that
in theory was meant to decrease fuel consumption and so lower
greenhouse gas emissions. Every time we object to the destructive effects of growth, capital accumulation and the escalating
competitiveness of capitalism, economists respond that the
problem lies in the inability of markets in their present form
to take into account the full production costs of a commodity
including harm and danger to health and the environment. The
only solution, they say, is to translate all perils and losses into
monetary terms through suggested instruments like carbon taxes
or setting up markets to trade in carbon emissions. These fiscal
and financial policies are marketed to us as magical solutions
that will inevitably and spontaneously lead to the retreat of
fossil fuel consumption and the magical appearance of sustainable alternatives. On application though, the residents of small
French towns and suburbs discovered that they were the target
of these policies not the producers of oil and automobiles who
enjoy various forms of government subsidy including the deployment of armies and the intensification of regional conflicts to

their advantage. (See the policies of the French government in Libya to protect the interests of Total, or the varied forms of political and material support given to Peugeot.)

Fear of the political and social change stemming from climate change lurks behind most of the political polarization we see in the West today. Voters from coal-producing areas voted for Trump, while large numbers of poorer UK voters, sensing that the EU will surely impose environmental criteria and policies whose non-negotiable cost will fall on them, voted to leave the Union. As in the rest of the conflicts on this planet, the crises predate the issue of climate change, but they are exacerbated by it, and then clothed in nativist and populist garb which creates further crises—the effects of which will be hard to deal with even if we find solutions for the environmental ones.

The common threat pushes us relentlessly towards separatist discourses. How easy to complain of Americans eating meat three times a day and their love of big cars and fast roads, or of Europeans who insist on insulating themselves from the changeable weather and exaggerate their heating and cooling even at the cost of increasing climatic volatility for the rest of the planet. The Europeans and Americans complain that more and more Indians and Chinese are catching up with the luxury-consumer lifestyle of the West. Everyone complains about Africans' fertility rates. And so it seems that the Bible story most aptly prefiguring the coming apocalypse is not the story of Noah's Flood but the story of the Tower of Babel: as a punishment for our pride in our technological prowess and our appetite to construct, consume and expand without limit, the Lord has confounded our tongues—we cannot communicate with each other, and so our fragmentation cannot be undone.

This situation, strange as it is, isn't new. Grasping it doesn't really need us to summon ancestral stories. During the Cold War, humanity lived in real fear of a nuclear war launched by

the two superpowers. This globalized paranoia wrenched every
internal or regional conflict out of its natural context and its
traditional limits and transformed it into a polarization point
between two camps. Polarization reached a pitch that made any
attempt to hold a neutral position or to defend common values
seem suspect; exploited by one party and treated as hostile by the
other (eg. the Non-Alignment Movement was regarded as closer
to the USSR camp, and the Human Rights Movement closer to
the West).

In our communal consciousness we remember the Cold War
as though it were an alternative—under the umbrella of mutual
deterrence—to another World War. And it's true that there
was no World War III, and no nuclear bombs were launched
after Nagasaki, but recent studies claim twenty million casualties of the battles of the Cold War, a third of the casualties of
WWII and ten times the casualties of Hiroshima and Nagasaki.
Moreover, the problems of the Cold War conflicts are still with
us today—three decades after the official end of the war.

In the Cold War era it seemed that we were faced with two
competing ideologies. But climate change appears to be the
result of how contemporary life is lived, and may be even the
result of a basic tendency in the human psyche. The capitalist
system dominating the world is so solid and well-established that
it seems as though we'll need a miracle to free us of it—or fix it.
Thus we see the spread of the Biblical imagination in its modern
secular manifestations. From a discourse that relishes the idea of
the coming extinction and talks of how we, as humans, deserve
what's about to happen to us, to the search for magical solutions
like clean, inexhaustible energy, or a technology that can capture
CO_2 from the air—even though nothing in science or technology indicates that this is possible. Of course there are those
who imagine fleeing the planet altogether, and there's a lot of
talk about Mars. The crisis doesn't lie, therefore, in our awareness

of the coming danger but in our failure to imagine alternatives for how we organize politics and the economy. This helplessness comes after two full centuries of valiant attempts to resist capitalism.

But climate change, like cars and fossil fuel technology, is a human invention which we can modify and change without miracles or prophets, by tackling the patterns of consumption and the forms of inequality that have led to it and motivate the battles fought around it. This long history of resistance has maybe not led to major victories over capitalism, but it has again and again succeeded in trimming it and improving the conditions of life for the majority. And what's more important is that this resistance is the only proposition able to unite people globally and to take the place of fights and conflicts. We need to find hope in the journey in search of salvation, for the journey itself can end our state of fragmentation and conflict. It might also ameliorate the effects of the catastrophe or at least impose modifications on capitalism—as did, for example, the movements of the Left which led to the welfare states after World War II.

This is a global problem. The individual whose scope of action is extremely limited and localized cannot solve it except by creating novel ways of organizing across continents. To achieve these forms of organizing we need first to extricate ourselves from absurd quarrels and reject every form of ugly nationalism. We need to reclaim the arena of local action, not as a space to hoard miserable gains but as a space to discuss a better future for everyone.

The crisis, for certain, is not a crisis of awareness, but of surrendering to the inevitability of inequality. If the only thing that unites us is the threat, then every person or group will move to defend their interests. But if we meet around a hope in a better future, a future where we put an end to all forms of inequality, this global awareness will be transformed into positive energy.

Hope here is a necessary action. Our rosy dreams will probably not come to pass. But if we leave ourselves to our nightmares we'll be killed by fear before the Floods arrive.

Published on 26 June 2019 in *Mada Masr*

ON THE ANNIVERSARY OF RABAA

15 August 2019
@Alaa: Only the innocent feel guilt.

VENGEANCE IN VICTORY:
A PERSONAL INTRODUCTION

I.

When I was released from prison I was congratulated over and over again by friends and family for making it out in good health. Maybe they were relieved because it's assumed that prison is supposed to destroy your health. Maybe they were just looking for something positive to say. Either way, I don't mind treating coming out of prison with minimal physical damage as an accomplishment; it wasn't easy and required an obsessive degree of attention, effort, anxiety—and cost.

Our digital world has no shortage of haters who resent my intact health, who believe that the purpose of prison is to destroy a person. This worried me—not because they're wishing me personal harm—but because they took my condition as evidence that all talk of other prisoners' declining health is a lie. I was particularly shocked by posts equating me with Abdel-Meniem Aboulfotouh.[84] Is there any context other than prison in which a body in its fourth decade is compared to one in its seventh? Your aunt gets allergies in the spring, or your grandfather's rheumatism acts up in winter; one kid gets sick constantly, but his sister rarely does. Our lives are full of this and it's a given that our bodies differ, each with its own features, quirks, and history. My family said nothing about my health for sixty months, while Aboulfotouh's family and lawyers were raising the alarm about his from the start. Add age and the impact of solitary confine-ment to the equation and there's simply no comparison. But as

---

84 Presidential candidate in 2012. A physician, ex-Brotherhood member, and a respected and popular opposition figure. Arrested in February 2018 and remains in prison.

soon as someone is locked up behind bars, he becomes a docile body without history, peculiarities, or individualized needs, just like all the other prisoners. His voice, and what that voice says about the body, has no weight.

II.

That day, the temperature drops at night and with it the scurrying of the insects in the kiosk inside the walls of Doqqi police station where I spend every night on probation. I fall into a deep sleep, after two weeks of tossing and turning. I wake up early, feeling good. I start my morning exercises, then I leave my kiosk of solitude and head to the bathroom, optimistic about the new day. I'm trying to get used to ignoring the details of life in a police station. I don't want to know what's happening around me. I've completely lost my curiosity about the workings of the Egyptian state, especially the organs that rule our bodies.

While my mind tries to ignore my surroundings, my shoulder registers some anomaly and the muscles begin to cramp. My release is less than an hour away.

Hoisting my bedding onto cramping shoulders I walk out to my car on autopilot; that's where the bedding will be stored for the day. My eye sees the heightened state of security: automatic rifles at the ready, armoured personnel carriers. My mind ignores the details, but my heart tightens, and the spasm radiates up to my neck. With difficulty, I drive to where I'm going, it's nearby. I join a breakfast in a friend's home teeming with children and joy, but the pain in my body keeps me from getting really involved. Two hours later, I finally notice dozens of messages from concerned friends, some of them warning me not to talk or comment. Something has happened during my enforced seclusion. Something about me? About us? Who does the 'us' refer to? Family, friends, revolutionary comrades? I glance at Twitter. Morsi is dead. My mind finally grasps what my body has known since dawn.

The formal, state-sanctioned language of the news sites
repulses me, but on social media I'm assaulted by debates and
discussions about the 2012 elections, the 2013 demonstrations,
and our position in both. I want to yell at them, at my friends,
my comrades: this story isn't about us, idiots! My body says
maybe, but there *is* a story about you that's imprinted on your
body. Something dreadful is coming.

III.

The first lesson you learn in prison is: *don't get sick*. The obses-
sion takes hold of you, however healthy you are, whatever your
conditions are like. It's not because Egyptian prisons are packed
with tough guys. On the contrary, you find spaces of compassion beyond your fears and expectations. The danger in Egypt's
prisons is from the intense bureaucracy and outsized paranoia.
Medical treatment or surgery requires a series of arduous steps,
starting with persuading your jailers that you're not lying or
bluffing or feigning illness. The doctor is typically a police officer
or the son of an officer, and he will not write a medical report
without consulting both the prison inspector detective and the
prison warden. Orders for transfer to a hospital, or for treatment
or surgery, or even for lab tests, are secondary to security, logis-
tical, and bureaucratic considerations.

The ultimate catastrophe is a night-time emergency after
the prison is locked down. A prisoner has no way of alerting
his jailers other than shouting. Banging on the iron doors is
the easiest way to make enough noise to draw the attention
of a sleeping guard, but it's also a severe infraction because it's
associated with prisoner riots. It doesn't matter if your cellmate
is dying. You can yell, and maybe your voice will be heard, or
you can try to revive him yourself. If he dies, no one will be held
accountable; if you bang on the doors, you and everyone on the
ward will be punished.

If you can get the attention of the guard, it will take several long minutes for him to get the keys, then hours will pass as policemen, guards, and prisoners examine you in order to diagnose the severity of your case and whether it's worth waking up the officer on duty. You will then wait as the officer decides whether the situation merits further action: a call to the warden or the head detective. They in turn must decide whether it's worth alerting the high command, at which point finally a decision can be made to summon a doctor from the nearest Prison Authority hospital. Maybe the doctor's speciality and expertise will align with your emergency. Maybe the prison clinic and pharmacy will be equipped to handle your case. Theoretically, in the absence of such happy coincidences, the situation may be brought to some higher command to transfer the emergency case to a prison with a well-equipped hospital—or an external hospital. But transfer orders are so complicated that during the sixty months I spent in prison, I didn't hear of a single case in which a prisoner was moved to an intensive care unit at night. I did hear of and witness several deaths.

Aboulfotouh and Ahmed Douma are not placed in solitary for harsher punishment or to destroy their health and minds. On the contrary, from the point of view of the Prison Authority leadership, these are privileged inmates who enjoy better conditions than the average prisoner. The purpose of solitary is to insulate the prison administration, Prison Authority leadership, and the National Security officers responsible for 'seditious elements' against claims that a political prisoner was able to make contact with the outside.

Prison officials are single-mindedly obsessed with preventing any contact with the outside world, although prison regulations clearly provide for visitation rights, communication, and the right to knowledge. The idea that political movements can be steered from inside prison has no basis in reality—in fact, it defies logic—but it is a fiction often repeated by regime mouth-pieces and their media outlets. As such, fiction or not, the powers that be could hold their own men responsible for it. So these men take care to prevent outside contact. Whether the risk is genuine or not is not important, nor is the effect of these pre-cautionary measures on prisoners' well-being. What's important is to appease the political leadership and protect one's position and influence.

Mohamed Morsi's fate was governed by this logic. The state of his health, according to official reports, was not determined by the results of medical tests and his vital statistics, and certainly not by his own narration of his pain. The state of his health was officially decided the day the press reported that he was eating roast duck in his cell.[85] As soon as that story spread, pre-emptive denial of any health problems became official policy, and no medical team subject to state orders could say otherwise. After all, the prison doctor consults the warden and the head detective before writing his report. If the presidency actually wanted to know the real state of the former president's health, it might have needed to fly in a medical team from abroad.

IV.
This day was not exceptional. Although the police station goes on high alert for reasons that don't make sense to a civilian like me—like, say, when the national team is eliminated from the African Cup—this incident did not draw the attention of the sovereign institutions. The deceased was not an ex-president. I don't remember when I saw the news, probably in the early morning. I ignored it. I tried to ignore all depressing news. I didn't look at the name of the victim. But at the end of my day,

---

85 A fabricated story pushed by state media designed to imply both the humane conditions inside Egypt's prisons, while also suggesting the Brotherhood are so well-funded that they live in luxury inside.

as I was going back to hand myself in to the police station as usual, the pain began throbbing in my thigh. I had slept fitfully the night before, searching for a comfortable position. The day was full of errands and I was finding driving difficult. I stopped resisting and gave in to painkillers. The next day, I finally read the news of the burial and realized the tangled ties connecting me to Omar Adel, the young man with no prior history of illness whose heart stopped because of breathing difficulties in the isolation cells of the remand division of Torah Prison. I remembered the night I spent in the same disciplinary cells when I was 25, around the same age as Omar. They were trying to break a collective hunger strike. I remembered the Friday sermon given by a fellow inmate. He started by saying that being in that prison was the next-toughest thing to being in the grave. The disciplinary cells are, truly, like tombs. It was like Omar was buried alive.

V.

They escaped the worst of the carnage. They spent four nights of terror herded into the Cairo International Stadium and then being moved from one temporary holding place to another, their families dizzy with exhaustion looking for them among the corpses at the morgue and official hospitals and field clinics. When it was discovered that they were arrested and were to be transferred to prison it was a relief for everyone. Prison life is tough, but—in theory at least—it's a stable, safe place to be when chaos is sweeping the country. More importantly, they'd survived the bloodbath. There was only one stop left on their journey of horrors. One short trip from the Heliopolis police station to the Abu Zaabal military prison, and then they could rest. Those who had been there at the violent dispersal of Rabaa couldn't imagine that there could still be something worse.

The Abu Zaabal police truck slaughter stands apart in its unequivocal, stark clarity. A decision to throw a gas canister

designed to disperse large, open-air crowds into a group of confined, defenceless prisoners packed into a closed truck seems to
demonstrate an explicit intent to kill. But the fact is, what happened was random. Just pointless behaviour familiar to anyone
who has ever been transported in a police truck.

Every transport of prisoners is marked by long periods of
aimless—and of course, unexplained—waiting. Say you're
summoned to a court hearing. If you don't already know it in
advance, you typically will not be informed of your destination.
An order is given to move you to a cage for prisoners awaiting
transport. It's usually a long wait, even if the truck is there,
maybe because the security detail is not yet complete. You finally
get in the truck and the doors close. But it doesn't move, maybe
because a civil servant was late filing a report somewhere. Then
the truck moves, but stops suddenly, maybe in front of another
prison. An hour later, a fellow prisoner may get in, and if you
ask him, he'll swear that he's been ready and waiting for hours.

This is how it goes until you reach your destination, where
you'll also wait, maybe for the officers to drink tea. Who knows?
But all this is normal. Often the prisoners arrive after the judges
have left. It doesn't matter: you're a prisoner and your time is not
your own—and it's worthless anyway. It is the same bureaucratic
logic that determines any government interaction and drags it
out without rhyme or reason. The difference is, now you're confined to a suffocating metal box with no respite.

That day, the transport truck was left under the August sun
for at least four hours. More than forty bodies were stuffed into
a space not big enough for half of them, without ventilation,
without water. No cause, no reason. They were already inside
the high-security prison complex. But the arrival of a body to a
particular place is meaningless unless that body is attached to a
set of stamps and signatures needed to turn its physical presence
into an official fact. It was definitely possible for the transport

officers or the prison officers to end the prisoners' suffering by letting them out of the truck, or opening the doors and giving them a drink of water, or refusing to move a truck packed well beyond capacity, or refusing to move before the heat broke, or by completing the necessary procedures quickly, or any number of other options—starting with getting rid of this bizarre fleet of Swiss transport vehicles and replacing them with an ordinary, humane means of transport.

But the police are not tasked with respecting the needs of human bodies, not even the need for air and water. We know this by their refusal to allow prisoners fans or refrigerators in the summer and the regular cutting of water at midday. The only job of the police is to prevent escape and contact with the outside world. The officer is judged solely by his degree of control over prisoners' bodies.

The decision to toss a gas canister into a closed vehicle to control prisoners' screaming about their inability to breathe is, despite its monstrosity, unexceptional. In any case, the gas canister was thrown into the truck hours after the carnage within had begun. The massacre was not the consequence of a decision. It resulted from the application of common practice and long-standing policy that hears the prisoner's voice as gibberish and sees his body as an inanimate object. A prisoner claiming that he needs to breathe like any other living being is doubtless lying.

Most of us consider the five-year sentence given to the deputy warden of the Heliopolis police station and the one-year (suspended) sentence given to three officers for a misdemeanour offense to be a travesty. Interior Ministry personnel agree: it's a grave miscarriage of justice against men who did their jobs to the letter.

VI.
This time, I didn't notice the incident when it happened. I only learned of it from a *Mada Masr* bulletin the next day. It was a

news story about prisoners attempting to escape from al-Saff General Prison by setting their blankets on fire. A white-hot rage swept over me. I snapped at a friend—how could she unquestioningly accept the framing of the Public Prosecution and security sources? Burning blankets doesn't help you escape. It's usually an attempt at rebellion against conditions when there's no other possible route. What does a prisoner own besides his body and his bedding? If no grievance is listened to and no voice heard, the only space for mutiny is to burn your bedding or harm yourself.

Accusations of escape attempts are common, despite the rarity of real escapes. Charges of attempted escape are brought as a deterrent, used to inflict harsher punishment, since escape is the most serious crime a prisoner can commit. The allegation lets the prison administration justify excessive violence and makes it easier to get rid of a troublesome prisoner, either by exiling him to some far-flung facility or transferring him to a maximum-security prison.

Journalists have colleagues and loved ones in prison, and have long shown sympathy and solidarity with prisoners. The issue is not that those sympathies have changed—it's prison itself. When you're hidden behind its walls you're robbed not only of your will, but your voice. Since you are deemed officially unfit for society, society's trust in you recedes until it becomes normal for the press to report on an irrational escape attempt that stood no chance of succeeding without stopping to ask what consequences there might be on prisoners' bodies.

VII.

Mohamed Morsi died while on trial for a charge related to the prison breaks in the early days of the revolution. The state clings to an absurd narrative about a conspiracy by a handful of Hamas and Hezbollah operatives who worked in concert with the

Muslim Brotherhood to break out their comrades and free other prisoners to spread chaos and terror in the country. A broad swathe of regime opponents and the pro-revolution public clings to an alternate narrative, no less absurd, about a conspiracy by the Interior Ministry to allow dangerous criminals to escape and spread chaos and terror around the country in order to derail the revolution.

Both narratives are based on the assumption that the moment a prisoner is set free, he turns into a savage beast and embarks on a rampage of rape, pillage, and murder. This image contradicts the reality of Egyptian prisons, their demographics, and the nature of the charges brought against most of the prisoners in them. It's also illogical. Every prisoner will be released sooner or later. In fact, most will qualify for parole and be freed before they serve their full sentences. Obviously, only a fraction of crimes committed are actually prosecuted in court, and the Egyptian justice system is known for its frequent in absentia convictions and the inability or unwillingness of the security services to enforce them. Logically, we should all realize that the prison community represents a small sample of existing criminals at any given moment - with the 'dangerous' criminals at large outnumbering those in prison. Everyone knows there are innocent people in prison—but still the competing parties demonized prisoners even though they escaped at the peak of a revolution of popular rage against the security agencies.

I didn't understand the impact of this demonization until I returned to the remand division of Torah Prison in autumn 2011 and saw traces of automatic gunfire on the walls—both outer and inner. As in most Egyptian prisons, and following a pattern repeated throughout history around the world, the prisoners responded to news of mutiny, rebellion, and revolution outside prison walls with their own mutiny and rebellion inside. The revolt reached its peak after the radio reported that Abu Zaabal Prison had been opened, the doors of the cell blocks had been smashed and the prisoners had partially liberated themselves. In the Torah Prison complex, security forces regained control by firing live ammunition—indiscriminately and intensively—from surveillance towers. Dozens of prisoners were killed to contain the revolt. For days, the prison was controlled only by live fire from the surveillance towers, the inmates cut off from the world without food, medicine, or water.

Prisoners who escaped didn't do much better. Escapees from Wadi al-Natroun faced armed patrols and helicopters that mowed them down. Those who survived—for example, by hiding under the bodies of their friends—were dealt with by neighbourhood vigilantes, on alert to protect their homes from the hordes of marauding criminals spreading anarchy like a virus. The lucky ones were roughed up and turned over to the Army for prosecution in a military trial.

I met one prisoner who was set free by his guards. It probably because, after they lost contact with their commanders and supplies were interrupted, lower ranking officers were unwilling to risk taking control within the collapsing security situation. They were advised to turn themselves in to the nearest military detail. Those who complied were met with new horrors as they were rounded up, held and transported to military prisons and temporary detention centres, many on commandeered trucks not fit for humans. Unknown numbers died on those terrible journeys.

Mohamed Morsi's dramatic entrance to the revolutionary stage therefore coincided not with a call to al-Jazeera on a satellite phone—a trivial detail that for some reason became the crux of the alleged conspiracy—but with the wide-scale slaughter of prisoners. The only people who cared were their families.

VIII.

Every winter since my incarceration, I've been stricken with
pain in the muscles and joints on the right side of my body.
The symptoms might manifest in an isolated spot—usually my
shoulder—or extend from my leg to my neck, then recede as
my body accustoms itself to the winter cold. The roots of these
pains are in the night of my arrest. After my house was stormed
by special forces brandishing weapons and wearing bulletproof
vests, after my mobile phone and laptop were stolen, after my
wife was hit, after I was hit and mauled, I ended up on cold tiles
in an unknown location, barefoot and wearing only my pyjamas.
My hands were cuffed behind me and I was blindfolded with a
filthy rag. I spent the night tossing around to find a comfortable
position. Sleep resisted me but, exhausted, I gave in and lay
down on my right side, and the cold seeped into my bones.

Some twelve hours later, I found myself before the prosecutor and finally discovered that I was in the Cairo Security
Directorate. I insisted on being questioned as a victim, and in
fact, the interrogator did record the traces of blood, my swollen
eye, and my general exterior appearance, as well as my complaint about armed robbery (they illegally confiscated 'evidence'
without a search warrant). Then he sent me to a forensic medical
examiner. But he did not summon any members of the arresting
force for questioning and brought no charges, except against my
friends and me.

After questioning, I was moved to Torah Liman Prison. When
a new prisoner is admitted, he is denied visits for eleven days as
part of the intake procedure. Winter came early that year, ush-
ered in by hail. Photos of the rare snow on the outskirts of Cairo
were everywhere. Even after I was allowed visits, the administration refused to permit the entry of warm clothes, saying they
did not fit regulations. As a result, the chill I contracted from
lying on the cold tiles in the security directorate lasted most of

the winter. The tremors only disappeared when I learned the Directorate was bombed. That morning, I thought I heard an explosion and started awake at dawn. Then I finally got warm. Now the pain which used to haunt me every winter comes back at the peak of the summer heat with news of those bodies that are still in prison. Maybe I didn't come out with my health intact, as my friends and enemies presume.

IX.
The period in which you're denied visits is known as 'intake'. You typically spend it in a special cell: crowded and filthy, no consistent inmates, no cleaning implements, no healthcare capacity. From time to time, other prisoners collect leftover food and old newspapers to send to the intake cell as charity. Officially, under prison regulations and laws, this is a quarantine period. Theoretically, the isolation is to assess your health status and identify any contagious diseases. But the regulations specify no actual procedure to assess health. In practice, what concerns the prison administration is not your health but your class status, your connections and your resources. These will determine how you're treated and where you're housed. Everyone is subjected to violence in prison, but overt violence is usually rare; the walls, gates, locks, and hopelessness are usually enough to ensure the prisoners' compliance. The real purpose of intake is to break the prisoners' spirit, so that they accept a new life stripped of any will. It's also a chance for the marks of any physical coercion experienced during interrogation, arrest, or transport to fade.

The moment of entry is critical to breaking the spirit. If you're classified as someone without protection, you'll be vulnerable to extreme humiliation and violence from that first moment. The intensity of the humiliation will decline with time, but the terror of those first days will never fade. The cruellest form of humiliation for new prisoners is known as the Guard of Honour: where new inmates have to crawl between two rows of policemen who rain down kicks, punches and abuse on them.

Twice I saw the Guard of Honour go wrong.

The first time, an elderly man, likely with a bad heart, died in the middle of the Guard. No one had checked his health. A gloom settled over us prisoners, but the routine remained the same and we saw no authorities making inquiries. A prisoner's death generally requires only the simplest procedures. Perhaps those in charge imagine that simplifying procedures for the release of a corpse is an act of mercy.

In the second incident, a young man of high social status accidentally ended up crawling through the abuse of the Guard of Honour, likely because he didn't know the protocol of asserting his privilege, because of his mild manners and naiveté, his class was misdiagnosed and he was subjected to humiliation unacceptable under entrenched norms. An error that later required frantic apologies from the ranking officers.

In neither case, of course, did a prosecutor come to the prison to investigate, nor was anyone held accountable for this systematic torture. The Guards of Honour did not stop.

X.

Many prisoners exhibit symptoms of post-traumatic stress disorder after their release. The trauma is related less to violent experiences in prison than to the difficulty of adjusting to normal life outside. Prison is like one ongoing instance of violence that strips the prisoner of his social and functional capacities.

The Egyptian state has chosen, for reasons that can only be interpreted as sadistic vengeance, to complicate the process of integration and recuperation for growing numbers of its detainees by contriving a novel, extra-legal punishment deceptively called police probation or parole. The hardest thing about probation is that the ex-prisoner is required to be complicit in his own oppression. No special forces are dispatched to arrest you each night; you're not moved in a transport truck. You yourself cooperate with the authorities to ensure that your body is delivered for twelve hours of isolation.

I try to avoid entering the bathroom during probation lockup. The only accessible facility is a public bathroom used by everyone at the police station and civil registry, except officers. It's filthy, rarely cleaned (and when it is it's usually cleaned by a parolee, in violation of the law). The door doesn't lock, and it has no lights or faucets.

On probation, as in prison, going from outside the walls to the inside is always an anxious moment because of the search. The penal system only pays attention to your body during searches. For the jailer, the body is a potential hiding place for contraband. If a prisoner tries to protect his body by refusing a humiliating search, it's evidence that he's hiding something. If he does not object but seems nervous about the roughness of the search or its intrusion into sensitive places, it's evidence of the same. If a policeman fails to find contraband, it's merely evidence of the prisoner's cunning. Since the list of prohibited items includes rights stipulated by law as well as basic needs not provided by the jailer, every prisoner is necessarily a smuggler.

Enduring the weight of submitting myself—the tense daily search, the scrambling to be on time for lockup, and the attempts to control my digestion and regulate my bowel move-ments—consumes a large part of the day's energy. The result is a persistent anxiety that settles in my gut. Recently my body has begun disassociating from my consciousness. I don't feel hungry or thirsty and I forget to eat and drink. Going to the bathroom during the hours of freedom requires extensive rituals at specific times, and my mind and body become agitated if I don't follow them.

XI.

I remember at the beginning of my 2011 prison stint, before I was moved to the Torah Prison complex, I was in a small cell on a floor designated for 'security concerns' in the Appeals Prison. There was no bathroom in the cell. The doors would open once in the morning for fifteen minutes, as hundreds of prisoners thronged to filthy stalls without doors or curtains. After the first experience, I didn't eat for five days. It wasn't a hunger strike—I just didn't want to need the bathroom.

From the perspective of the Prison Authority, I am a privileged prisoner. Ordinarily, the entire body is vulnerable during the search. As a rule, the prisoner has no right or ability to control his body, including his bowels.

As in intake, during the search, everyone is vulnerable to humiliation, but class governs the boundaries of the permissible. When prisoners return from a court hearing or are suspected of possessing contraband or snitching, most of them are forced to publicly vomit and shit with the use of a bizarre concoction made of oil, water, detergent, cigarette ash, and other unknown ingredients.

My return to prison after the revolution coincided with the death of Essam Atta in the Torah Prison complex during a forcible search, after he refused to subject himself to this degrading process. The Prison Authority maintained it had information that he had a SIM card in his possession. When they failed to find it, it became necessary to search his cavities. His refusal was a sign of his guilt. The search turned into a beating and then he was restrained and the magic potion was pumped into his body. Even today, the Interior Ministry claims that such measures are part of an ordinary search— not torture and systemic humiliation. Essam Atta's body was at fault because it did not produce the alleged phone chip, despite the ranking policeman's instructions. Even worse, it refused to live despite the routine nature of the procedure.

XII.

For years, a group of prisoners, specifically detainees at the high-security section of Torah known as Scorpion Prison, were denied visits. Suddenly, two months before my release, the Prison Authority decided—or had a decision made on its behalf—to extend the visitation ban to all political prisoners. Since the official position is that all prisoners are ordinary criminals and there are no political prisoners, the press didn't report on the decision. And since we non-existent political prisoners are only allowed to read the state-owned papers, we didn't know about the decision. Visits just stopped. I didn't even know that the decision applied to prisoners other than myself because I was the only political prisoner in my cellblock. For a week, I was plagued by fears that some calamity must have befallen my family to keep them away. Then one day I was summoned to the administration at night. Without warning, I found myself in a transport truck accompanied by an armed security detail. A few dozen metres later, the vehicle stopped and I found myself in the notorious Scorpion Prison. It was only two hours later that I realized I was there for a visit. For five years, my regular visits had constituted no threat to public security, but suddenly I had become a problem that required forces, equipment, and commanders on the alert.

My mother finally entered the visitation booth on crutches. She hadn't been in a car accident as I'd imagined. She had spent a week camped out in front of the prison gate, holding a visitation permit issued by the Public Prosecution. Five nights in the open in the dead of winter caused a stiffness in her knee that required five months of treatment. Not one of the officers, generals, policemen, or general personnel detailed to secure this momentous event bothered to bring her a chair during the visit or while she waited. None of them were shamed by the elderly mother asking for the legal right to check up on her son.

Disregard for the laments of the body extends to the bodies of prisoners' families, just as legislation, regulations, and courts ignore the fact that prison is a punishment not only for the alleged criminal but for children, partners, siblings, and parents.

It wasn't surprising. When my sister and I had requested release from pretrial detention on the grounds of my father's illness they had treated us as liars They refused to believe that his health had deteriorated, even after he fainted inside the Torah Prison complex while standing in line for a visit. The denial continued even after he was admitted to a state-run university hospital, and after news of his illness and coma had become public knowledge, recorded in official documents.

Anger at the news that my father had died while my sister and I were detained sparked a wave of solidarity that resulted in a decision to permit us to attend the burial and funeral. The General supervising my transport did not understand the mourners' outrage at the deployed Interior Ministry personnel, their chants when we were returned to prison, or their banging on the cars carrying us. For him, my status as a prisoner pre-cluded any strong emotions on my part or sympathy from friends and colleagues. As a rule, doesn't the prisoner simply disappear from people's consciousness? Don't he and his family fade into a sea of identical bodies? Wasn't the concession by the bosses to let me receive condolences a generosity worthy of praise and gratitude?

The only lesson the Egyptian justice system learned was to never again permit prisoners to attend funerals.

XIII.

In the revolution's squares, we celebrated the death sentences handed down in the Port Said stadium killings case, but didn't notice the significance that it was only civilians that got tough sentences. But in Port Said, locals had a different reading. The families of the condemned men assembled in front of the prison, along with hundreds of the city's residents. The massacre was set in motion by ignoring the fact that the condemned had families and friends and, more importantly, a narrative different from that of the Prosecution—a narrative popular in the city after decades of marginalization. The authorities ignored the existence of any context which those imprisoned bodies used to inhabit, so the plan for transport and security—and even the decrees of judicial bodies—were drawn up as if to be applied to inanimate objects, not people. From the perspective of sovereign institutions, their imprisonment erased their existence; the executions were a fait accompli. So no one bothered to address city residents or plan for a restless day, or ready security plans to contain the anticipated anger, or even, at least, move the defendants outside the city before sentencing.

The scene changed from an angry assembly seeking to block the defendants' transport, to fights breaking out, to what seemed to be an attempt to storm the prison.

Security forces responded not with crowd-dispersal methods, but with indiscriminate gunfire. Dozens of people were killed and injured, including many far from the prison's gates and walls. It was no doubt a confusing moment that could be blamed on poor planning. But the next day's events left no room for doubt. The funeral processions for the executed turned into massive demonstrations. The display of popular solidarity alone was enough to demonstrate that city residents did not accept what had happened or the explanation that the dead were all thugs. They were martyrs for the whole city. Instead of respecting people's wounds, or at least being on guard against their rage, the police opened fire on a funeral procession, multiplying the casualties, and this time without the excuse of protecting the prison. Chaos spread throughout the city and the Army was deployed.

That day, President Mohamed Morsi was not preoccupied

with the victims, but with covering up the fact that the police
and army had acted without explicit orders from the political
leadership. He gave his 'I said I would act and now I have acted'
speech, claiming responsibility for a crisis created by others.
The Brotherhood Guidance Bureau stalled attempts by a local
Brotherhood leader to mediate the crisis.

That massacre sparked the first calls for the Army to remove
Morsi. But Morsi wasn't prosecuted, and of course, no security
personnel or agency faced any charges. A person can be prosecuted for walking out of prison or using a satellite phone, but no
one is tried for the killing of prisoners and their families.

XIV.

When I entered Torah Liman Prison for the first time, I noticed
a sign saying it was inaugurated in 1886, four years after the
defeat of the Orabi revolution. It was the first modern prison
built in Egypt, and its first inmates were Orabist detainees.
Although the state denies we are political prisoners, I was moved
to the solitary cellblock, where a sign at the entrance reads:
Political Cellblock 1A. It's an old building made of brick, not
concrete. We were told it was the oldest of the prison wards.
Political opponents of the state have passed through these cells
from the defeat of the Orabi revolution through to the defeat of
the January 2011 revolution.

Since the state was established, prisons have been used to hide
away dissidents and rebels and incorporate their bodies into a
single ignored and precarious body. Everyone who has ruled
Egypt—including liberal Wafd governments and the Morsi government—has used the same prisons, the same courts, the same
arsenal of laws. (I was sentenced with a cocktail of laws dating
back to 1914, 1937, 1945, 1998, 2011 and 2014.) Since the revolution erupted and the prisons were thrown open, the docile,
invisible bodies of prisoners have been fair game, their killing

a routine matter of concern only to themselves and their families. Since the defeat of the revolution, the state has stuffed the prisons fuller and built new prisons to absorb greater numbers while continuing to deny them any legal protection.

Sooner or later, most prisoners will come out of prison. But every prisoner is locked behind the gates with the possibility that they will stay there until they die. The indifferent reactions of the state and its mouthpieces to Mohamed Morsi's death demonstrate that the purpose of his imprisonment was not to find the truth, or deliver justice. If the purpose of his incarceration was in any way related to the supposedly high-minded goals of the criminal justice system, he would have been kept healthy enough to ensure his trial was completed. Those in charge of the system probably didn't want such a dramatic ending, although the plan was certainly that Morsi would never leave prison alive. What annoyed the authorities was that the world did not forget him before his death.

Sooner or later, most prisoners will come out of prison. But for all prisoners before whom the gates open, there is a chance they will have lost an irreplaceable part of their spirit and health. The indifferent reactions of the state and its mouthpieces to successive prisoner deaths demonstrate that the purpose of their imprisonment is unrelated to reform, reeducation, rehabilitation, or even deterrence. If prisons existed to protect society, attention to prisoners' health would be paramount. Their bodies, after all, will come into contact with those of their families and loved ones, and the consequences of their injuries would not be contained inside the prison walls.

After the dramatic, on-air death of the former president, and with our comrades disappearing every day into the black hole of prisons—some of them to be released only to the grave, others to come out to a world where their loved ones have already gone to the grave and left them behind, alone—can we really consider the story of prisoners' bodies a story only about prisoners? The story is not about prisoners' health, but the health of the nation. It's a story of tools of oppression passed down through the generations and a vicious vengeance that will be inherited. The total negation of the voice and body is the impetus of this vengeance. We think of vengeance as a wilful decision to pursue a feud and inflict pain, but, if you see and hear me, there's a chance for retreat and a truce; even if we don't take advantage of it, we at least remain on an equal footing. When the feud rages, you don't see or try to understand me. I become an object, something to be eliminated, destroyed, disappeared, negated, excluded; I become a symbol or a bogeyman, without a physical presence. Vengeance's legacy is the price paid by all bodies, and they continue to pay it even after the feud fades.

The prisoners who escaped in January didn't make it home, though their bodies may have. Although most of us ignored their slaughter and participated in their demonization, something in the prisons broke. They can no longer successfully seclude and discipline bodies; we hear the lament of prisoners, albeit faintly. The outlawing of the bodies of prisoners and their loved ones and the expanded construction and filling of prisons are merely an attempt to subdue rebellious bodies, even if their rebellion involved no more than declaring their pain.

Recently, letters have escaped the prisons calling for a settlement of the detainee issue at any cost. From the perspective of the political conflict, the letters demonstrate a defeat that threatens the Muslim Brotherhood's future, which is why its leadership's disavowal of the messages was expected and rational. But the smuggling of these letters, their circulation, and the debate over them created the opportunity for the narration and examination of pain. None of this works in the regime's favour. Now we must ask ourselves in all seriousness: how do we protect our children's bodies from the legacy of prisons? The solution does not stop with the release of detainees. It starts with release, but must end with an imaginative vision for the erasure of prisons, not prisoners.

Published on 28 August 2019 in *Mada Masr*

ON BDS

The attack on BDS is so absurd that taking a position against it requires stating the obvious as a form of action.

One thing that should be examined though is how this current wave of attacks isn't solely about *hasbra*[86] and deep-rooted German guilt but also about a form of xenophobia that masquerades as a disciplinarian form of liberalism.

BDS is an act of solidarity with the Palestinians. Resisting the anti-BDS campaign is about issues that affect all democracies.

Published on 24 September 2019 on Facebook

---

86 *Hasbra* is the Hebrew word for 'explanation', which is also understood as meaning 'propaganda'.

FIVE METAPHORS ON HEALING

I. REBIRTH

'Every parting gives a foretaste of death, every reunion a hint of the resurrection.'
—Arthur Schopenhauer

'You must be ready to burn yourself in your own flame; how could you rise anew if you have not first become ashes?'
—Friedrich Nietzsche, *Thus Spoke Zarathustra*

For most of its history, humanity has grappled with two certainties: that life is suffering, and that innocence, once lost, can never be regained. Yet both scripture and myths reverberate with tantalizing alternatives of death and rebirth, sacrifice and resurrection: variations on the phoenix in which the burning of the old and the emergence of the new from its ashes give us a chance to break the cycle of fate, either in the form of a blank slate or a return to roots—a continuity of the self after getting rid of wounds, impurities and sins. Pain is the price to be paid for redemption.

II. AMPUTATION AND CAUTERIZATION

'One is always in the position of having to decide between amputation and gangrene. Amputation is swift but time may prove that amputation was not necessary—or one may delay the amputation too long. Gangrene is slow, but it is impossible

to be sure that one is reading one's symptoms right. The idea of going through life as a cripple is more than one can bear, and equally unbearable is the risk of swelling up slowly, in agony, with poison.'
  —James Baldwin, *Notes of a Native Son*

The body, not the soul, is the locus of pain. Homo sapiens is but a rational animal. Modern medicine, with its rationalism, terminology, methods and machinery, is able to cure all pain. Medicine originated in surgery. In acts of precise violence. A precision that might dictate the removal of an entire diseased organ, not because the organ is disposable but because it's not essential. As long as you are alive and in possession of your mental faculties, you're fit. Who among us has not dreamt of a decisive delivery from pain? And if the pain lingers after surgery, fear not for these are ghost pains, mere delusions caused by your nervous system. Just be rational about it. If it worries you that your imagination and your mind are one and the same, there's psychiatry for that. Trust the experts and relax. Amputate, then cauterize, and before that anaesthetize. And after the deed is done, the painkillers, rehabilitation therapy and patience will see you through. Life will go on.

III. RECYCLING
  'We are building the new order out of the bricks the old order has left us.'
  —Vladimir Lenin

'His eyes are staring, his mouth is open, his wings are spread. This is how one pictures the angel of history. His face is turned toward the past. Where we perceive a chain of events, he sees one single catastrophe which keeps piling wreckage upon wreckage and hurls it in front of his feet. The angel would like to stay, awaken the dead, and make whole what has been smashed. But a storm is blowing from Paradise; it has got caught in his wings with such violence that the angel can no longer close them. This storm irresistibly propels him into the future to which his back is turned, while the pile of debris before him grows skyward. This storm is what we call progress.'

—Walter Benjamin, 'Theses on the Philosophy of History'

Suffering is not sacrifice and the body is not a machine. The pain is not yours alone; every individual belongs to a social class and these classes emerge as history marches on. You can become an agent of history, instead of its victim. Make of your pain a revolution, your suffering is resistance. Destroy the sources of pain, and with the ruins of the old we shall build the new as an act of collective agency. This is inevitable, for history follows a logic as deterministic as the laws of the material universe. You just have to recognize the right moment when it comes, and pick the right faction.

IV. HAUNTING

'Capitalist societies can always heave a sigh of relief and say to themselves: communism is finished since the collapse of the totalitarianisms of the twentieth century and not only is it finished, but it did not take place, it was only a ghost. They do no more than disavow the undeniable itself. A ghost never dies, it remains always to come and to come-back.'

—Jacques Derrida, *Spectres of Marx*

They will not eject you from history as long as you can still speak; they will not banish you to the past as long as you can still listen. But which present do you inhabit?

Haunt the dreams of your comrades, and the nightmares of

your enemies; live in a future that never came—be a spectre, a memory, and a herald. Remind them that the current state was not inevitable until it came to be. Do not occupy yourself with the question of why this very possible future failed, leave the victorious to grope for answers. Be the question, and do not heed your impotence. A ghost has no need for material presence or action, you just need to shimmer.

V. REGENERATION

'For salamanders, regeneration after injury, such as the loss of a limb, involves regrowth of structure and restoration of function with the constant possibility of twinning or other odd topographical productions at the site of former injury. The regrown limb can be monstrous, duplicated, potent. We have all been injured, profoundly. We require regeneration, not rebirth, and the possibilities for our reconstitution include the utopian dream of the hope for a monstrous world without gender.'
   —Donna Haraway, *A Cyborg Manifesto*

There can be no return to paradise lost, for we were not born innocent; there can be no resurrection for we are not holy, and our sacrifices were not consciously made. No surgery can cure us and no medicine, for the decision to amputate is not ours, and no clinical research was conducted to explain away our ailments. There will be no rebuilding as the land itself can no longer withstand any more clearing. Let us postpone the wandering of our souls till after death, for each one of us is haunted by comrades who departed, and it would not do to leave them desolate before their time.
   If we are to be treated like animals with no agency, so be it. But we shall bypass cattle and livestock, ignore pets and domesticates. We shall look to the lizards, starfish and

earthworms—those beings that can regenerate after any injury, no matter how grave. We shall accept that regenerated organs may not be identical to what was lost. They could appear to be mutilated, but look closer and you will see the beauty in monstrosity, for only the monstrous can hold both the history of dreams and hopes, and the reality of defeat and pain together. The monstrous need not forget their old injuries in order to lose their fear of acquiring new ones.

Written in the Kiosk of Solitude,
Doqqi Police Station
Published on 26 September 2019
in *Mada Masr*

Two days later Alaa was arrested by State Security plainclothes officers inside Doqqi Police Station.

In September 2019 some small street protests had erupted, triggered by a building contractor revealing details about government corruption, details shocking even to a populace that expects a high level of corruption.

Seeing these small protests as a critical security failure, Sisi re-organized the division of power among his security agencies. State Security, Mubarak's feared domestic security force, had been sidelined to some degree since failing to prevent the outbreak of revolution in 2011. Now, they are placed in full control of operations again, and a massive sweep of activists begins.

Alaa is one of dozens of targeted arrests, among thousands of people arrested randomly from the street.

On 10 October 2019, Alaa's sister, Mona, wrote on Facebook:
"After a long day at state security prosecution Alaa Abd el-Fattah was just returned to Torah Maximum Security 2 an hour ago, Alaa reported to the Prosecutor the following:

1. He was blindfolded as he was brought to prison, forced to strip off all his clothes except his underwear, beaten up and verbally abused as he walked through a corridor into the prison.

2. The beating stopped for a moment as he was spoken to by the prison doctor, who asked him if he had any medical conditions. Alaa told him he has a history of kidney stones and that he needs clean water. The beating resumed afterwards.

3. He was also threatened by an officer—he could not identify him as he was still blindfolded—who told him he hates the revolution, and that this prison was built to break the likes of him and that he won't get out of here.

4. Alaa was robbed of all his belongings and the clean clothes we got him, even the slippers.

5. Today right before he was transferred to the Prosecutor he was threatened and told not to speak about what happened or the prison conditions.

Alaa reported officially all the violations in detail, he is now again in the hands of those who assaulted and threatened him . . . He is at imminent risk of further assault and torture.

We—his family—are now in front of Torah Prison gates, we are staying here until our visit in the morning—we obtained an official visit permit—until we can see him and make sure he is safe.

Help us and speak up for him

#FreeAlaa"

STATEMENT TO THE PROSECUTOR

Alaa is being held in preventative detention, a way of imprisoning people that does not involve them going to trial and instead needs only to be renewed every fifteen days by a prosecutor.

Deprived of pen and paper, newspapers or radio, cut off from the world, with prison visits now conducted through glass and over a monitored phone, conditions have never been worse.

But Alaa now invents a new mode of public address: turning his renewal hearings in front of the Prosecutor, which are little more than a formality, into a public platform. His lawyers would take notes as quickly as they could, then reconstruct them as best they could for his family to publish online.

When Alaa appeared in front of the Prosecutor for the first time, on October 10, the news of his beating and threats were the most urgent public communication and the notes to his first statement were subsequently lost.

It is now 7 November 2019.

I understand that several international bodies have issued statements denouncing the violations I've been subjected to, along with Mohammed Baqer,[87] Israa Abdel-Fattah,[88] and all those who were detained in the latest sweep. Statements were issued by the European Parliament, the UN Special Rapporteur on Arbitrary Detention, the UN Special Rapporteur on Human Rights Defenders, and the UN High Commissioner for Human Rights. These statements come at a time when Egypt needs all the international support it can get on the crisis of the dams

---

87   A human rights lawyer, and Alaa's lawyer, who was arrested while representing Alaa.
88   A journalist, activist, and co-founder of the 6 April Youth Movement.

being built on the upper Nile, starting with the Grand Ethiopian Renaissance Dam. The respect for, and protection of, human rights is one of the most important elements of a state's soft power. So, it's more appropriate at a moment like this that the state, rather than committing such violations, should concentrate its efforts—and our efforts—on garnering international support for Egypt's position and its demands regarding the Renaissance Dam crisis, as this is a real, crucial and urgent challenge.

Torah Maximum Security Prison, where I am incarcerated, is full of detainees from various organizations. I knew about the death of Abu Bakr al-Baghdadi when I heard rejoicing from some cells and shouts of condemnation from others. So, when you deprive all these prisoners of books, newspapers, and magazines, even government newspapers which are your instrument for promoting the state's narrative, and you deprive them of radio and even of using the prison library: what do you expect they'll be like when they come out? Isolating them like this guarantees they're not exposed to any different ideas, so what's the point of detaining them? Whose interest does it serve? This doesn't produce any reform or rehabilitation. If you deny us music the vacuum will be filled with 'Salil al-Sawaram', deny us news and the vacuum will be filled by *Dabiq*.[89]

My mother has filed several complaints with various official entities about the conditions of my detention: I am denied exercise, books, newspapers, or the use of the prison canteen. I am denied books and newspapers despite presenting a court ruling to the prison authorities that I had previously won about this same issue.

The current prison warden, who was deputy warden during my previous term, and saw me getting books when I was serving

---

89 'Salil al-Sawaram' is an ISIS song used in propaganda videos; Dabiq is an ISIS magazine.

a sentence, rather than in preventive detention as I am now,
said that it's the Prosecution who are responsible for depriving
me of my simplest and most basic rights. So, I demand that
the Prosecution explain this and respond to it. I also urge the
Prosecution to inspect the prisons, to go and see for themselves
what the conditions are like. I'm not talking just about my
condition, which—despite all I'm being subjected to—is better
than many others. My conditions are but a drop in a dark sea of
injustice. Some people have been denied visits for several years.
The Prosecution should go to the prisons, investigate, and perform its duty in lifting this injustice.

Delivered on 7 November 2019
at State Security Prosecution Headquarters

STATEMENT TO THE PROSECUTOR

Today, 9 December 2019, I have a complaint regarding the conditions in Maximum Security Two, in the Torah Prison Complex, where I'm being deprived of my rights—as stated in the official prison charter—mainly regarding maintaining our health during the winter season. I'm still not getting my two hours of exercise, I don't get any exposure to the sun, I'm deprived of hot water or any way of heating water for bathing. The prison administration didn't provide us with standard issue mattresses or pillows, so the cold seeps into our bones from sleeping on a concrete bunk with no bedding.

But, more importantly, I'm being deprived of the written word. I'm not allowed books or magazines, to subscribe to a newspaper, or use the prison library.

After two months and ten days of repeated complaints, and after my family sent reports and requests and complaints to all the authorities responsible for prison oversight or for monitoring the performance of the Ministry of the Interior, it's clear that this goes beyond a denial for security reasons, but rather reveals a phobia or a hatred for the written word.

This phobia has unfortunately taken hold of the Egyptian state, and has spread through it. I see no logic or reason for my detention except the written word, especially since my arrest coincided with that of prominent academics and researchers, and preceded that of journalists known for their professional integrity.

The way that phobia of the written word dominates the state's institutions—whether decision-making or security institutions—is strange since the founding fathers of Egyptian culture,

like Rifa'a el-Tahtawy, contributed to developing curricula for
military schools, translating texts for them, and that was the
engine of Egyptian culture pushing society towards modernity.[90]
And until not too long ago it was understood that the criteria
for joining these institutions included awareness of, and the
ability to articulate, ideas. In countries of the civilized world,
these institutions are staffed by experts in various disciplines who
have practical experience and theoretical grounding that enable
them to analyse situations and make decisions. In military command you'll find experts in environmental science and resource
management while in the police you'll find social sciences and
psychology.

For a long time it was like that here, too. But suddenly
there's hostility from the state and an attempt to produce clones
unthinking and incapable of debate.

This is harmful to society, basically, because the authorities
that currently run things—whether we like it or not, whether
we're with them or against them—are the consciousness that
manages and determines this society's destiny. So if this consciousness is closed off from thinking, from the word, from the
ability to debate and collect knowledge—this will have an effect
on society and cause serious damage.

We need to embrace the right to have and exchange information, to allow everyone to freely express their opinions without
fear. This alone will yield serious benefits for society, not just
prisoners.

---

90 In the nineteenth century, Mohammed Ali's Egypt went through a sustained effort to
modernize the state and its institutions, which involved significant knowledge transfer
from Europe with a strong educational component. This was mainly led by Rifa'a el-
Tahtawy, who was sent on a five-year mission to France, and upon his return, started a
busy career translating books on science, philosophy, and history; developing curricula;
establishing schools and colleges; and establishing the first newspapers. All these efforts
were state-sponsored.

[At this point Alaa spoke on how modern civic legal language contributed to the evolution of modern standard Arabic but the notes are unclear.]

When I demand my right to read and write, I am not demanding a luxury. Rather I'm asking to be allowed to live in this age, in this century, to be allowed to maintain my ability to contribute what I can to resuming the now-faltering advancement of the Egyptian state. If the Prosecution supports the enablement of my right, it would not be out of trust, but by virtue of the judiciary still being the one authority invested in the written word, that the judiciary cannot escape the use of the written word because it's very authority is practised through it. We need to restore the importance of the word, to spread the right to the word as something that's not inimical to society, but is in fact vital to its development and progress.

Delivered on 9 December 2019
at State Security Prosecution Headquarters

2020

STATEMENT TO THE PROSECUTOR

First: nothing in my prison conditions has changed; I'm still deprived of exercise, fresh air, books, newspapers, a radio and hot water. The complaints that I and my family have submitted still stand.

As for the accusations against me, I've requested in all previous hearings that the Prosecution actually complete my interrogation.

I'm confused: this isn't the first time I stand in front of the State Security Prosecutor, nor is it the first time I'm imprisoned because of my political positions, but it *is* the first time that I don't know the nature of the charges, or the events, for which I'm in prison. For example, when I was accused in the case of the protest at the Shura Council I didn't deny the charges, but argued that the Protest Law violated the Constitution.

I know that there are hundreds of cases, like mine, that are not being referred to the courts.

I don't understand the political motivation for detaining me this time. I've explained to the Prosecution that I've spent five years in prison, and that since my release I was serving a probation sentence which put me in a police station for twelve hours of every day, and that the nature of my family and professional responsibilities have kept me completely removed from any public work of a political nature.

Cut off from any reading material or world news I am left only with the question: 'Why am I in prison?'

The only explanation I can come up with is that the security apparatuses have a certain conception; a conception built on a history and, after the revolution, on continuous campaigns of defamation.

I'm in detention as a preventative measure because of a state of political crisis—and a fear that I will engage with it. It's clear that I'm detained here today because of previous positions I've taken. I don't deny these positions, but I believe that right now Egyptian society is exhausted from its multiple problems and poor administration and that the security apparatuses are no longer able to understand me, or what goes on in the minds and the hearts of people like me.

So today I'm trying to give a summary of the nature of my political thinking, and what I might wish to call for. I hope that this will help clarify the facts and define the shape of the investigation.

Since I came out of prison last March and followed the amendments to the Constitution I've felt that the country is in a crisis; a crisis set in motion by the President, but that extends beyond him. The conflicts, polarization, terrorist activity and grinding economic crises that have taken place over the last few years have resulted in a situation where the various components of the political class do not trust each other, and any trust between the political class and the people has been lost. Every institution in the country now engages with crises through a security mindset only, so it's difficult to see how the current system can last. The future is now open to a number of grave scenarios that require all of us to give up on our plans and postpone our dreams and put aside any idea of a knockout victory that can solve these chronic conflicts and complex crises.

What I call for, therefore, is now completely different. Despite my radical opposition to the person and the administration of President Abdel-Fattah el-Sisi, I am no longer of the view that we should seek an immediate end to his rule. I find myself closer to the ideas expressed by MP Ahmad Tantawi in his 'Return to the 2014 Constitution' initiative to establish the principles of the devolution of power and limits on presidential terms—these

being a higher priority than the person, background, or programme of any particular president.

In fact, after accepting the defeat of the 25 January
Revolution I find it hard to imagine how Egypt might catch
up with established democracies that don't allow candidates
from the military to stand for civilian positions until a certain amount of time has passed since retirement from active
duty. My hope is that our choice of president next time will
be through elections in which the current regime and the
military establishment can compete—as long as there's trans-
parency in the transition. Presidential term limits should be
set, the military establishment should choose its candidate of
continuity, who should quit the military, be appointed Vice
President, and tasked with communicating with the opposition
and understanding civil society. All political forces can debate
their choice of candidate and the mechanisms of choosing this
candidate without fear—unlike the Amal Coalition who were
looking to prepare for parliamentary elections and have ended
up in prison.[91]

Having returned to prison, and having met detainees from
across the Egyptian political spectrum, I find that the prisons
themselves have become a crisis threatening the future of
the nation. The Constitutional Court ruled in 2012 that the
clauses for executive detention in Emergency Law are unconstitutional—so open-ended pretrial detention is an illegal
workaround. As long as it's possible to indefinitely detain anyone
who doesn't see eye to eye with the ruling system and as long
as the instruments of criminal justice are misused as a tool for
handling political, economic and social crises, any ruler, whoever

---

91   The *Amal* Coalition or, the Coalition of Hope, was a newly formed political alliance
     looking to field candidates in the 2020 parliamentary elections. Several of its most
     prominent members were arrested, including former Member of Parliament Zyad
     Elelaimy; journalist, Hisham Fouad; and Hossam Moanis, former presidential
     candidate Hamdeen Sabbahi's campaign manager.

they are, even if it was my own lawyer, Khaled Ali, will soon see their rule descend into oppression and despotism.

Let the starting point be to use normal rather than exceptional procedures from within the judicial system, in combination with initiatives like those sponsored by the Minister of Justice and MP Ahmad Tantawi such as: to limit imprisonment on remand to short periods immediately preceding a case coming to court; to expedite rulings on the unconstitutionality of infamous laws such as the laws dealing with 'terrorism', or 'protest' or 'congregating' or 'thuggery'; to respond to the rulings of the Administrative Court in regard to not depriving certain groups of the right to conditional release. These procedures alone could end the majority of miscarriages of justice in Egyptian prisons. The remainder can be considered case by case while prison regulations are adhered to, nobody is subjected to cruel or insulting treatment, and the youth who have drifted towards violence as a result of a polarization that they didn't create, but inherited, are reined in humanely.

It's possible to improve the relationship between the people and the institutions of state simply by adhering to the recommendations of the United Nations Human Rights Council's Universal Periodic Review, which Egypt has ratified. It's interesting that the state complies with every demand of the International Monetary Fund, but baulks at the recommendations of Universal Periodic Review: perhaps Egypt could negotiate some debt relief as part of a human rights structural adjustment programme?

When I'm released from prison my most radical demand will be that Egypt adheres to what it has voluntarily chosen through three parliamentary sessions, once during the Mubarak era and twice during Sisi's rule.

As for the issue of democratic transition—which is first and foremost necessary for the stability of the nation and to restore it to a healthy condition, before it being the demand of any political or opposition group—I find myself for the first time responsive to the idea of a gradual transition, because the extent of the crises, the polarization and the mutual absence of trust require it. It's possible to use what remains of the President's second term—according to the 2014 Constitution—to liberate civil society and syndicate organization, then to run local council elections according to a simple mechanism such as direct elections with proportional representation of lists in each unit. Decentralization can then proceed gradually through elections for precincts and governorates instead of jumping directly to experiments like electing mayors and provincial governors. At these ground-level activities there will be an opportunity to build strong parties and an opportunity for the institutions of the state to learn how to interact with politics, politicians and society fairly, without cronyism, trials and arrests.

But, in the end, the crisis goes deeper than mechanisms for transitions of power, and though it's natural that there are different opinions and theories at play about our chronic problems it's dangerous to leave our problems to political debate and competition, to factions defaming and misrepresenting their opponents, or claiming that the crises can be easily solved, by launching slogans instead of programmes. We need to find a mechanism for talking frankly and honestly about our chronic crises and setting the rules for political competition.

I suggest a series of National Conferences where stakeholders, political leaders and technical experts are brought together to discuss the major issues facing our country today: water, food, development, justice and reconciliation. Instead of convening youth conferences in Sharm el-Sheikh, National Conferences could set an agreed-upon national agenda for how to confront our crises as we cannot afford to leave everything to polarization, and the opposition should not be forced to use structural issues to score political points. The Grand Ethiopian Renaissance Dam is a perfect example of such an issue.

The first in such a series of National Conferences could be convened on justice—which the judiciary has repeatedly called for.

When it comes to justice and reconciliation, from our point of view, we the victims of oppression, I would suggest that it's necessary to postpone everything that's too heavy a burden on the existing institutions and concentrate on the future, until circumstances allow for the procedures of transitional justice and far-reaching constitutional reform. Yes, I would ask that we sacrifice our dreams so that our children may still have dreams of their own. And I would ask those on every side who have lost loved ones to postpone the retribution that is their right in exchange for a guarantee that there will be no more massacres or bombs or assassinations.

This is a summary of my thoughts, thoughts I discovered in prison. If there's anything in them that requires legal accounting, and even though I've not had the resources to formulate them properly or offer them to public opinion, I'm ready to stand before a court and answer for every word. Or to submit to a detailed interrogation if the Prosecution requires any clarifications. If my words and ideas are not legally liable, then the duty of the Prosecution is to submit their investigation and desist from accusing me of creating or joining terrorist organizations— which could anyway only be made up of the peaceful dissidents, human rights activists, thinkers, writers, politicians, students, football fans and others whom I have met in prison or in prison transports.

Delivered on 22 January 2020
at the State Security Prosecution Headquarters

STATEMENT TO THE PROSECUTOR

This is my last hearing in front of the Prosecution, and for several hearings now I've been requesting that the investigation be completed, along with other requests and complaints about my detention conditions, and the situation regarding my son.

First, on the detention conditions—and here I'm presenting a complaint for the ninth time to the Prosecution, my lawyers have filed complaints with State Security Prosecution, and my family have presented complaints directly to the Prosecutor General at his Office of Human Rights Affairs.

As for the charges I'm facing, my situation has become absurd beyond even a novelist's imagination: over the course of ten hearings to renew my detention, the Prosecution has not confronted me with details of the investigation, or any evidence, or witness testimonies, or even explanatory details of the charges against me. So I have ended up guessing the political reasons for my detention, and acknowledging them. I don't know whether the Prosecution is reluctant to pursue the investigation, or incapable of dismissing it.

It seems that the decision about whether or not to release me lies beyond this building.

This is unfortunately a systematic practice affecting hundreds, even thousands, to circumvent the Constitutional Court's ruling on the unconstitutionality of administrative detention, so cases just stay open for years without referral to court.

Practically, I am a captive, not a defendant; Torah Prison Complex is a detention camp, not a prison; and we are captives of a system that was dedicated to protecting the authority of a person or a regime, but now has become a burden on the regime itself. Actually, the state institutions have become dedicated to protecting and covering up for repression, and repression has become an end in itself, which severely threatens the future of this nation.

Nevertheless, I will not tire of addressing the Pros-ecution seriously, filing complaints, appeals, and reports, and complying with the investigation procedures, because one decision to dismiss a case, or drop charges, or a serious inspection of a prison, or investigation of a violation or a disappearance, even by one investigator, may present a lifeline for a nation that has been deprived of justice for too long.

Finally, I would like to thank the Prosecution for their patience, and for their humane treatment and handling of my ordeal and that of my son, and for allowing Khaled to visit me here at the Prosecution headquarters. The look of human compassion I see in their faces when Khaled has come to this building has been a glimmer of hope.

I take pride in every word I have put on record during these ten sessions, I pray that God may accept them in the balance of my good deeds, and that the people may count them in the measure of my struggle.

Delivered on 5 February 2020
at State Security Prosecution Headquarters

THE PANDEMIC HAS REACHED
OUR PRISONS

The pandemic has reached our prisons. It made no distinction between guard and prisoner. It entered our cells and made no distinction between political and criminal prisoners. It stormed our detention camps and made no distinction between Islamist and secularist.

The pandemic has come,
Homes have become shrines,
And cells have become shrines
So you, who stand on the verge of the pandemic,
Raise the banners of truce.[92]

For the pandemic has come to prove the absurdity of our disputes, and the modesty of our conflicts before Divine Will, to prove both our helplessness and the weakness of our adversaries before the force of nature. The pandemic has come to remind us that safeguarding the lives of all is a necessity, unattainable except by joining hands in solidarity. The pandemic has come, and none have survived except those societies that closed ranks and mobilized joint efforts, driven only by their survival instinct, their celebration of life, and the single goal of securing the future.

---

92 Alaa is writing after Amal Donqol:
   You, who stand on the verge of the massacre
   Raise the armuor
   Death has fallen, and the heart has scattered like a rosary
   And blood has flowed over the cloak
   The homes are shrines
   The cells are shrines

The pandemic has come, crushing in its path all those who seize on their petty gains, and all who dwell on the sins of the past. It has come as an omen and a testament, as a trial and a choice for all of humanity. The sensible have answered that what comes next must not be like what went before.

And so we call on every sensible person in Egypt (and they are—God willing—the majority), and all the active forces in the community: either we survive together, or we all suffer irreparable and unlimited loss.

Our destiny is one, whether we like it or not, for the safety of the prisoner is necessary for the safety of the judge's son, and the safety of the detainee is necessary for the safety of the officer's mother, and the safety of the captive is necessary for the safety of the family of the one who gloats over his misfortune. We are all equal before the virus, nothing but hosts for its spread and reproduction. All security solutions are invalid, and all instruments of repression are powerless.

The Egyptian Captives' Forum launches this initiative, calling for an open political and human truce, during which we voluntarily freeze all political conflicts and disputes and devote ourselves to confronting the pandemic. The Forum hopes there will be serious engagement with this initiative from all forces, currents, parties, and movements representing the entire Egyptian political spectrum—which is fully represented in the prisons and detention centres.

The Egyptian Captives' Forum also appeals to all the 'grown-ups' in Egyptian state institutions (and they are—God willing—many) to interact positively with this initiative, to put an end to security-focused management, to set aside repressive procedures and replace them with collective management and solutions based on science.

We also propose the establishment of a crisis management unit made up of the Armed Forces, the Medical Syndicate, and the

National Council for Human Rights, with international support from the Red Crescent, the Red Cross, and the World Health Organization. This unit shall manage and mobilize all the efforts and resources of Egyptian society, and unleash its potential energy to safeguard the future and confront the pandemic.

The Egyptian Captives' Forum also calls on the leaders and senior members of our judiciary to join this initiative, by working towards unleashing all the experience and energy trapped in our prisons or exiled abroad: doctors, nurses and volunteers. And by mercifully considering the mothers, the sick, and the elderly, whose lives are at risk because of the political crisis, and re-aligning the resources and efforts wasted in litigation and in sustaining the prisoners, the captives, and their families.

The Egyptian Captives' Forum emphasizes the urgency of ending overcrowding in prisons by the wide and comprehensive application of amnesty, parole, release on medical grounds, and the authority to suspend penalties and release detainees. These are necessary procedures to protect all of society, and all the more reason to completely clear out the illegitimate detention centres, as did the countries that have succeeded in controlling the spread of the pandemic.

Finally, the Egyptian Captives' Forum places its confidence first in God, and second in the people, and launches its initiative hoping it receives a widespread, deep discussion, and committed adoption. For the pandemic warrants the dedication, sincerity, and unity of the Egyptian community and, indeed, of the community of humans.

Finally, we ask you all to pray for us. For the homes are shrines, and the cells are shrines, and we stand on the verge of the pandemic.

Save us before you can no longer save yourselves.

Published on 9 July 2020 in *Megaphone*

A HANDWRITTEN NOTE

'Hi, I've not seen your letter yet, so I can't respond. And I don't know which one of you is here but I think it's Mama. I'm a bit worried at the thought of you waiting out there in this rain. It looks like the whole place has drowned – as usual. But honestly, when it was raining it was joyful and the smell of the wet dust was good and the sound of people raising prayers was inspiring. You miss being part of nature and the climate but this rain is making itself felt through the walls.

I hope you're all well. My health is good, that's all I can say. The day of my birthday was a bit dramatic and I couldn't celebrate but the banana cake made up for things a bit. I try to energize my head in the absence of books by remembering stories from history, sometimes by chattering on about science. My imagination can't really engage with post-release dreams but, you know, one tries to find reason for optimism in the ebbing of the right-wing wave in the world, and to believe its effects will reach us. Of course I'm used to Gramsci's method regarding the pessimism of the mind and the optimism of the will, but there's such negation of the will here that I need to train myself into an optimism of the mind before I mess up my colleagues.

That's all. I'm generally fine and I love you and miss you.'

November 2020

2021

I. THE SEVEN COURSES OF CHANGE

Our crisis is not limited to our persons, nor is it about our detention alone; it's the crisis of a whole nation, and there is no path to salvation except political change, starting at the top of the system.

So, what are the possible courses of change?

And which of them is more beneficial for the country and the people?

Human historical experience tells us that the courses of change are limited to seven:

Divine intervention

The death of the dictator usually opens the door for some change and some respite. In some cases, such as Spain and the Philippines, it brought about comprehensive reform and a democratic transition.

Foreign intervention

Usually, foreign intervention is not advisable, but we can't dismiss some cases where diplomatic intervention led to a democratic transition, such as Western support for democratic movements in Eastern Europe after the fall of the Soviet Union.

Voluntary change

It seems impossible, but there are historical cases of systems that chose change in response to changing conditions. Mahathir Mohammad in Malaysia is the best example of voluntary transformation. In Peru and El Salvador, the debt crisis caused the military to relinquish power and start negotiations with political actors in search of solutions.

Military coup

There are two kinds: a palace coup, in which the leaders of the ruling junta overthrow the man at the top and replace him, or a coup by mid-ranking officers, who take control of the army and use it to control the state. We've seen both examples, in Egypt's coups of 1952 and 2013. We could also consider Abiy Ahmed's ascent to power in Ethiopia the result of a palace coup.

Military insurgency

This is not a coup, but an uprising by soldiers and junior officers. In Egypt, the Orabi Revolt is an example. Portugal achieved a democratic transition after a military revolt was joined by the people, and transferred power through elections.

Popular uprising

No explanation needed. The effect of the people storming into the political arena with their bodies is unequalled in achieving change. And the experience of the January revolution is present in our minds, despite the defeat.

Organized revolutionary action

Organized groups take the place of popular action to compensate for the difficulty or lack of correct conditions for a popular uprising. The best example is South Africa's National Liberation Movement, where the organized struggle resulted in the end of apartheid.

So, which of these routes—in your opinion—suits us? Which of them can lead to positive outcomes, and achieve what we want?

II. SIX MAJOR CRIMES IMPEDING CHANGE

Our country didn't arrive at this impasse through a mere political dispute or routine despotism, but as a result of major crimes, open wounds, and raging conflicts, the effects of which are all ongoing. Major crimes are different from others in that the question of criminal liability becomes less important than the need to address the effects of the crime. These crimes, therefore, are the concern of everyone who seeks change and reform.

The Crime of Massacre

The military has committed many massacres since the launch of the revolution, but the dispersal of the two sit-ins is a defining moment, to the point where we may call this the 14 August regime. No one has been spared the aftermath of Rabaa except its martyrs; even those who ignore or justify it are paying its price today with this instability.

The Crime of Detention Camps

These are not prisons and we are not defendants. The large numbers indicate that the aim is not just oppression, but the eradication, firstly, of the Islamist movement, and then of any form of opposition. Our prisons aren't even comparable to the political detention centres of the past, but are closer to the crimes of colonialism in its mass detention camps.

The Crime of the State Abandoning the Law

You might think that forced disappearances and extrajudicial killings are part of the same scene as the expansion in detentions and the spread of death sentences. Unjust legal procedures, however, can be ended through legislation or other constitutional tools. The state's total abandonment of any adherence—however formal—to the law destroys the citizens' faith in the institutions of state, in the idea of the law, and in the state itself—which makes it hard to imagine a future.

The Crime of the Sinai Campaign

Things have escalated to the point of military conflict in the homeland—a disaster in itself. Add to the marginalization of the people of Sinai and we are in danger of a schism in society where each section of the people can only imagine one type of victim. The greatest crime is the use of scorched earth policies and collective punishment by both parties—noting, of course, the difference in resources and responsibility.

The Crime of Demonization

This is our crime, even if it intersected with conspiracies and incitement. Tolerating the demonization of the Islamist movement, smearing them, going along with calling them derogatory names like 'sheep', all this paved the way to the massacre. At the same time non-stop sectarian incitement led to the tragedy of burning and blowing up churches. How do we live together in peace and safety in the shadow of this antagonism?

The Crime of Lack of Rigour

All the above led to crimes classified under international law as crimes against humanity. As for this one it's the crime of the revolutionaries, the reformists and the politicians. Let's be honest with ourselves: none of us were up to what happened, so all of us have to be responsible for mending the effects of what happened. Is it realistic to demand that the effects of the above crimes are erased and to ask for a guarantee that they won't be repeated? Can this be done? And under what conditions?

III. FIVE AXES OF POLARIZATION

We were divided after unity. We competed after cooperating. We differed after agreeing. All this is normal, and can be positive if our plurality and diversity are well handled. But, instead, we pushed on with polarization, and the axis of our alienation was political identity: secular and Islamist. Our disagreement was not about policies or decisions, and we lost ourselves to a useless division. To call for change is to call for a return to politics, to opinion and counter-opinion, debate and disagreement. We can't properly manage our disagreements if we narrow them down to one axis that is non-negotiable. So, what are the other axes of polarization that we have neglected?

The Freedom Axis

Individuals and groups hold diverse views about the nature of personal and public freedoms. What's legally permissible? What's criminalized? How does society regulate the behaviour of the individual? How does the state regulate the pathways of entities and groups?

The Economic Axis

Economic systems vary according to the role of the state and the role of the market. Which is more suitable for our country, central planning or individual initiative? Who leads development, the public or private sector? Which are the most important activities, trade, manufacture, or knowledge industries? What's the role of agricultural production? What's the effect of tourism? These are the issues that preoccupy free nations.

The Theory of Change Axis

Positions vary between the revolutionary who wants radical change, the progressive who wants to use the instruments of the state to expedite the development of society, the reformist who calls for gradual progress and moderation, and the conservative who seeks the stability of the structure and identity of the state, and demands of its leaders only competence and integrity.

The Worldview Axis

No one disputes that the destinies of all countries and all peoples are linked. But we vary in our conception of how to interact with the world: some believe in competition while others believe in cooperation, some favour alliances based on a common identity while others prefer alliances based on shared interests. Some adopt a transnational ideology, others an internationalist one, and yet others are more comfortable with a local outlook.

The Modernity Axis

Many of the outcomes of modern technological developments are malign. We differ in our understanding of modernity and how to engage with it. Some look for solutions in authenticity and tradition, others are keen to compete in the modernity race, and still others have faith that answers are to be found in the instruments of science and technology. The problematics of modernity, contemporariness and authenticity are rich: they shouldn't be trivialized, and it's not helpful to ignore others' views on them.

Is it possible to go back to the unity of January? And was it in fact a real union that engaged with and understood the roots of our differences and diversity? Is it better to rise above our polarizations - or understand and acknowledge them? Is our diversity a blessing or a curse?

IV. FOUR CORNERS OF THE POLITICAL COMPASS

We were polarized as if our society was composed of just two teams, but, as we've seen above, the actual axes of political polarization are no fewer than five, and political positions can be broken down to right, left, and centre. So, does our unity require studying all possible groupings?

When Egypt came under colonial occupation, a diverse national movement emerged, it cooperated a lot, diverged a lot, and clashed occasionally. Its components—based on intellectual roots, types of political and partisan organizations, and candidates for office—are four:

The Islamist Corner

This is the largest in number, and has the longest experience of exclusion and marginalization. Egypt is the heart of this ideology and this global project.

The Pan-Arab Corner

The Egyptian state—as with the rest of the Arab republics—has been shaped around the idea of Arab nationalism, so this idea is widespread in society and among senior state officials and technocrats.

The Liberal Corner

Has been well-established in Egypt since the 1919 revolution, advocating a constitutional state, rule of law, and liberties. It's the trend most compatible with international norms.

The Socialist Corner

Because the issues of poverty, development, and economic independence are the most pressing, this trend has been reinvigorated despite its relatively small size. It is also the most connected to opponents of the global system outside the Arab world.

Our current tragedy stems from the notion that it is possible to exclude one of the points of the compass. Let us first agree that exclusion is—in practice—impossible, and the effects of the attempt are destructive to the nation. But, to understand the depth of what we have in common, we need to realize that—unlike in free societies—our national movement forms a minority in society. If all the constituents of the national movement were to get together they would still not represent the national community, for citizens have been forced out of political life by decades of despotism and corruption, to the extent that the electoral turnout—after the revolution—did not exceed 50 per cent.

The national community is divided, politically, into four corners, which have become more pronounced after the coup:

—Those supporting the coup, seeing it as protecting the country's interests.

—Those that agree with the coup and seek to reform the system through cooperation, negotiation and political participation under its control.

—Those disapproving of the coup and seeking to change it through constitutional struggle or a revolutionary movement with reformist demands.

—Those disapproving of the coup and seeking to end it through revolutionary struggle and revolutionary demands.

What's really weird is that all four corners are represented in the coup's prisons today. So, is it time to experiment with unity? And what does it take to fully represent the people?

V. THREE NECESSARY SACRIFICES

It's cost us years of our lives and we thought of them as the price of freedom, but as the prisons fill up, we have to ask ourselves if the road to freedom really passes through them? And what's the price that hasn't yet been paid?

When faced with great ordeals we need sacrifices greater than individual heroism and group steadfastness; we need the sacrifices of entire generations, and each generation has a role that stems from its responsibilities:

The Older Generations

Normally, leadership is assumed by the older generations, a harvesting of long years of work and struggle. Since the coup we have watched our old icons fall, and few have managed a gracious ending. The nation needs icons to preserve links with the struggles of the past, and elders to transfer experience. The older generations need to give up their role and leadership in exchange for a dignified ending and the safeguarding of the memory of the nation.

The Middle Generations

We are usually concerned with holding fast in the face of the pressures and temptations of the world. We are occupied with protecting ourselves from being swept away by the current, with holding on to the cause. We are far more cautious than the younger generation, for we have less chance of rectifying our mistakes. But a preoccupation with purity is not necessarily the best attitude for a generation responsible for children and, soon, grandchildren. What should occupy the middle generation is that we should not pass on the conflict to our children, that we should protect our grandchildren from the effects of the ordeal, even if that means sacrificing purity and heroism in exchange for the courage to engage with the opponent and to push for compromise.

The Young Generations

Most of the sacrifices and all of the victims have come from among the young. It's in the nature of youth to be bold, but in our layered ordeal insisting on a pre-laid plan complicates things more and expecting a return on every sacrifice deepens the crisis.

The most difficult sacrifice is giving up your dreams and ambitions, and as usual the young will pay the heaviest price. Today we have to give up our dreams in return for a secure future where a generation that has not yet come of age can dream without limit and pursue their ambitions without fear.

Are we up to this sacrifice? Or has experience not matured us yet?

VI. TWO NARRATIVES ABOUT THE PAST FOR THE SAKE OF THE FUTURE

If unity around the future is the condition for change, then it is necessary to reach a common understanding of the recent past. But what understanding is possible between factions that have disagreed to the point of blood and honour? The six crimes were not small, nor were they committed without complicity, albeit silent. The attempt to understand the motives of each faction might renew the conflict and reinvigorate the animosity. So perhaps it's better to start with the not-so-recent history, in an attempt to understand how we arrived at the moment of revolution in the first place, before agreeing on an understanding of how we lost it. Any society needs broad agreement around the understanding of its history. This contributes to maintaining social stability, and integrates the experiences of successive generations in a logical sequence that is instrumental in understanding the present moment. Usually, the understanding of history is split into two narratives:

The Main Narrative
This is the mainstay of the wider consensus, and forms the imagination of the majority of society. It is adopted by the mainstream, and is voiced in school curricula, in national museums, in film and drama. A stable society seeks a main narrative that is objective and does not conceal realities. But our country is built on a despotism that fears truth—its main narrative is ambiguous and confused, based on exclusion and on an attempt to fabricate a unanimity devoid of any dissenting opinion. The task of wrenching the main narrative away from the regime will not be

achieved by championing a particular ideology, nor by denying the history and accomplishments of the modern state, but by being objective, and reaching wide agreement on the major events.

The Alternative Narrative

This narrative brings together the experiences of the marginalized, the opposition, and the minority groups. The alternative narrative does not seek facts that contradict the main narrative, rather it seeks to take in the excluded voices, to document the missed opportunities and the aborted ventures. The alternative narrative is not ashamed of defeats, for it is not the story of the strong and the victorious. Each group may produce its own narrative, but:

—Can we influence the main narrative, the imagination and the perception of mainstream society, without a unified alternative narrative?

—Is it possible to come up with a historical account that combines the experiences of the Muslim Brothers, say, with the experiences of the Nasserist trend, named after the dictator responsible for repression and murder of the Brotherhood's leaders?

—Can we arrive at a historical account that respects the experiences of all, and the sacrifices and pains of all, and acknowledges the facts and the events impartially?

—And can we overcome the conflicts of the present and the recent past if we carry on fighting over a history that was over before most of today's citizens were born?

VII. UNITY

If unity is the condition for change, then why were we broken? Weren't we united in the January revolution? We revolted against despotism, we were united behind a clear idea of what we refuse. But we did not share a common analysis of priorities or of the nature of the tasks after the fall of the regime, not to mention a lack of alignment around plans to get through the nation's chronic crises.

If freedom is our goal, then freedom—in a diverse society—requires democracy, and democracy requires opinion and counter-opinion and competition for power. But democracy needs rules to regulate it, conventions to protect it, and wide consensus around values, interests, and alliances, for there are things that don't change with the alternation of power even in the longest-standing democracies.

As for democratic transition, it needs more caution and wider consensus, because the conventions governing democracy have not yet taken root, the institutions' adherence to law and the constitution are not complete yet, and the sharpness of disagreement in budding democracies threatens the whole democratic course.

Democracy, in the poor and developing countries of the south, has its peculiarity, and the required economic development needs long-term plans that should not be modified with every election. In the United States, alliances don't change with every election, and in India the ruling party changes but the course of the food programme does not change—nor does the space programme. In Tunisia, whenever the disagreement intensifies, the competing sides go back to the negotiating table, so that the venture is not aborted. But in Egypt we neglected to stabilize democracy and reinforce the rule of law in institutions and in free society, and we entered the revolution believing that we knew the answers and that crises are easy to handle, and so rushed into competition and confrontation.

We need to renew the inclusive national agenda so that it goes beyond its minimum—the demand for change—and reaches its highest common denominator: actual plans for development.

Escaping the triangle of despotism, corruption and discrimination requires institutional and administrative reform that must be built on total, detailed agreement that leaves no room for dispute or competition. Division here will only benefit the enemies of freedom.

As for the triangle of poverty, ignorance and disease, escaping it requires economic development. Its main features have to be agreed on. But it would be good to expand the agreement to cover plans and details since the effort to implement them involves the whole of society, not just those in power and in politics.

And there's no possibility of escaping these two deadly triangles unless we achieve major objectives, such as the independence of our national decision-making, the stabilization of domestic security, food sovereignty, and water security. These objectives cannot be achieved without a concorde that includes the military elites, the state's senior administrators, and national experts.

The inclusive national agenda is not a theoretical issue, and it cannot be postponed till after the change—it is actually a condition for change, for it is impossible to achieve democracy without agreeing on its meaning and prerequisites. Agreeing only on what we reject is not useful. The opacity of future plans can only lead to loss of confidence between the parties and greater antagonism; it makes it easier to acquire enemies.

Claiming that problems are easy to solve, or brushing aside other people's priorities results in the masses dispersing with the first difficult test.

1. Are we able—under this repression—to engage our minds and our imagination in conceiving a future that brings us together around specific plans to grow the economy, reform the state, develop society, and liberate the individual?

2. Would this unified agenda gain wide circulation and popular acceptance, to be an effective instrument in bringing change?

3. Would it be possible to draft a comprehensive agenda that would bring the competing parties closer together, neutralize the antagonists, and reassure those afraid of change?

PALESTINE ON MY MIND

In the beginning, it was on me to pass on the news. Most of my wardmates are not allowed visits and none of us are allowed newspapers, so my weekly visit had become the primary source of information. News of the Zionists' protracted electoral impasse and the 'Deal of the Century' kept rolling in. I remember trying to analyse and share the news quickly, broadcasting it by shouting through the hatch in my cell door. That was probably when my wardmates first got to know me. In any case, Palestine, was always on my mind.

Then came the pandemic, cutting off visits and the news along with them. I protested with a hunger strike that lasted thirty-seven days. I told my cellmate about the time I visited the Empty Stomachs solidarity sit-in tent in Gaza. I've been on hunger strike four times since then, and each time I remember the Palestinian captives' strike. Palestine's always on my mind.

Despite the defeats, I'm still grateful to the revolution for all it gave me. For one, I was able to visit Palestine twice. I never say I visited Gaza, not only because Palestine is indivisible, but because anyone who visits Gaza cannot but realise that they're in the metropole of Palestine, its beating heart. There, you swap the Palestine of dreams, metaphor, and poetry for the Palestine of flesh and blood and tears and sweat.

To isolate me from my wardmates, or perhaps to contain me one week into my strike, I was moved to another ward where newspapers were allowed. After six months of being denied the printed word, I held a state newspaper in my hand. The first thing I see is a photo of a Palestinian child wearing a cabbage leaf on her face in place of a surgical mask. I scan for news of the pandemic and try to imagine how the world has changed, try to imagine how my son, Khaled, is coping with the closures, the social distancing, the masks and swabs. I always take pride in the fact that the first stamp on his passport (and the last on mine before my imprisonment) is from the Rafah border crossing. Khaled was born at the height of the revolution and visited Palestine before he was even one year old.

On that first visit, I spoke of my family's attempts to live a normal life under exceptional circumstances with no end in sight. I thought that was the Palestinian experience, so I ended my speech with the words 'I am Palestinian.' Words that seem so naive now that the whole world is living in exceptional circumstances with no end in sight—so did we all become Palestinians? Of course not. Only the children of Gaza are photographed wearing cabbage leaves instead of masks. I'm not Palestinian and have done nothing worth mentioning for the cause, but when visits started up again and Khaled came in wearing a mask specially designed for the sensitivities related to his autism it *did* look to me like that cabbage mask. I'm not a Palestinian, but I am an Arab, and Palestine's always on my mind.

After my hunger strike ended, I was returned to my original cell. My wardmates gave me a big welcome. It was Eid al-Fitr, and we passed the night talking and singing. Then they asked me to sing. I'm not a very good singer, but I contributed for the first time with something other than news and analysis and sang 'I Call Out to You'.[93] Palestine's on my mind.

After Eid, I was banned from writing to my family. More accurately, I failed to stay within the fuzzy, ever-shifting red lines that govern what subjects are permissible for correspondence.

---

93 'I call out to you/I clasp your hands', a solidarity poem written in 1966 by Nazarene poet, communist and politician, Tewfik Ziad. It was set to music by Ahmad Qabour and performed for the. first time by the Lebanese People's Chorus in a field hospital in Beirut in July 1975 at the start of the civil war. Since then it has accompanied struggles and protests across the Arab world.

My last letter had not made it through because I wrote of my concern for my sister Mona's health in the pandemic, wondering if her immune system might have been affected by all the teargas she inhaled during the early days of the revolution. I don't know if the offense was the reference to the revolution, even in a negative context, or if it was the teargas that annoyed them. I do know that the quantity of tear gas fired at revolutionaries in Egypt is comparable only to that used against Palestinians in Jerusalem and the West Bank and that its long-term effects haven't been studied properly. Palestine's always on my mind.

My mother started a sit-in in front of the prison gates—closed, they said, because of COVID, and it ended in her and my two sisters being assaulted and Sanaa being arrested for the third time. My prisonmates are embarrassed to tell me the bad news, so I hear it late. I try to comfort them—and myself—by describing Sanaa's stubborn, defiant personality. I tell them she was named after Sanaa Mehaidli, the Bride of the South.[94] Through the hatch in the cell door I tell the story of an argument we had when I refused to drop everything I was doing and wouldn't let her skip school exams to go to Gaza together after the resistance demolished the separation wall along the border.[95] I guess back then I thought the siege wouldn't last.

By 2012, our roles were reversed: at the first opportunity I put the revolution aside and travelled to Palestine. Sanaa, who'd had a friend die in her arms in the clashes after the storming of the Zionists' embassy, couldn't understand how anyone could take a break from the revolution.

But at the end of that year, with the onset of bombing on Gaza again, Sanaa left immediately. She entered without a

---

94 16-year-old member of the Lebanese resistance who drove a Peugeot 504 into an Israeli army battalion in southern Lebanon in April 1985 and exploded it.

95 In January 2008 Palestinians destroyed the barrier separating the Palestinian and Egyptian halves of Rafah and flooded into Egypt. They stocked up with goods that they needed because of the Israeli blockade then went back home.

passport or official stamps and went off the radar entirely until
the war was over.

Since I'd been talking through the hatch about Sanaa I got
a message brimming with affection from my neighbour Anas
[el-Beltagy], who is as dear to me as are all his siblings. He was
born the same year as Sanaa so I find it hard to accept he's not
a boy anymore but a man almost in his thirties. That night I
dreamed of Asmaa, his martyred sister, instead of Sanaa, my captive sister, and woke up to sing 'On my Mind There's a Song',[96]
for Palestine is always on my mind.

While telling my family's history, I discover that a new
neighbour, the mysterious Amm Seif (who had hijacked a plane
to demand the female prisoners' release),[97] had met my father
in southern Lebanon when they had both joined the resistance.
What twists of fate: two Egyptian Seifs, both communists,
meeting in the camps in Lebanon. One returned to Egypt, went
to prison, and came out a lawyer and defender of the weak. The
other stayed with the resistance and the PLO—until the PLO
moved to Ramallah and the resistance moved to Gaza, leaving
him alone with no battlefield, camp, or rifle. He returned
to Egypt, a stranger in a strange land, lost until a revolution
restored him to life. When the revolution was in retreat he
tried to resist with 70s fedayeen tactics—so they branded him a
lunatic and threw him in solitary in Torah's Scorpion 2 Prison.
I'm blown away by the twists in destiny's road—but not surprised that they intersect on Palestine's threshold. For we are
Arabs, and Palestine's always on our mind.

Visits resume, but have been reduced to twenty minutes, once
a month—again because of the pandemic. I'm back in touch

---

96 By Marcel Khalife from a poem by Mahmoud Darwish about seeing a young woman, a
    childhood friend, martyred.
97 In 2016, Seif Mustafa, 58, hijacked an Egyptair plane flying between Cairo and
    Alexandria and diverted it to Cyprus.

with the news. The Deal of the Century is moving ahead full
steam, the UAE isn't content with normalising with Israel but
is pressuring Sudan to follow suit, exploiting their fragile political and economic situation. The Arabs are not rising up. After
a year in prison, I meet Rami Shaath in the courthouse lockup.
He's in prison for his activism with the Boycott Divestment and
Sanctions (BDS) movement. We spend the whole day talking
through the wire mesh dividing our cages, exchanging news. I
tell him I'm worried that the Palestinian cause will be finished
off. With a very Palestinian wave of the hand he gives me the
good news that the number of Palestinians in historic Palestine
has exceeded the number of Israeli Jews for the first time and
that, despite Arab weakness, the BDS campaign is raising a new
generation of solidarity activists around the world.

He tells me that reconciliation between the Palestinian
factions is imminent, and I talk about how the changing demographics in the US might erode the usual identification with
Zionism, but I imagine it will be a decade before this comes to
fruition. Rami is optimistic. But me, I remember our betrayed
spring, the siege on the embassy, the open crossing. I remember
our chant—*the people want to end the siege*—and yours: *the
people want to end the division*. I wonder if the people taking
part in the Great March of Return and launching incendiary
kites have heard these chants? In photos they look very young
and seem completely disconnected from the moment when we
thought that the road to Jerusalem ran through Cairo. Anyhow,
whether I count on optimism of the intellect or optimism of the
will, Palestine's always on my mind.

We start a cultural program. When it's my turn, I shout out
lessons on contemporary history and politics, beginning with
the history of the rights movement in Egypt. I explain the
movement's solidarity with the Palestinian cause. In contrast
to the global human rights movement which was embroiled

in Cold War debates, the local movement was always militant. I remember my father's criticism of the feeble positions
on Palestinian rights taken by institutions like Human Rights
Watch. Then I hear about their latest report on Palestine, which
explicitly condemns Israel of the crime of apartheid—even in the
'48 territories. Maybe Rami was right, and change is imminent.
The point being: Palestine's always on my mind

Ramadan returns. It's been a year since my hunger strike. The
pandemic continues and won't be ended by vaccinations. We
expand the cultural program for Ramadan to include battles
from Islamic history, but on the tenth plans change and I am
tasked with narrating the October War.[98] My prisonmates are
expecting a narrative different from the one they learned in
school and saw on television. I have a dilemma: how do I explain
to prisoners of the current military rule the complex history
of the Egyptian military? How do I relate the confusion of the
last days of the war without minimising the victories of the first
days? How do I wade into the labyrinth of Camp David, this
tunnel that we've never got out of?

I begin by clarifying that this army never shed Palestinian blood
(but a voice inside me nags that it did shed Egyptian blood).

Try as I might, I'm unable to present a coherent historical
narrative that combines the suffering of the Islamist movement,
the ambitions of Arab nationalism, and the achievements of the
secular elite. Division, once entrenched, is difficult to overcome no matter how good the intentions. News comes of the
impending announcement of Palestinian reconciliation and I
allow myself some cautious optimism. It's easy to reach a consensus on Palestine, and it's always on my mind.

My compatriot[99] and administrator of the cultural program

---

98   The October War of 1973 started on 6 October, which coincided, that year, with the
      tenth day of Ramadan.
99   Meaning from the same town as Alaa's paternal family.

suddenly initiates a new ritual—a midday anthem—and for some reason he settles on 'My Homeland'.[100]

Every day he sings it to us. Why this song, I ask him. No response. It's just Palestine on the mind. What kind of national anthem is this, so full of questions and sorrow? Too beautiful to be an official national anthem; an anthem to the dream rather than the glories of leaders and ancient history.

In the last ten days of Ramadan, news arrives of Sheikh Jarrah and al-Aqsa. Something is happening, something will happen. Then we hear that the Murabitoun at al-Aqsa[101] are asking for help from Gaza! Despite our isolation, we quickly understand that something is different this time. Every night prayers go up for our people in Palestine. My wardmates are occupied by news of the missile capabilities of the resistance. I try to point out the importance of the movement inside '48, in the West Bank, Jerusalem, and on the borders.

I pace back and forth in my cell, repeating as if possessed 'the whole national territory' over and over to myself. No, sorry, that's not it, the battle is still long, I mean the whole national *movement*, I mean all of the national components, I mean the full mobilisation of every strand of the people, the full mobilisation of every strand of the people, the full mobilisation of every strand of the people.

But why *not* the whole national territory, every piece of the nation's soil, its dust? Are we not made of this dust, and to it we return? And here it is now, the whole national territory rising up, supported by Gaza—who recycles the dust of her ruins and

---

100 'Mawtini', 1934, by Palestinian poet Ibrahim Touqan, set to music by Lebanese composer, Muhammad Fleifel, is the unofficial national anthem of Palestine. It is hugely popular in the Arab world and was adopted as the national anthem of Iraq in 2003 after the fall of Saddam Hussein.

101 The *Murabitoun*—those who remain fixed in a place—are a . . . fluid group of Palestinian residents of Jerusalem who volunteer to remain within al-Aqsa sanctuary twenty-four hours a day to protect it from a take-over by Israeli settlers.

builds anew. Anyone who has been to Gaza learns that Palestine is the people before it's the land or the shrines; that Palestine lives in its metropole not just in the songs and poems.

The Egyptian Left's perpetual fondness for the old 70s songs has long annoyed me. In the police transport trucks I prefer the company of young prisoners singing Cairokee instead of Marcel Khalifa and Sheikh Imam. I wonder what the youth flying incendiary kites out of Gaza listen to? Probably not Sheikh Imam. Still, I find myself singing 'Hey Palestinians, I Want to Travel to You' with Amm Seif. I'm a dinosaur, yes, but I'm an Arab and Palestine's always on my mind.

Tableyya[102] time comes. I have to write a letter under the direct supervision of the prison administration. I'm supposed to avoid any talk of politics, and I shouldn't reveal how much I've learned of the news through our conversations between cells, floors and wards. But Palestine's on my mind and forces the issue. I write down this thought that's taken hold of me: I regret not having fled to Gaza when I had the chance.

My father was released before the case of the 'armed communist organization' was referred to trial. My earliest childhood memories are of our family hiding out on the Mediterranean coast. We hid until my mother's pregnancy with Mona was certain. Then my father turned himself in. He spent five years in prison. When he came out he had the option to leave the country, but he picked up his life and resumed the struggle. When he died he was buried in his homeland among his students and comrades. He never regretted the decision.

My ordeal didn't start with this prison stint; it began three months after the massacre, in November 2013. I was released twice in 2014 and never thought of fleeing the country. I thought I would follow in my father's footsteps: I'd pay the

---

102   The *Tableyya* is the weekly package of items sent in to prisoners from their families: the food they will eat, laundered clothes and any toiletries or medications that are allowed in.

price willingly, get out, go back to my family and my professional life and resume the struggle. But after five years in
prison—for a demonstration!—I was not freed, but released to
probation which required me to spend all night—twelve hours
of every day—in the police station. Every time I complained
of the cruelty of this punishment, someone would remind me
that Mahmoud Darwish went through something similar and
declared that the night was theirs and the day his. Palestine's
always on the mind. But it seems the Egyptian regime didn't like
the deal and, just six months later, begrudged me the day and
sent me back to prison.

'Why didn't you run?' my cellmates ask.

'To where?' I reply, 'Gaza?'

All the other escape routes seemed too dangerous, but why
didn't I seriously consider escaping to Gaza? Had I let the news
coverage of Gaza as an open-air prison blind me to the truth of
what I'd seen with my own eyes, and written in my own article?
Gaza is besieged but it has not been taken captive, and the difference is enormous.

If I were free in Gaza instead of locked up in Cairo, I would
read books, play with children, enjoy the company of women,
walk on the beach, work and make a living. I'd teach and I'd
learn. I would live and be alive this moment. I would have
breathed the dust-cloud of the whole national territory as it
moved instead of trying to analyse it from afar. I regret not
escaping to Gaza.

I know it's naive. I know I've not lived under bombardment,
that visiting a siege is different to living under it. I know that
this idea that's taken hold of me is only a sign that I'm getting
old. Yes, I long for you, Palestinians, but I also long for a time
when my will had not been torn from me, when my defeat was
not complete.

I sign off every letter with a drawing for Khaled. My drawing's

no better than my singing, but autism pushes us to communicate without words. From memory I draw a photo taken of us in
Gaza. We were in Khan Younis and the barrier was in the background; a group of Egyptians, all looking at the camera, Khaled
on my shoulders. As the photo is taken, Khaled turns to look at
the fence and points to the horizon stretching out behind it, the
only one preoccupied by the Palestine beyond.

I ask his mother to play Reem Banna songs for him. I return
to my cell humming 'Garden of the Spirit'.[103] For some reason, I
never listened to Reem until I went to prison, and I fell in love
with this song. In Torah Maximum Security 2, there's no music,
no woman's voice. If music was not banned, I'd listen to her
everyday. I've never seen Mount Carmel, I don't know the sea
at Haifa or Yafa, I only know the sea at Gaza. No one sings for
Gaza, but they ask for her help.

There are cities that inspire poets and musicians and so become
immortalised in depictions that might not reflect their reality.
Free Jerusalem; tranquil Alexandria, Bride of the Sea; Beirut, the
Sheltering Tent—the symbols seem more real than the cities. But
Gaza and Cairo are both cities that resist romanticisation and so
elude song. No one sings to Cairo, but it is the capital of the Arabs.
No one sings to Gaza either, but it remains the indisputable capital
of Palestine. Both are always present in a crisis.

The day Cairo was liberated we thought that Jerusalem was
near and so sped toward Gaza. The road to Jerusalem looked like
it ran through Cairo—but what is certain is that it must pass
through Gaza. Jerusalem is not too proud to ask Gaza's help—
maybe Cairo should now show a little humility and do the same.

My generation was raised on scenes from the Second Intifada
and launched itself onto the scene with student demonstrations

---

103 Reem Banna (1966–2018), Palestinian singer. In 'Carmel el-Roh' she sings of the
     loneliness of the prisoner and wishes him the breezes of the sea at Yafa and Haifa to
     blow against the cold and the heat of his cell.

in support of Palestine. One movement followed another until this generation led a revolution. Yes, the roots of the revolution lie in the solidarity demonstrations with the Second Intifada, for we are Arabs and Palestine's always on our mind.

Every year some half a million students in Egypt graduate to university, and more than a third of them end up in universities and institutes in Cairo. This year they all saw the whole national territory rising up in revolt.

It is estimated that there are some 60,000 political prisoners in Egypt. All the prisons of all the Arabs combined could not contain the students of Cairo, if Cairo only realised that it's living under siege, not in captivity.

Do I have the right to dream of escaping to Gaza? Do I have the right to dream of a road to Cairo that passes through Gaza? Does a captive have the right to ask for help from the besieged? I know that these questions show how ancient I am, but I'm an Arab and Palestine's always on my mind. And, in my defence[104] I'll say that I refused to be humiliated in my country, and I never lowered my banners, and it should count that I stood in the face of my oppressors: an orphan, naked and barefoot, and my solace is that the tragedy I'm living is but my share of yours. I call out to you: you are always on my mind.

Published on 7 September 2021 in *Mada Masr*

---

104 The lines until the end are Alaa's re-arrangement of lines from Tawfiq Ziad's 'Unadeikum' ['I call out to you'].